I Came –
I Stayed

I Came – I Stayed

The True Story of My Life with Cerebral Palsy

Arlene Sollis

I CAME – I STAYED
THE TRUE STORY OF MY LIFE WITH CEREBRAL PALSY

Copyright © 2014 Arlene Sollis.

All rights reserved. No part of this book may be used or reproduced by any means, graphic, electronic, or mechanical, including photocopying, recording, taping or by any information storage retrieval system without the written permission of the publisher except in the case of brief quotations embodied in critical articles and reviews.

iUniverse books may be ordered through booksellers or by contacting:

iUniverse
1663 Liberty Drive
Bloomington, IN 47403
www.iuniverse.com
1-800-Authors (1-800-288-4677)

Because of the dynamic nature of the Internet, any web addresses or links contained in this book may have changed since publication and may no longer be valid. The views expressed in this work are solely those of the author and do not necessarily reflect the views of the publisher, and the publisher hereby disclaims any responsibility for them.

Any people depicted in stock imagery provided by Thinkstock are models, and such images are being used for illustrative purposes only.
Certain stock imagery © Thinkstock.

ISBN: 978-1-4917-4272-3 (sc)
ISBN: 978-1-4917-4271-6 (hc)
ISBN: 978-1-4917-4270-9 (e)

Library of Congress Control Number: 2014914027

Printed in the United States of America.

iUniverse rev. date: 10/09/2014

This book is dedicated to my Father and Mother, who worked so hard to help me overcome my disabilities

and to

Diane Snider, my life-long friend

Table of Contents

No.	Chapter Name	Page
1.	Before Me	1
2.	My Early Arrival	9
3.	Home Again	17
4.	My Early Education	22
5.	My First Subway Ride	41
6.	Shoveling Snow	43
7.	After Graduation	44
8.	My First Teaching Job	52
9.	Camp Freedom	88
10.	Spain and Portugal	96
11.	Hartford, Connecticut	101
12.	YWCA Tour of Western Europe	110
13.	Norfolk, Virginia	113
14.	The Norfolk Therapeutic Recreation Program	126
15.	Norfolk Continued	129
16.	My Brother	134
17.	Sarah and Me in Great Britain	138
18.	Teaching at the Endependence Center	147
19.	Norfolk Community Service	149
20.	The Anchorage – Housing for the Mobility Impaired	151
21.	Planning the Big Move	154
22.	From Walking to Crutches to Wheelchair	161
23.	Norfolk – The Wards Corner Incident	165
24.	Tampa, Florida	170
25.	My New Life in Tampa	178
26.	Our Swimming Pool	187
27.	My Hip Ordeal	193
28.	Another Big Move	214
29.	Writing This Book	232

List of Pictures

Picture Name   **Page**

Frances Morgan and George Sollis 1
Our Duxbury House, Summer 1937 2
Ice House Sign Year 2009 3
The Sagamore Bridge 7
My Father and Mother 9
Me at Age Two 17
Dickie Eaton and Me 17
Me in the Swing 18
Me and Crow 19
Me in My Sandbox 19
Me and our dog 20
My Mother, about 1942 20
Me on Trike 23
Uncle Jim's dog 25
Me and Marie 28
Philip and Me 31
Duxbury HS Grad 1955 40
United Cerebral Palsy 56
Me and Nursery School Children, Danielle and Stephen 63
Johnny April's Popsicle Stick Lamp 92
Johnny April at Chappaquiddick Beach 93
Eleanor Marnock and Johnny April at Mr. Pinney's Picnic 94
John Morgan, Minerva, and Kathy 134
Sarah and the Yeoman at the Tower of London 139
Stonehenge 140
Me, Connie, and Sarah feeding Ring-Tail monkeys at Dublin Zoo 141
Sarah and Me at the Zoo 142
Volunteer Achievement Award 149
LaVerne and Me 150
A Wheelchair Accessible Kitchen 151
The Stove and the Oven 152

The Sink	153
Mayor Fraim's Letter	169
Lucky	172
Diane and Emogene at Lowry Park Zoo	178
David, Me, and Diane	179
Darlene and Diane at Busch Gardens in Tampa	179
Karen, Lorraine, and Arlene at Tarpon Springs	184
No Sidewalks on Williams Road !	186
Arlene Getting Out of the Pool	187
Getting Out, Stage Two	187
Me in the Pool	188
Kathy Yeomans Using the New Pool Lift	190
Resident of the Year Award	192
Monticello	195

ACKNOWLEDGMENTS

Without the help of many friends this book would not have been possible.

I would like to thank Lorena Morgan, my cousin, for the many hours she spent working on my old photographs. Many had to be restored and cropped and sized to fit the size of the pages of the book.

I am so grateful for my neighbor Lucien Yeomans, who worked so diligently helping me to format the pages, and edit the manuscript. He also took the picture for the book cover and is in the process of preparing it for publication. I often called him when things went wrong to help me to get back on track. Anytime, day or night he would come to my rescue when I needed help.

My old high school friend, Paul April, came to my rescue when I didn't have a picture of the popsicle stick lamp that his brother John had made many years ago. He had the lamp and took a picture of it and sent it to me.

Another high school friend, Darlene Hiller, who lives within an hour's drive from me, came down about every other week to help me with the typing, proof-reading, and editing.

I am most grateful to my Aunt Sheila Morgan for having read and critically reviewed the first draft of this book, and for her many suggestions regarding accuracy and improvement.

The pictures of the Accessible Kitchen are courtesy of Bob Horan, of Virginia Beach, Virginia.

Before Me

The Year was 1930. People were struggling to get back on their feet after the start of the Great Depression the year before. My parents were no exception.

Mother was working as a sales clerk for Hudson's Dress Shop in Boston, Massachusetts while still living at home with her father and stepmother and four younger brothers.

She had been seeing my father for quite some time. They had met at Revere Beach Amusement Park the year before.

He was in the Merchant Marines and was out to sea a greater part of the time. He had applied for advancement but was turned down because he was blind in one eye due to an accident during early childhood.

He had asked my mother to marry him several times and said that he would leave the Merchants Marines and find work locally. If she had needed more time to decide, he would take the next ship out and would be gone for several months.

But she accepted, and they were married on September 28, 1930. Little did they know that the ship my father did not sail on was never to return. It was lost at sea somewhere in the rough waters of the North Atlantic.

So it was that Frances L. Morgan and George R. Sollis would begin their lives together, a marriage that would last for forty-eight years through hard times and good times. They settled in Duxbury, Massachusetts, a quaint little pilgrim town eight miles north of Plymouth. It was my dad's birth place and he knew he could make a living from the bay. At one time he owned thirteen dories. He would rent them out to clam diggers and collect two dollars a week for each dory that was rented. He would average about twenty

Frances Morgan and George Sollis

dollars a week which, back in those days, was enough money to keep a roof over one's head and food on the table. It didn't matter too much what the weather was like. People just knew they had to depend on the bay and they would go out when the tides were right, even if the temperature dropped below freezing. The men would put on their heavy black rubber boots and coats and head out to the mud flats in the hopes of a good day's dig. The winters were very hard. The days were short. And most of the time the clam diggers could only make one tide a day. Sometimes a snowstorm would come up or very strong winds and heavy rains which would make it impossible to work.

With the longer days and warmer temperatures it was often possible to catch an early morning tide as well as the early evening one. By mid day the sun would be out and it would get very hot, eighty to one hundred degrees, even in New England. The heat, combined with the humidity, made for very unfavorable working conditions and many would head back to shore before they had their quota for the day.

My dad had to make sure all of his dories were accounted for at the end of the week. He did all of the repairs needed to keep them in useable condition. The bottoms had to be scraped to remove the seaweed and barnacles that collected over time. They had to be painted. The oars and oarlocks had to be in working order at all times.

When they were expecting their first child, my parents knew they would need more than just the two room house they were renting on Park Street. After shopping around for several weeks, they came upon a house on Tremont Street less than a mile from where they were living. The house had been taken over by the bank as many were at that time. The bank wanted to sell it to get it off its hands for a price of two thousand dollars with no down payment. But my parents were not ready to accept the responsibilities that went with owning a house. The bank told them that they could rent it until a buyer could be found. For the moment that was just fine.

Our Duxbury House, Summer 1937

The house was set on three quarters of an acre of land, half of which extended to include the Mill Pond at the foot of the street. There were no other houses in sight at that time. It was on Route 3A, the shore route from Nameloc Heights to Quincy. There were lots of trees, mostly cedar, white pine, birch and spruce with a few maples and oaks. There was even a pussy willow tree growing in the front yard near the pond. During the summer the front yard was a blanket of yellow daisies. In autumn, just before the trees lost their brilliantly colored dresses of all shades of yellows, oranges, and reds, the view around the pond was just so magnificently breath taking. People passing through would stop to admire the view and take photographs.

There was another very unusual picturesque sight on this pond that caught the eyes of many passers-by. It was the old icehouse. It was owned and run by a man by the name of Roger Cushing. He later built his Cape Cod home directly across the street from it. This icehouse was one of the very few left in New England. It was unfortunate that it burned to the ground, I think sometime in the 1960s. As are

Ice House Sign Year 2009
Darlene Hiller

many old barns and homes in the area, it was left weather beaten, having never been painted. They usually turn charcoal grey with age. Now-a-days people put a protective sealer on to prevent the outside from drying out from over exposure to the hot sun of summer, and snow and rain that would rot the shingles. In winter, Mr. Cushing would wait patiently for a long cold spell when the temperature would drop into the teens and remain there for several days, more like two weeks. He kept checking the thickness of the ice and when it was just right, he and his crew headed out with their heavy equipment, sometimes working into the wee hours of the morning. I was never permitted on the ice while the men were working. But if they were out during the day, I would watch with fascination from our living room window. They cut each block a certain size to fit on a conveyer-like ramp that was operated by hand, somehow using pulleys to get the ice to the top of the chute where it would be dropped into the ice-house for proper storage. The ice was carefully layered in sawdust which acted as insulation from the heat of summer.

Sometimes, for something to do on a hot summer afternoon, my friends and I would accidentally on purpose wander into the icehouse to get cooled off. We would come home covered in sawdust. Mother never said anything. We had to take the outside hose and get it all off before we entered the house.

I have only one regret here, and that is that I never took any pictures of the icehouse and neither did my parents.

Our house itself was rather small. The original house had two rooms, a cellar and an attic with two rooms which became our bedrooms. The kitchen was in the cellar. It had a set tub for a sink. That was used for doing dishes and laundry and even bathing. It had a potbelly wood burning stove which was used for cooking as well as for heat during the winter months. There was a small pantry here. There was a back room where the icebox was kept. This had a dirt floor and because of this, the room stayed very damp and dingy. The kitchen had two very small windows on the barn side which allowed some outside light in but they could not be opened and a larger one on the street side. I don't think this one could be opened either.

There was a sunroom which was added to the cellar and faced the pond. My parents used this room for a dining room. They did most of their entertaining there. There was an outside door on both the front and back side of this room. In the main part of the house, were the living room, and another room on the backside which was the main entrance. I have no idea what this room was used for when my parents first moved there. There was a sun parlor which was also added sometime after the house was built. It went the full length of the house and faced the street, and it had a front outside door with a small porch. This room was originally used as a tea room by its previous owners.

I have no way on knowing whether or not the back porch was a part of the original structure. It seems to me that it was. It also went the full length of the house with the main entrance to the house in the middle of it. The roof was level with the lower part of the back window of the attic, my bedroom.

The bathroom, if you could call it a room, was to the left of the entrance. It was no wider than its door. All it had was a toilet and a very small wash basin with running cold water only. The toilet tank was above the toilet and had a pull chain for flushing. This room had a very small window over the toilet.

The other room was the sitting room. The doors to both the attic and the cellar were there. The stairs to both were very steep and narrow. To use the attic steps, one had to go up and down on tip toes or turn sideways. Luckily, in all the years we lived there, nobody in our family ever had an accident on them.

My parents had their bedroom up in the attic in the front room. It had plenty of floor space. But because of the slant in the roof, these two rooms appeared much smaller. There was a very small closet over the stairs where my mother hung blouses and kept her shoes. The only other closet in the house at this time was in the smaller bedroom, and it too was very small. These two rooms would get unbearably hot in summer, and uncomfortably cold during the winter months, since there would be very little heat getting to them. The sun parlor was originally built as a tearoom. It had many windows across the front and pond side with a front outside door, which we would never use. I don't know why, but it was eventually nailed shut. The entrance was through the back room. There was a window in the sitting room facing the street and looking into the sun parlor. The door was often kept closed during the winter months to keep the main part of the house warm and cozy.

There was also a large barn that would serve as a workshop, a garage, and later, a boathouse. It had two big doors that swung out and hooked to the front of the building when fully opened, to prevent them from blowing in the wind. When they were closed, they were secured at the top and bottom. The barn had a small door on the house side, which was kept padlocked most of the time. Just inside this small door there was a trapdoor which led to the cellar which had a dirt floor. This part of the barn was very dark and dingy, since it had no doors on it. It would later become a chicken coop and even later still a duck coop. Both of which were short lived. The upper part of the barn later served as a boat house, and also a workshop from time to time also.

The outside appearance of the house and barn did not change much over the years, but there were many improvements made to the interior of the house. There were two additions to the outside of the barn. One was when my mother got her own car, and the other was to put our boat under cover during the winter months.

The year my parents moved into their new home was anything but easy for both of them. Mother gave birth to a baby boy. They named him George William after his father and Grandfather Morgan. My dad was a junior and he hated it when his aunts and uncles would address him as Junior instead of using his first name. I don't think the baby ever made it home from the hospital. He was very ill and passed away several months later. Years later, when I would ask my mother for the details all she would tell me is that he had died as an infant. My father never mentioned the baby to me either. He would use a shaving mug with the initials G.W.S. engraved in gold lettering on it. I still have this mug tucked away amongst my family treasures.

That winter the temperature would drop to below zero for more than a week at a time. My parents spent most of their waking hours by the wood burning stove in the kitchen trying to keep warm. Most of my mother's time was spent preparing meals and doing dishes, that is until the water pipes froze

At this point, my father decided he'd had enough of living in the cellar. He knew neither of them could live this way much longer. He knew he had to do something, and quick. He told my mother to pack her heavy clothes and a blanket for the car, a model A Ford. He was taking her to spend a week with her father in Belmont while he built a new kitchen upstairs in the back room. He would put in a cooking stove and a sink, the first of many remodeling jobs the house would undergo.

The wood burning stove remained in the cellar, and the room served as my father's workshop for as long as we owned the house.

Shortly after my father completed the new kitchen, my grandfather came for a visit. He measured for new kitchen cabinets. He was in that business. He brought them the next week and together, he and my father had them up within an hour. Mother painted them. A drop-leaf table was brought up from the cellar, so now they had an eat-in kitchen in the main part of the house. Life began to show signs of improvement after a rocky start.

My father's first big construction job came in 1934, when construction of the new Sagamore Bridge began. The original bridge was built in 1912, two years prior to the opening of the Cape Cod Canal. The Federal Railroad Administration acquired the canal in 1918 after a German submarine opened fire on an American tugboat working in the area three miles off the coast of Nauset Beach, Cape Cod.

In 1928 Congress ordered the Army Corps of Engineers to widen and deepen the Cape Cod Canal to accommodate the increased ship traffic through the canal. They were also put in charge of building the two road bridges and the railroad bridge connecting the Cape to the U.S. mainland.

President Franklin D. Roosevelt signed emergency legislation that authorized the Public Works Administration, (PWA) to finance and build the three bridges on September 6, 1933. Work began three months later.

My dad had *read about the project in a Boston newspaper and had been following its progress for seve*ral months. Then one day in the spring of 1934 he and another young fellow decided to take a drive to the construction site to see for themselves just how far along the work had come, not knowing what to expect.

When they got out of the car, a man greeted them and asked them if they were new on the job. My dad told him he wasn't working there. The man told them if they wanted a job to come back the next morning prepared to work a ten-hour day as long as the weather held out. So this was how my dad got his first big construction job on the Sagamore Bridge.

The Sagamore Bridge
Wikipedia

He stayed with the project to see its completion in June of the next year. This bridge was built over the original drawbridge, which was demolished following the completion of the new one. This new bridge was a 135 foot clearance to accommodate any large ships and naval vessels, and its length was 1,408 feet from end to end. With the predicted increase of motor traffic to and from the Cape, the new bridge was built with four lanes, double that of the old one.

My dad would tell me years later, when he drove my friend Holly and me to Provincetown on a day's outing, how he dropped his lever when he was working on the bridge and he was so high up that it disappeared in thin air; he couldn't see it when it hit the water. He also told me that when the three bridges were dedicated and opened on June 22nd, 1935, he and my mother were on hand for the ceremony. He just had to be one of the first to make the round trip on both the Sagamore and the Bourne bridges. They are only one and a half miles apart along the canal.

Years later, my mother's cousin John LaCarte and his wife Millie bought a house in Buzzard's Bay overlooking the Bourne Bridge. My parents and I would spend some weekends with them during the summer. My dad would hitch up the trailer with the outboard motor boat on it to the back of the car. My dad and I were early risers and we often took a ride through the canal before anyone else was up. The view from the boat was just so breathtaking and so beautiful. He took me under all three bridges. One Saturday morning we were fortunate enough to watch the railroad bridge in operation. It had to be lowered because a train was headed for the Cape. We were gone longer than usual that morning. The rest of the house thought we had gone fishing. My dad told everyone of our adventure and said I wasn't satisfied just to see the train pass on the bridge, I also wanted to watch the track being raised. I think he enjoyed it as much as I did. That day Mother told me I would have to get breakfast for my dad and me and leave the kitchen as I found it.

My Early Arrival

My Father and Mother

My parents were settling into their new home. With the kitchen now in the main part of the house, a stove with an oven was installed, a refrigerator with a small freezer on top was given to them and a small drop leaf table and two matching chairs were brought up from the cellar. They now had a workable eat-in kitchen. My father built a counter top along the outside wall and installed a set of drawers for storage under the counter. This was a start in the right direction towards modern living. My mother liked to cook and bake and my father liked good food so any improvements to this room were welcomed.

By this time they were expecting their second baby. It was due to arrive before Thanksgiving. Mother was very anxious and very worried, but at the same time hopeful that everything would go well. So it was that I was born on October 18, 1935. I came one month earlier than expected. The doctor did not know until the next day when my skin started to turn yellow that something was not right. I had jaundice, a condition quite common in newborns where the still developing liver may not yet be able to remove enough bilirubin the from the baby's blood. Too high of a level can sometimes cause deafness and cerebral palsy.

The Rh factor was unknown at this time but it could have been the cause of my condition. I do have a different blood type than my mother. This could have caused a sudden buildup of bilirubin in the blood resulting in a lack of oxygen to the brain.

The doctor waited until my father got to the hospital before he broke the bad news to them. What he told them was that I was very sick, just like the baby that died. He said that if I lived, I would never talk or walk and most likely never live to see my tenth birthday. He advised my parents to put me in a state hospital and that he had already made arrangements for my transfer. Mother told the doctor that she wasn't leaving the hospital without her baby regardless of what was wrong with me or how much care I needed. She just wasn't going to send me to a state hospital to die like her first baby did. So it was that I got to come home with my mother.

Before we left the hospital, my mother was given a set of instructions and told to keep me on a three-hour feeding schedule for a certain length of time. This meant she had to get up in the middle of the night to feed me regardless of whether or not I was sleeping. If I was asleep, my mother woke me to feed me when the clock said it was time, but if I was already awake and fussy, she had to wait until the clock said it was time to feed me. This three-hour feeding schedule was very tiring for my mother. She wasn't getting much sleep at night and I was taking most of her time during her waking hours.

At some point during these first few months, Nana Brown, my father's mother, came to live with us. She was a tremendous help to my mother. She took over a lot of the household chores so my mother could better tend to my needs and get a little rest during the day. I was a very fussy baby and cried a lot. Before Mother brought me home from the hospital, I was put on a feeding schedule. Like most mothers of that time, mine thought the doctor knew best, and she stuck to it. If I was asleep and the clock said it was time to feed me, she awakened me. Sometimes I took the full amount of formula. But most of the time I fell back to sleep and Mother just put me back to bed on a half-emptied bottle and, no doubt, a half-filled belly. On the other hand, if I woke up earlier than I should have, Mother just had to let me cry it out until the clock told her it was feeding time again. My grandmother tried rocking me, but most of the time I kept on crying until Mother fed me. Most of the time, I spat up some of the formula shortly after I was fed. So I guess I was never really satisfied. Nana tended to most of the household chores and prepared most of the meals. My dad was still making a living from the bay and doing odd jobs for people in Duxbury and the neighboring towns of Kingston and Marshfield, so meals had to be planned around his work schedule which was not very easy. We didn't have a telephone and would not have one for many years to come. So if he was on a job or having a good day in the bay, there was no telling what time he would be home to eat. There were many times when my mom and Nana would have to eat before he got home. This was a way of life for our family until World War II, when my father went to work at the Boston Naval Ship Yard.

By the time I was eight months old, and still not sitting up unsupported, my parents grew very concerned and took me back to see our family doctor. It was at this point that he became a little concerned also. He recommended that they take me to the Children's Hospital in Boston, a fifty-mile drive from Duxbury. He would make arrangements for me to be seen by a team of pediatric specialists. He told my parents that these doctors were the best in all of New England and that if there was anything wrong with me that they would know and be able to advise my parents as to what steps the doctors would need to take toward my treatment and just what to expect as far as my progress would go.

By the time my first birthday rolled around, I still was not progressing as well as most babies of the same age. Mother grew increasingly concerned that maybe she wasn't doing enough for me, or that what she was doing was not the right thing. She began spending more and more time on my exercises, but this really didn't help. Sometimes the longer she worked with me, the less cooperative I would become. And the more frustrated we would both become. All she knew was that all of her friends who had babies older or younger than me were not having any of the problems with their babies that she was having with me. My grandmother told my mom that she was wearing both of us out and reminded her that my exercises were only to be done twice a day, not six times a day.

During the winter months the sun parlor was not used much as it had no cellar under it and it would cost too much to heat. The entrance to this room at this time was through the kitchen and the door was kept shut as was the window in the living room. All four of us lived in two rooms from November through April. Nana Brown slept on the studio couch in the living room and I slept in a crib which was taken to the sun parlor during the day. Mother thought I would catch cold if I slept upstairs, as these two rooms were not heated either. On really cold days, my dad lit a fire in the wood burning stove in the cellar in the early evenings after supper. This helped to keep the living quarters comfortably warm until the family retired for the night. Their bedtime was very early, I think 8 pm. I don't recall when my parents bought their first radio, but whenever it was, they listened to it faithfully every night for about two hours until they bought their first television in 1954.

By the time I was two, I had begun to crawl well enough to get about the house. I would put both hands in front of me and drag my body behind. A strange way of crawling, but at least I was beginning to get about and explore the kitchen cupboards and under the sink. I could not yet pull myself to a standing position.

At some point around my second birthday, my parents took me to Children's Hospital for a follow-up visit. The doctor was pleased with the progress I was making. But he told my parents that the leapfrog crawl had to be corrected before I could ever learn to walk. He had the physical therapist show my parents what I was doing wrong and then showed them the proper way most babies learn to crawl. She put me on the mat on the floor and positioned me on all fours and began by moving my left arm and right leg and then the right arm and left leg. She told my mom that for the first few weeks, she would need help with this exercise, one person to move my arms and the other to move my legs. After a few sessions, the brain would take over this pattern and I should be able to master this crawl. The therapist also told my parents to buy me a walker and keep me in it for as long as I could tolerate it. This would put me in a standing position to help strengthen my leg muscles.

Mother had earlier learned that when the doctor said to do these exercises twice a day, he meant twice a day and not five or six times a day. She set up a time to work with me each day and stuck to the schedule for the next two and a half months. Nana Brown was still living with us and she was a big help to my mother. They seemed to work together well. Mother told me many years later that she never had to ask for help. My grandmother just knew what to do, and pitched in at the right time. Needless to say, she assisted my mother with my exercises every morning after breakfast and when the household chores were done and again after my afternoon nap. All their efforts were beginning to pay off. Shortly before Christmas, I was crawling correctly without assistance.

My parents did buy me the walker that the therapist at Children's Hospital said I needed. At first, I rebelled and screamed when I was put in it. No doubt, I must have been afraid of it. Mother would take me out of it, calm me down and try again in a couple of hours. After about the third or fourth day, the screaming stopped when I was put in it. Mother decided, for the first few days at least, to put me in the kitchen while she prepared the evening meal. She talked to me a lot and sang some of those silly nursery rhymes. Then one day she saw that I was pushing myself backwards in the walker. She was so excited. She called my grandmother in to show her what I had done. Now all I needed to do was to learn to go forward. It was several more weeks before I discovered how to do that. Mother established a daily routine with me. In the mornings she put me on the floor or in the playpen and in the afternoons after I woke up from my nap she put me in the walker until suppertime, or until I started to get too cranky. One Sunday afternoon while my mother and grandmother were preparing supper, they heard my father scream from the cellar. Mother dropped whatever she was doing and by the time she got part way down the stairs, my father had me on his lap on the cellar floor. He was shaking so bad he couldn't talk. I was screaming at the top of my lungs. The walker was at the foot of the stairs, nobody said anything. They knew what had happened. Their main concern at that moment was how badly I was hurt. He told my mom later, that when he heard the thump, thump, thump on the stairs, he turned and grabbed the walker midway before it hit the bottom of the stairs and the wall in front of me. He then gently lifted me out. He thought I was more scared than hurt. My mother wasn't so sure. When they got me calmed down, mother began checking for broken bones and bruises. Fortunately there were none.

My father wasted no time in making sure no such accident would ever happen again. The next day he bought a latch and hook for the inside of the cellar door. That hook was never removed. When I was a teenager I asked him why the hook was there. Nobody ever used it. That was when he told me the story of how I had fallen down the stairs when I was two years old.

By the first of November, my mother decided that she wanted to have Thanksgiving dinner at home. She invited her grandparents, Grandma and Grandpa Foster. They were both in their eighties and wanted very much to meet their first great-grandchild. They lived in Lawrence where my mom grew up. It was about a two-hour drive to Duxbury.

My mother had done all the baking the day before and had gotten up early to prepare the vegetables, get the turkey in the oven. She set up the gate leg table in the living room so that when her grandparents arrived, she would have time to sit and chat with them a while before dinner. They were due to arrive around 11 am, and dinner would be served at 1 pm or thereabouts.

The day was sunny and unseasonably warm for that time of the year. After the guests had arrived, mother set up the playpen in the front yard and put me in it while my father and great grandparents were outside taking advantage of the Indian summer weather. I had just learned to pull myself to a standing position with the aid of the playpen's vertical bars. I had not yet learned to sit back down gracefully, and would just let go of my grip and plop down, usually landing on my fanny. My mother padded me well so I wouldn't get hurt. She felt that if I got hurt, I might not try to stand. All and all, it was a great Thanksgiving. We didn't see much of my great grandparents. I remember visiting them once when I was around five years old. It must have been around Christmas time because the weather was very cold. They had a big house. Each room had at least one chime clock in it, and none of them struck at exactly the same time, and no two sounded exactly alike. Oh, yes, I had my favorite, the cuckoo clock in the kitchen. I asked my father to buy me one like it. He said "Now, my Pet. That clock would make your mother cuckoo and you wouldn't want that, would you?" We all had a good laugh over that. I never asked him again.

We were to spend the night there. I was to sleep in the spare bedroom in the main part of the house. My mother put me to bed at my usual bedtime. I lay awake listening for the next chime of the clocks. I tried to guess what clock was chiming and which one would be next. I was still wide awake when my parents checked in on me before they retired to the attic bedroom. My mother was quite upset that the sleeping arrangements were not going to work. My dad didn't say a word. He picked me up and carried me up the back stairs. It was the one and only time I ever remember sleeping with my parents.

Mother said she couldn't sleep with the window closed, she needed fresh air. She asked my father to open it, which he obligingly did. What he didn't tell her was that it did no good because there was a storm window on the outside. At breakfast the next morning, we all had a good laugh over the incident.

In December of my third year, my parents decided I was old enough and well enough to make the trip to my grandparents in Belmont for Christmas day. My grandmother was pregnant and the baby was due shortly after the holidays.

On Christmas morning, my mother bundled me up in my new snowsuit, hat, mittens and scarf and my father drove us to spend the day with mothers' family.

My grandparents' house was quite large, with many rooms with thick carpet on most of the floors. By now I was crawling pretty well, so mother felt at ease leaving me in the front room while she went to the kitchen to assist my grandmother with the dinner. With so many people around, there wasn't much of a chance of me getting into something I shouldn't. I must have explored every niche I could find. My mother came in to check on me every half hour or so. If she didn't see me, she wanted to know where I was. Once when she checked in and asked "Where is Arlene?" Everybody looked up at her and to their dismay they all said at once "I don't know." When everyone called my name, I didn't answer.

The search was on. I think one of my uncles found me curled up asleep, way back in the coat closet on the boots and rubbers. I must have gotten tired and found a dark quiet place for a snooze. My father gently lifted me out and carried me to the sun parlor and laid me on the sofa. I guess I gave everyone a Christmas scare.

With the holidays over, it was now time for my next visit to Boston Children's Hospital. My parents were not prepared for what the doctor's next plan of treatment was to be. They listened carefully to what Dr. Cruthers had to say and the options he was giving them. He told them that they could continue on the same path of therapy they were using but it would be very slow. He really wanted to admit me to the hospital, so I could get more extensive treatment. At first mother said "no". I had never been away from home before. I think she thought that something bad would happen to me and she didn't want to lose me. But my father repeated what the doctor was telling them, that the hospital had special equipment to help me, and the therapist could try out different things until she found what worked best for me. Dr. Cruthers told them that it would be for only a short time and then I could go home again.

My mother had tears in her eyes, but she finally heard what my father was telling her. She knew he was right. That day they would go home without me. They were told to come back the next week for a progress report and if they wanted to take me home with them, no one would stop them. My parents did go back the next week. My mother was quite surprised to see how well I had adjusted to my new surroundings. She saw me through a one-way window. I could not see her. I was in the playroom with some other children. Most had more problems than I had. But we all seemed happy. My mother felt a lot better about leaving me there this time.

I didn't see my parents again until sometime in the spring when they came to take me home. My father was the one who had tears in his eyes as we left the hospital. He had carried me in several weeks earlier. Now I was leading both of them outside. He wanted to pick me up and hug me. But he waited until we all got to the car. I was a very different child from the one they left behind a few weeks before. I could now walk and I was talking much more. My father told my mother "There's no stopping her now". And I guess he was right about that.

Home Again

When I first came home after spending three months in Boston Children's Hospital, my parents were very surprised at all the things I had learned to do besides just learning to walk. I was potty trained. I was feeding myself with a spoon, even though I still had some difficulty doing it.

My mother would often be in a hurry and try to help. But I wanted no part of her help. I told her I was a big girl now and could do it all by myself. She knew she had to allow more time at mealtime. Not only was I walking, but I was also climbing onto chairs to fetch for things that were otherwise out of reach. I got my hands on a bottle of iodine that was accidentally left on the kitchen counter. Somehow, I managed to get the top off. I spilled it all over me, burning my lips pretty badly, and ruining the dress I was wearing.

Me at Age Two

My walking gait was and always would be very awkward. I fell a lot. One day I was outdoors in the front yard. Nana Brown was keeping an eye on me. She hollered to my mother that I had fallen. Mother asked if I was hurt. Nana said she didn't think so.

Dickie Eaton and Me

"Well then" mother replied, "she will get up when she gets ready". My mother had the right idea. Over the years I would take many falls and then move on.

My mother always made sure I had playmates, boys as well as girls. Grace and Gene Eaton had a boy named Dicky. He was a year older than I. They lived on Landing Road, near a little beach. We all spent many hot summer days playing in the sand and at the edge of the water. We also spent a lot of time playing in our back yards.

Irene Glass came to our house often. She had three girls, all older than I, and by now Patty had been born. Irene made donuts, and once or twice I remember her making pizza. That was a real treat! One time I must have been angry about something. Barbara, a year older than I, went crying to her mother that I had pulled her hair. My mother told her to pull mine right back. That ended my hair pulling.

Blanche and Norman White had four boys. The youngest, Joey, was my age. Our favorite place to play was the crawl space under Island Creek Hall (a small community recreation facility) which was next door to their house. I kept as far away from their house as possible. The family had chickens and I was attacked by their bantam rooster a couple of times. I was afraid of the thing. Joey and I were later in the same class in high school.

My father built me a swing on our back porch. I out grew the swing of course, but the hooks from which it hung were still there as a reminder of the many hours of use it got from me and the neighborhood children when my parents sold the house many years later. This swing was replaced with a hammock which the whole family enjoyed during the summer months.

I was around three years old when my parents bought me a wicker doll carriage. Pushing it was a real problem as it tipped over quite easily, and I lost my balance and fell often.

Me in the Swing

My dad solved the problem by putting a heavy lead weight at the foot end under the carriage. I played with dolls, but I much preferred trucks and trains over dolls and a tea set.

One summer when I was around five or six, a crow came to our house for an early morning visit. It would sit on the back porch railing. At first nobody paid much attention to it. One morning my father called me to the back door so I could see this bird that came every day. When I started to open the door, the bird flew away, only to return the next morning at the same time. I thought he might be hungry and ask my father if I could put some food out for the bird the next morning before he came. For several days I stood at the door talking to our visitor. Then one morning I put food out. But this time I stayed on the porch near the railing. Before long, the crow and I became good friends as you can see from this picture.

Me and Crow

My father built me a sandbox under the pine trees in our back yard. He put real beach sand in it from Duxbury Beach. At the beginning of each summer season, I rode to the beach with him to get fresh white sand for it. He also built one for my Uncle Philip, who is two years younger than me. My grandparents had a small fenced in and gated play yard so we wouldn't wander into the street.

Me in My Sandbox

Me and our dog

During the 1940s, if my mother wanted to visit any of her friends during the day, the only way to get there was on foot, since we lived in a rural area and there was no public transportation. Even though we lived on a main road, there were very few houses nearby and many of the side streets weren't even paved at the time.

My Mother, about 1942

Even though I could now walk, like most children of five or six years old, I got tired very quickly and had to stop to rest along the roadside. My mother was always in a hurry to get to where she was going. So when my father found this big old wicker carriage at the town dump and brought it home, my mother was delighted with it. This meant that she would be able to walk longer distances. She just put me, and often our pet dog Frisky, in it when she wanted to spend time with her friends who lived a mile or two away. It didn't really matter much how cold the weather got as long as there was no snow on the roads. She would bundle me up in a snowsuit, mittens and hat, and wrap a blanket around me before she headed out.

My mother introduced me to books before I could ever walk or talk. She spent a lot of time reading to me every day. After I heard a story or poem a couple of times, I could predict what was going to happen next. My mother would sometimes be tired or in a hurry and would try to skip over a few pages. But I never let her get away with it. She learned not to start a story that she didn't have time to finish. She read all of the Brothers Grimm fairy tales, and introduced me to many children's bedtime Bible stories. I think she was very happy when I learned to read by myself.

My Early Education

By the time I was five years old, I was doing everything the neighborhood children were doing and maybe even more. Sometime before school opened in September, mother took me for the first grade readiness test. But even though I passed it with flying colors, mother was told that because I was handicapped, I would not be able to attend classes there. The town of Duxbury was only responsible to provide me a tutor for three hours a week. My mother felt this was not enough. But it was better than nothing.

The school arranged an appointment for my mother and me to see a teacher on Standish Shore, by the name of Mrs. Clark. She ran a private kindergarten. Just maybe she would be willing to take me on for the three hours.

When mother and I arrived, Mrs. Clark greeted us warmly. She had cookies and milk for me and tea for mother and herself. When I was finished eating Mrs. Clark showed me to the playroom so mother and she could talk. I learned from my mother many years later that Mrs. Clark would take me only if I didn't have "*fits*". My mother told her that I did NOT have epilepsy.

So it was that mother drove me there for my lessons three afternoons a week, rain or shine, for the next school year. Even though I was learning to read and knew some basic number concepts, my mother felt that there was something that was not right with this education program. I needed more than what Mrs. Clark could provide for me. When I graduated from Duxbury High School in 1955, Mrs. Clark was one of my special guests.

At some point, my mother must have written to the State Board of Education. But I really don't know just how my parents found out about the Massachusetts Hospital School. The school was located in Canton, about a 45 minute drive from home.

I remember when I was seven years old my parents took me there for psychological testing to see if I was a candidate for the school's education program. I remember telling my parents that the person administering the test must think I am awfully dumb. Children with below average IQs were turned down. Needless to say, I must have said the right things at the right times, for a change. That September I was enrolled there. I would spend the next six school years away from home and my parents again.

The school was set up to meet the educational and medical needs of its students. The hospital had a girls' floor and a boys' floor. At the time I was admitted, every student was admitted to the hospital and lived there until it was felt that he or she was ready to be moved to a cottage. Some students never made it to the cottages due to their medical needs, which required skilled nursing care.

I was assigned to the young children's ward which slept eight or ten of us. We slept in over-sized cribs. I did not like this. The second night I was there, I threw my pillow and coverings on the floor, climbed over the side, and fell asleep under my bed. When the nurse came in, she put me back in bed. I would get out again almost as soon as her back was turned. This went on for several nights. I complained that

Me on Trike

I was a big girl and I was not going to sleep in a baby's crib. I was soon moved to another ward where I slept in a big girl's bed. My parents were not permitted to visit me for the first two months to give me time to get adjusted. My birthday is in mid-October. My mother was not about to let it go by without taking me for cake and ice cream. My parents went to the main office and I guess my father gave the person at the desk a hard time. She finally reluctantly let my parents take me out for the afternoon. I had to be back by four o'clock. My parents had bought me a tricycle during the summer and they thought I should have it at school, so they brought it with them on their first visit. At first the hospital staff told my parents that I could not have it because there was no place to store it. My father told the head nurse that he was leaving it there for me to ride and she would just have to find a place for it. On nice days I was permitted to ride it to and from school. I had it for about three years until I outgrew it. I was not permitted to let any of the other children ride on it. I did not like this as I was used to sharing everything with the neighborhood children. When I confronted my mother about it, she told me I had to obey the rules of the school even if I disagreed with them. I was one of very few who got to go home for Thanksgiving weekend. My parents saw to that too, even if they broke the rules.

For the first two years I was there, I attended classes in the morning only. I had music one afternoon a week and a craft program also, which was actually an occupational therapy program. The craft program taught woodworking, sewing, and leather craft, as well as many other things.

I was going on eight years old when I entered first grade. The classes were very small, six to ten children to a room. The school building was long. The students entered their classrooms from the walkway outside. The hospital building was the farthest away, about a ten or fifteen-minute walk. These walkways between the main buildings were boarded up during the winter months to keep out the snow and cold winds of New England. Many students used wheelchairs, carts or crutches. So these walkways had to be kept cleared at all times.

Religion had its place here also. I attended Mass each Sunday. An altar was set up in the big recreation hall. A local priest came to say the service, and some nuns came to give us catechism lessons. We also had a four-legged visitor every so often. The head doctor's dog, a German shepherd, would wander in. We also had another visitor– a pet squirrel that we all fed. Once the squirrel climbed up on the altar, and the priest said "I guess God's creatures want to hear Mass too." My parents came to see me make my First Communion at the end of that first year I was at school. I was confirmed there a few years later by Cardinal Richard J. Cushing of Boston.

The school provided us with all the latest movies, including the news reels and cartoons. The only thing that was missing was the popcorn. They were shown on Friday night. We all looked forward to a night out.

By now the United States had entered into World War II and I had several uncles who were stationed over seas, so these news reels always captured my interest. My Uncle Jim, my father's youngest brother, had left his dog in our care and I just loved this dog. Uncle Jim was a military policeman in the Army. He occasionally sent home a trunk full of things for the family. I remember once he sent me a set of building blocks from Germany which I play with for many years. I still have a couple of small keepsakes he sent my parents from Germany and France, with their names on them.

Uncle Jim's dog

My mother's oldest brother, Richard, was in the Air Force. He was stationed in England. The news reels showed a lot of airplanes getting hit by the enemy. These news reels were very scary for me. I was nine years old at the time. I would close my eyes and cover my ears so I wouldn't see or hear them, but somehow this didn't work. When I got back to the dorm and went to bed, I could still see and hear those planes far into the night. My Uncle Bradford was in the Marines. He spent a lot of time in the jungles of the Philippines. Those news stories were very graphic also and scared me. There was a small Army base in Plymouth and when I was at home during the summer months, I would watch the big army trucks pass by our house just about every day. One of my mother's cousins, John LaCarte, happened to be stationed there. He spent a lot of his free time at our house.

I was almost ten years old when World War II ended, and I was so happy when all our relatives were safely home for the Christmas holiday.

My Uncle Bradford stayed in the Marines as a reservist, but none of the other relatives wanted any part of military life after the war ended.

My uncle Bradford's brother, Philip was too young for World War II. He later joined the Marine Corps as a Reservist.

When the circus or the Ice Capades came to the Boston Gardens, the school was closed for a day and everyone was loaded onto buses and driven into Boston to see the show. For some of the children, these trips were the only time they ever got to leave the school. Many were wards of the state and the school was the only home they knew. I also remember once going to the Boston Children's Museum.

By the end of my second school year, I was transferred out of the hospital to one of the four cottages known as NGC. I really don't recall what these letters stood for, but we girls called it Nice Girls' Cottage. There were eighteen of us ranging in ages from six to about twenty and the two house mothers, matrons as they were called back then. They were sisters and they lived upstairs with us. Their names were Ada and Ellen Suddon, two elderly spinsters. The building was a large two-story wooden structure with a large cellar. Our sleeping quarters were on the second floor. It was one big room partitioned into sections, but with no doors on the partitions. Each section slept four and had a single large chest of drawers and a wardrobe for our clothes. Even though the room had two sets of stairs, we used only the back one which we entered from the dining area. It was an open stairway and I often slid down the banister when nobody was looking, When we were old enough or physically capable enough, we were given household chores to do. Each month we were assigned a different chore and there was no switching with anyone else, like it or not. When it was my turn to sweep the cellar floor in the winter, I was more than happy. There was an outdoor glider which was stored there during the winter months. Needless to say, the floor hardly ever got swept. I kept the broom by the glider and as soon as I heard the upstairs door click I picked up the broom and dashed to one end pretending to be hard at work. I did sweep it clean on the last day so that the next girl wouldn't complain that I left it dirty.

The older girls decided that it was time I learned to iron my own clothes for church. Thank heavens they let me practice on rags first. Otherwise, my mother would have been very upset if she saw scorched places on my clothes. We used flat irons back then. They had to be heated on top of the coal stove. It wasn't long before I got the hang of it and did pretty well. I was very happy when we switched to electric irons a year later. I learned how to properly set the tables for meals and make a bed. I was too tiny to reach the big set tub in the kitchen to do dishes, which made me very happy.

We children had a lot of free time. We played outdoors much of the time. There were swings and a monkey gym for both the boys and girls to use, which were located in a field between the boys' and girls' cottages. There were also three seesaws on one side of my cottage which I think us girls abused terribly. Sometimes we would push so hard we bounced them right off the bar. Nobody ever got hurt however. I liked to climb the big oak tree that was in our front yard. Sometimes I would ask someone to pass me my book after I got settled in. I spent a lot of time up here. It was quiet.

On days when we had to stay indoors, we did jigsaw puzzles and played a lot of board and card games. My parents kept us well supplied with games and puzzles. The matrons, if they had a free moment, would join us. I think we had every board game that was ever made at that time.

One of my favorite things was collecting pictures of movie stars and trading them with the other girls. I kept them in a big box. They were arranged alphabetically with the ladies on top and the men underneath. My parents kept me supplied with movie magazines when they came on Sundays to take me out for the afternoon. I found them years later when I was cleaning out the cellar closet just before my parents sold the Duxbury house in the mid 1970s. They were tucked away in the back of the closet waiting for me to discard them. None of us were angels, including me. I remember once in the springtime catching grasshoppers and putting them in a jar. I brought it to the table at lunchtime and unscrewed the lid. Everyone went wild when the grasshoppers started hopping all over the table. When the matron asked which one of us was responsible for the uninvited guests, nobody squealed on me, therefore nobody was punished for doing it. I knew better than to try that again.

In the fall, all the window screens were taken off so we could wash the windows before the storm windows were put on for the winter. One Indian summer morning three freshly baked cakes were set on the table by an open kitchen window to cool. I happened to pass by them and decided to help myself to one of them while nobody was around. Four other girls and I had a feast under the big oak tree. While we were having lunch that day, we eyed the cake that was placed before us. The pieces were cut much smaller than usual. We five thieves got more than our share. The matron mentioned that some dog must have walked off with one of the cakes. We never got that opportunity again.

I was one of the more fortunate children there. My parents insisted that I spend all of the holidays and the ten weeks of the summer vacation with them. In 1948 when I returned for school, my parents were told to take me to C-4. The building I had been assigned to for the past two years had been closed. It was going to be demolished to make way for a new modern structure. This wasn't the only change that was made. Most of my roommates had been transferred to other schools and I never saw any of them again. My best friend, Marie Elizabeth Clancy, was one of them. I have tried several times to locate her through the internet but so far I have turned up nothing.

Me and Marie

I did not adjust well to my new living quarters, most of the girls were older than I, and most of them had more physical limitations than I had. Many used wheelchairs or carts to get about. I felt so alone and so out of place. I spent more time on my studies, which was not a bad thing. My parents bought me a radio and I spent hours listening to music and the afternoon soap operas. I learned to knit and embroider, and my parents kept me well supplied with yarn and things to sew. None of the puzzles and games we had in the other building ever made it to C-4 and I never asked my parents for new ones. There was a big parlor on the main floor. It had a victrola and a lot of records. I began playing all the marches and waltzes. I think I just about drove everyone crazy. But I didn't really care. I was doing my thing, like it or not.

One day I was coming back from school. I was crossing the lawn just outside of the cottage. I tripped and fell and landed on a piece of broken coke bottle. When I went to get up, I noticed my dress was wet with blood. I managed to get inside and sit in the parlor. Blood was dripping everywhere. One of the girls called for help. The matron tried to stop the bleeding but she couldn't. She called the hospital to tell the doctor that I was coming. She put me in a big wooden wheelchair and had one of the older girls push me to see the doctor.

He was waiting for me. He took one look at the knee and knew it would require stitches. He told me it would hurt a little. So I was prepared for a painful few minutes. Much to my surprise, when he started stitching the wound it didn't hurt at all. In fact, I chatted with him and watched the whole procedure. When he was done, he told me to stay off my feet and come back in ten days and he would remove the stitches and I would be as good as new.

When I got back to the cottage, I checked the calendar to see just when ten days was. I was surprised but delighted to see that it was on the day of the school's big spelling bee. I would just plan to be at the hospital all morning.

On the morning of the spelling bee, I headed straight for the hospital. By now I had gotten pretty good at pushing this big old wooden wheelchair around the campus, so I didn't need anyone to go with me. As I was passing the recreation hall where the event was getting underway, I looked up only to see the principal of the school. She told me I was headed in the wrong direction that the spelling bee was to begin in a few minutes. I replied that I was ***so sorry*** I had to miss it, but I had a doctor's appointment at the hospital to have the stitches taken out of my knee. She had to let me off the hook. My plan worked that time.

By the end of the fourth grade I was doing quite well in my studies. The only real problem was that the teacher taught me to print using all upper-case letters, and it took me forever to do my homework. For some unknown reason I was never taught cursive writing. My papers always looked so sloppy no matter how much time I spent on them. I could knit and I could sew. But I just could not write legibly. This problem did not change very much over the years, even though I did teach myself cursive writing a couple of years later. It did help some, but not all that much.

I had successfully completed the fifth grade. My parents knew I was very unhappy at school. I hated living in C-4. I was not getting along with most of the girls and I avoided the matrons as much as possible. I followed the daily routine of eating, studying and sleeping, and that was the extent of my day. There was no recreation. And the only time I was allowed to leave the campus at all was on Sundays when my parents came to take me for ride and on school vacations when I went home. At home I went to Mass at Holy Family Church and took the bus with the neighborhood children to the movie theater in Plymouth on Saturdays. I would sometimes walk to a friend's house, and sometimes I stayed for lunch if she was having something I liked. If she wasn't, I often invited her back to my house where I could make something we both liked. I often visited the lady who lived just up the hill, or the one who lived about a five minute walk through our back woods. Some Sundays Patty Glass and I walked to the Miramar, a nearby seminary, to attend church. After the service we would wander to the back of the church to pay a visit to the monkey that was kept there. Then we would go to the small grotto and light a couple of candles. The grotto had two entrances. The upper one had very steep stone steps leading to the beautiful little altar, and the only light was from the candles. I guess God was watching over me. I never had an accident on these steps. One summer Nana Morgan had rented a cottage on Mullens Ave, also in Duxbury. I often took the short cut through the woods across the street from our house to get there. Sometimes my mother would send me on ahead to tell Nana to be ready in an hour if we were going off somewhere for the afternoon. Or maybe I was to ask Nana and my Uncle Philip, who is two years younger than I, to join us for supper.

One summer when I was about twelve, Philip came to spend several weeks with us. Nana Morgan was quite ill and spent a lot of time in and out of the hospital. Philip and I got along very well together most of the time. Sometimes Mother would let us walk through the woods to the beach on Landing Road when the tide was in. At low tide this beach was a mud flat and not very suitable for swimming. Sometimes Mother would pack a lunch and drive us to Duxbury Beach. At this beach it didn't really matter much whether it was high tide or not. There was a bay side and an outside beach here. The water was much warmer on the bay side so sometimes we would start our day here and stay until the tide got too low and the mud flats started to emerge. At this point we would pack up our things and cross over the narrow strip of sand dunes to the outside beach. The water was much colder here. But we kids didn't seem to mind it. We had to walk quite a distance to get to the water. Once in the water, especially on the incoming tide, we had to be very careful not to get caught on a sand bar as neither of us could swim. The water between the sand bar and the beach could rise very quickly and be over our heads. I always was, and still am, afraid of being over my head and not being able to touch bottom. I never want to be any more than waist deep. I think I never learned how to swim because of my fear of the water. I can

Philip and Me

float on my back but I don't feel at all safe doing that.

Later on in my life, I attended a swimming class in Norfolk. The instructor was determined that we were all going to pass the class. On the last day we were required to use the deep end of the pool. I was terrified. When my turn came, I froze. The instructor had to get into the pool with me. I didn't want to let go of the ladder. Somehow she got me into a floating position and let go of me long enough to pass the class. I never went near the deep end of *any* pool after that.

One day while Phil was with us, he and I were playing with beanbags on the back porch. It was a rainy day and I guess we ran out of things to do indoors. He accidentally bumped into me and I fell against the porch railing breaking open one of the boils I had on my thighs. This hurt. I screamed and picked up the nearest thing I could lay my hands on, which was a hammer, and started after Phil, who by now was at the other end of the porch. He was about to come after me with a brick. Mother heard the commotion and came running to our rescue. She told Phil to go sit in the sun parlor and read a book while she tended to my oozing boil. She kept us separated until supper time. She knew I needed time to calm down from the incident. It took most of the summer to get rid of all the boils. Once they cleared up I never had any more.

None of these things were possible at school. The only places I was permitted to go was to school and back to my cottage. I once wandered down to the barn to see the cows, pigs and chickens, and I was caught. I was grounded for a week and sent to bed right after supper with no radio to take the curse off the punishment.

At the beginning of the summer vacation of 1949 I told my mother that *I was not* returning to *that* school in September. I had said this many times before and my mother had ignored these remarks. But this time there was something in my voice that she could not shake off. She knew the time had come to think about another school placement. She was very much against sending me to the public school even though she knew all the teachers from working in the public school cafeteria. As a last resort, she went to see the parish priest, Father Manning to see if he had any ideas. He told her of a new Catholic school that was opening up in September in Plymouth. The classes would be very small, six to ten students to a room. Some of them would be boarding at the school and transportation would be provided for all the others who needed it. He told my mother to go home and think about it, and if it was something she and my father thought I could handle, to let him know and he would arrange for Mother Superior to come to talk to my parents.

My mother said nothing to me about trying to find another school for fear that if things didn't work out she knew I would be very upset about it.

My mother knew first hand that I would be getting a good education in a parochial school, but she was worried that I would fall behind and get discouraged.

My father, on the other hand, felt that the competition would be good for me. He told my mother that she could not shelter me from the big world forever. I had to learn to face the real world sooner or later. And if I failed at something, I would have to pick up the pieces and move on.

One afternoon in early August, two nuns came to the house. Mother sent me outside while they talked. I had no idea why the nuns were there. The only nuns I knew taught catechism after church service on Sundays. In a few minutes, my mother called me in and told me to have a seat and listen carefully to what the sisters had to tell me. She introduced them by name, and they talked with me for a few minutes. Then my mother asked me how I would like them for my teachers. I still had no idea what she was talking about, until one of the sisters said "You will be coming to our new school in Plymouth. We will be picking you up on the Wednesday after Labor Day." I turned to my mother and asked if what I just heard was true. I didn't need any reply. When my father came home from work that evening, I couldn't wait to tell him all about the afternoon's event. I was so excited I could hardly talk, and he could hardly make out my words. He and I sat on the back porch talking until Mother called us in for supper. He told me that he and Mother had been working on a plan to bring me home from boarding school for almost a year. He said that my mother was against putting me in public school because she knew how cruel other children could be, and she didn't want to expose me to that. But when they heard of the new Catholic school in the area, they thought the nuns would have a better way of handling the children should such a bad situation occur.

When I asked my mother for some new clothes for school, she told me I wouldn't need any because all the children would be fitted for uniforms as soon as school started. The only thing I needed was new shoes.

When I finally brought the uniform home about two weeks after the start of the school year, my mother was delighted because we both knew what I had to wear every day and it saved a lot of time in the morning. All of us girls wore navy blue skirts and matching pullover vests made of wool, and white short sleeve cotton blouses, navy blue wool knee-high socks, a red cardigan sweater for cooler days, and navy blue berets which we wore when we all filed to St. Peter's Church for Mass every first Friday of the month.

I had one uniform with four blouses in the two years I was there. Mother kept the skirt and vest cleaned and pressed. These were sent to the dry cleaner's during Christmas and Easter breaks. My socks were darned at least once before they were discarded because I wore holes in the toes or heels.

I had a very long day. Classes began at nine o'clock. I was one of the first to be picked up in the morning. I remember having to ride all the way to Marshfield to pick up a couple of girls before picking up more girls on the other side of Duxbury on the way to Plymouth. I had been riding about one and a half hours before I even got to school. Classes let out at three o'clock. I was one of the first to get home in the afternoon. Needless to say, I had no time for anything but homework. And I did have plenty of that. Most of us had not attended a Catholic school before now, and we had a lot of catching up to do. In most subjects we were a full grade behind. Most of us had not had much religious training either and we had to learn many of the everyday prayers almost over night.

Perhaps the most difficult for me was learning English grammar. I had no writing skills at all when I entered Sacred Heart School. So this was like trying to learn geometry without having learned the basic math skills. I spent most of my Saturdays just reviewing the lessons of the week until I was sure I knew what I was doing. Mother was a big help to me and spent many hours each week going over my lessons with me, making sure I learned what I was being taught.

I am most grateful for having had these lessens drilled into my brain. The nuns gave me a solid foundation to build on. And I took every opportunity to learn.

Sometime during the summer of 1951, my parents received a letter from Sacred Heart School telling them that I would no longer be attending classes there. The reason was never made clear to my parents. But I read between the lines. I just could not write well enough or fast enough to keep up with the rest of my class, and the sisters did not know how to handle the situation. When I was given written assignments during class time, I just didn't have enough time to complete the work and had to turn in half finished papers. What I did was right for the most part, but I rarely had time to finish anything. If I tried to hurry, my handwriting became very scribbly and impossible to read. I think the teachers saw this as a real problem, one to which they had no solution, and rather than try to work things out, they decided that they would just tell my parents that the classes were all filled up, and there was no room for me.

When the fall session of 1951 began, I still had no school placement. My mother was still working in the Duxbury school cafeteria and knew all the teachers and many of the students. She was very late getting home on the opening day of school. I thought she might have stopped to have tea with one of her co-workers so I didn't pay it any mind.

I was sitting on the back porch reading when she drove in and got out of the car. My mother then greeted me with a firm tone of voice and a half smile, saying "Arlene, you will catch that red and white school bus that goes by here every morning at 7:15." I was overjoyed. With tears streaming down my cheeks, we both went inside. Mother made a pot of tea and we sat at the kitchen table talking about why she was late getting home from work.

Mother told me that she had been to see the school superintendent, Dr. Everett Handy, early that morning to learn about how I could best continue my education at home. He told my mother that he saw no reason for home schooling if I could walk and climb a flight of stairs, which I could do quite well by holding onto a railing. He himself had a prosthetic leg and was very much aware of my mother's concerns about how the other students might be mean to me.

Dr. Handy met with the high school teachers in the teachers' room at lunchtime to tell them that I would be coming to school the next day. He told them of my mother's concerns. He told them that he was meeting with the principal, Rodney Wood, and my mother after lunch and together they would map out which classes I would take and which teachers I would have. He told them that if there was any trouble at all from either the teachers or the students, he would take strong disciplinary action against them, meaning that the teachers could lose their jobs or that the students could be suspended from school for a time.

I reported to Mr. Wood's office the next morning as I was instructed to do by my mother. We chatted for a few minutes about my courses and the reasons he had decided to put me a grade ahead in most of my classes. The reasons were that the parochial school was so far advanced in most of the subjects. I would be taking eighth grade math but everything else would be high school freshman classes.

Before he sent me to my home room, Mr. Wood called one of my new classmates, Rose Coffin, to the office, and asked her to show me around the campus and help me in the lunchroom. She and I would become good friends throughout high school and beyond.

I took home economics all four years of high school, not because it was an easy course to pass, but because I really enjoyed it. I liked to sew and cook and towards the end of the first year, I managed to master the electric sewing machine with the knee control. The foot control just did not work for me. My teacher, Mrs. Marston, must have had the patience of an angel. I learned to lay out patterns, but I just could not manage to use the scissors to cut them out. Either she or one of the other students did that for me, modern day reasonable accommodation, I guess.

These classes were held in a separate building from the rest of the high school. It was once a one room schoolhouse that had been moved there from the Island Creek section of town. It had a large kitchen which went the full length of the front of the building. It also had another very large room, part of which was partitioned off to resemble a living room with a sofa and a couple of easy chairs. This part of the room could also be converted into a dining area. Here we were taught proper etiquette, which was hardly ever used, but at least we knew how to set a table for a formal affair if we ever had to.

These classes also provided us with quite a lot of time to socialize and get to know each other. It is here that I met Diane Doyle, and we became lifelong friends. She, like me, had just transferred from another school. Because our school was so small and not many of us took home economics, all of the high school grades were grouped together to make one nice-sized class with no more than three or four from each grade. Diane and I stayed with the program all through high school.

I had one minor problem my first few days of school. It took me longer than three minutes to get from the home economics class to my English class. I had not one but two flights of stairs to climb and my class was at the far end of the building. And not only that, I had to wait at the foot of the stairs until all the students had come down before I started up because I needed the left hand railing for balance. My English teacher did not like it because I was always late for her class and she let me know it every time. After putting up with her for three weeks, I decided I had enough of her nasty remarks, and I asked to be excused from my previous class ten minutes early. I was in my English class seat before the room was even emptied. I could tell that she didn't like this either. But I didn't really care.

I was doing very well with very little effort and I really liked having so much free time to study what I wanted to learn. I remember one time when the class had to read ***A Tale of Two Cities*** from our literature book. When I discovered it was a condensed version I took it upon myself to read the full length novel my parents had. I compared the two books. I never read another condensed version of anything after that experience. They just were not the same as the original stories. I think I may have gotten some extra credit for this. I felt sorry for the rest of the class because they missed so much of Dickens's style. I had a hard time with the exam because I wanted to write in more details than the teacher required.

On the first day of my second year of high school it was discovered that the class had been given the wrong literature books the year before and we were about to read the same books over again. The teacher decided to try something different. She got permission to substitute the *Readers' Digest* for it. I think the whole class enjoyed that experience very much. I know I did.

During my sophomore year, I started going to all of the basketball games, most of which were played on Friday nights and did not interfere with my homework schedule. And my parents did not have to transport me either as the school provided all of us with a bus driver, Mr. Herrick Sr. He owned the garage that serviced all of the town's school buses. He not only drove us all home, he made sure we got in safely by driving us right to our door if we had a long walk in from the street. He always waited until I put the porch light out before continuing his route. It was a very small school and I knew all of the players and cheerleaders. Many of them were in my class. It gave me a sense of belonging, something I had not experienced before now. Until that time, I felt like an outsider trying to fit in somewhere. I still like basketball and I follow the women's college teams on television.

By now, I was spending a lot less time at the books and still doing quite well. For the next two years I made the Honor roll most of the time with very little effort. My parents seemed to be satisfied no matter how I did. I guess they thought I was doing my best and that was all they expected of me. Knowing how they felt made me more determined than ever to satisfy myself and nobody else. My classes were a combination of business and college courses, or what is known today as general studies.

I remember taking everyday law with Mr. Snipe. I found it very interesting and was doing well, making straight A's in it. But a month into the course, I noticed that all my homework papers were coming back marked with "A" with no corrections or comments on them. Because of this I suspected he wasn't reading my papers. And to prove my point, one day I passed in a paper with answers from the last chapter in the book. Sure enough, it came back the next day with a big letter "A" across the top of the paper.

I was very angry and wasted no time in letting him know that I would not tolerate such a thing. I didn't care if I embarrassed him in front of the whole class or not. I told him I wanted to earn my grades and did not expect them to be handed to me on a silver platter. I think I could have gotten him fired. But I gave him a second chance. Needless to say, I had no more trouble with that problem.

It wasn't until I got to high school that the school nurse, Miss Susan Carter, did a routine hearing test, and we realized that I had some very severe hearing problems. I could not hear softer sounds, I lacked sensitivity to higher-frequency sounds, and I had great difficulty recognizing different words and sounds.

Miss Carter told me that she didn't know how I had covered it up so well. She alerted all of my teachers and told them to make sure I took a front row seat in all of my classes. I always did this anyhow, so I didn't have to make any seating changes. None of my classmates ever knew that I had a hearing loss.

Miss Carter also recommended that I go for lip reading lessons. The school made all of the arrangements and my mother drove me to Brockton, a 45 minute ride one way, once a week for about ten weeks. By then, mother and I agreed that this was a waste of time as I had already been lip reading without realizing it for quite some time. I think we all do it to some degree. Besides that, hardly anyone ever spoke as slowly or as distinctly as this teacher did.

My senior year was very hard for me— not academically, but emotionally. While most of my classmates were preparing for college or to enter the work force after graduation, I could not make any plans for my future. I knew I had always wanted to become a teacher. But I also knew it required a college degree and my parents just could not have afforded the expense. I also knew that the Department of Rehabilitative Services (DRS) would not sponsor me because it considered me unemployable.

My parents wanted me to do something with my sewing skills and were hoping that I would set up a shop of some kind in town. There was already a fabric shop there, but I could not use scissors well enough to cut fabric to do alterations, so I could not see how this was going to work out for me. I told Mrs. Hendrick, my home economics teacher, that as much as I enjoyed sewing, I could not see myself spending the rest of my life seated at the sewing machine day in and day out. She knew what I meant. She knew I would become very bored with this very quickly. While I enjoyed sewing as a part time activity, it was not something I wanted to do, or could make a living at. She saw this when our class got the job of making the high school choir robes. Most of us were very happy to see this project come to an end.

Office work was out of the question as I did not have enough coordination in my fingers to type, and I still use one finger at a time, even on the computer keyboard. I think it is called "Hunt and Peck". I also tried using the adding machine but I had the same problem as I did with the typewriter. Worse, I kept losing my place when trying to add long columns of figures, and I hardly ever came up with the right answers. I became very frustrated with this one day and walked out of the room in tears, never to return to the adding machine again.

I remember when my senior class started planning its last get-together before graduation, a dinner party and a dance. I usually went along with whatever the class wanted to do. I just didn't go to the dances. I didn't much care what the students did after school hours.

But for some reason this time it bothered me that I was being left out. Out of the clear blue skies I said "Hey, you guys, I thought this was supposed to be a class outing. You all know I don't dance." All eyes turned to me in surprise. Mrs. Churchill, our home room teacher, was surprised too, and after a few seconds said "Yes, that is right. I think we all forgot that Arlene has a part in this class too". This is how we all got to go to Nantucket for our senior class outing.

A few days before graduation we had a dress rehearsal. I was so upset because no matter how hard I tried, I just could not keep my cap from falling off. I hated being the only one there without a cap.

Duxbury HS Grad 1955

When I got home that afternoon, I told my mother to take my father's new suit back to the store because I was not going to graduate. I threw my cap across the kitchen floor and it landed in the cat's milk.

She knew something had gone wrong at school. But she had no idea what it could be. She picked up the cap and wiped the soured milk off with a towel and we went into the living room. By then I had calmed down a little. Half in tears, I told her I just could not keep the bloody cap on my head and I was not going to be the only one not wearing one. She tried putting the thing on my head, but it just fell to our feet. I said, "Now you see what I mean". She spent an hour adjusting it to make it fit a little better. But nothing really helped much. Then, just as she was about to give up on it, she remembered something. She said "Do you remember the hats you wore to church as a little girl?" She took out some thin white elastic and said "Let's try this. It's going to have to be tight, but I think it will work." She took my cap from me and started sewing in a piece of elastic on one side. When she got it basted in place, she placed the cap on my head and pinned the elastic to the other side making several adjustments until at last I could parade around the house without the cap falling off. When we were both satisfied, she stitched it permanently. It was a little uncomfortable, but it **did** work. I think I had a red mark under my chin where the elastic had cut into me for about a week after graduation.

My First Subway Ride

During the summer when I was about fifteen was one of the very few times that I would spend at my Grandmother Morgan's. She was living on Hammond Street in Cambridge. It was just a few blocks from Harvard Square. It had rained for the first couple of days of my visit. My Uncle Phil was then thirteen and I was two years older. We were running out of things to do to pass the time of day. My grandmother decided that on the first warm, sunny day we got, she would pack lunches for the both of us and send us to the Boston Public Gardens (known as 'the Common'). Phil could take me on the swan boat. I had never done that before. I had read *The Ugly Duckling* many times and my mother had told me about the swan boat but never did get around to taking me there.

Phil and I set out on our adventure around 10:a.m. My grandmother told us we had to be back in time for supper. Phil asked me if I had ever ridden on the subway train. I told him that it would be my first time. He told me I would have to pay attention to where we were going because I was going to have to get us home for supper.

When we got to the subway entrance, he explained that we would be riding in the dark some of the time, and outside in daylight some of the time. I guess he didn't want me to get scared of the dark. My first impression of the station was that we were in one of the bomb shelters like I had seen in World War II movies of England. For a fifteen year old country girl it was a scary place. When we got to the platform, and before the train arrived, Phil told me that we would have to move quickly as soon as people got off and before the door closed. He more or less pushed me into the last car on the track and led us to the outside platform of the car. We rode underground in the dark from Harvard Square to Park Street, in what seemed like an eternity to me. It took maybe fifteen minutes. I was counting the stops so I would know where to get off on the return trip later. I was very happy to see the sign that read "Park Street" so we could get off the train. We made our way to The Boston Public Gardens. We went on the 'Swan Boat'–it was the first time I had ever ridden in it. The swan boat was driven by a 'paddle-wheel'. The wheel was turned by foot pedals–like on a bicycle.

Afterwards, we went over to the edge of the pond and had our bagged lunch. I don't think we ate much of our lunch. We fed it to the bird, one bite for me and one for the birds. I did manage to get us back to my grandmother's in plenty of time for supper.

I think it was during this visit that my grandmother took me to the Harvard Museum of Natural History to see the glass flowers. There are over 830 different plant species here. They are so life like. I remember the water lilies looked like they were freshly picked from our pond. This exhibit was crafted in Germany and I think it is the only one like it in this country.

Shoveling Snow

It started snowing on Saturday evening and continued until daybreak Sunday morning. My Uncle Herbie had come by with the big state snowplow sometime in the wee hours of the morning and plowed our long driveway out all the way to the garage.

Early that morning my father and I went out with the shovels to finish the job. We had to make a path from our back porch to the garage, and another from the front of the porch to the driveway, so I could get to the street to catch the bus for school the next morning.

We had just finished making the path to the garage. My father had cleared a space in front of the big doors large enough to swing them open. He had gone inside to fetch a bucket of rock salt and sand mix to spread at the head of the driveway so he and my mother would be able to get out the next morning to go to work. Just then, a car pulled into the yard, and a man got out and went in to see my father. I paid the man no mind and kept on shoveling the front path.

A few minutes later the man left. My father came over to me and said "I hope he gets stuck". I looked up at him in disbelief of his unkindly words. Then he told me why the man had come. He had come to tell my father that he was going to have him arrested and sent to the Plymouth County Jail for child abuse for *"Making your poor handicapped child shovel snow and God knows what else"*. My father told him that he **never** makes me shovel snow. I just enjoy doing it. And besides, it is good therapy, as it helps me with balance and strengthens my muscles. My father told the man to mind his own business.

The man did get stuck. His car wheels were just a-spinning, and he was dancing the Irish jig with the car. It took him a good fifteen minutes to get out of our yard and onto the street. My father and I laughed so hard our ribs hurt. After the man was out of sight, my father spread the rock salt and sand mixture at the head of the driveway. We never saw this man before and we never saw him again.

After Graduation

The summer after graduation my parents were planning to take me to a camp in the Catskill Mountains. The camp was for physically disabled children and adults. My parents thought it would be good for me to get away for a couple of weeks. The Kiwanis Club of Duxbury sponsored me for the two weeks.

The camp was run by a physical therapist and a speech therapist. One of the campers, Ruth Gardner, said to me one day "I think you need a little help with your speech and why don't you take advantage of it while you're here?" I made an appointment with the speech therapist that afternoon and it was discovered that I could not make the 'ch', 'sh', 's', 'z' and 'j' sounds properly. Part of this was due to the fact that I had never heard them. I was unaware that I had any problem with my speech until then and I learned that it was due to my hearing impairment.

That summer I learned to row a boat. I also learned to float on my back. The camp did not have a swimming pool at the time so we swam in a stream that was very cold because the water flowed down from the mountain. The weather was quite chilly in the morning when we first got up. We wore sweaters and light-weight jackets to breakfast. After breakfast we shed the jackets and an hour later we shed the sweaters and were in the water. At supper time we put on a sweater. After supper we had to put on our jackets. That is how quickly the mountain weather changes.

I met campers from all over New York and Massachusetts. One of the campers I met was Holly Shiffman of New York City. She and her mother lived in the Bronx. Her mother, Mrs. Shiffman, was director of United Cerebral Palsy of New York at one time. Holly had cerebral palsy and was also legally blind. She worked with her mother in the cerebral palsy office doing the filing. She also attended the Institute for the Crippled and Disabled, as did many of the other campers. Holly told me about some of the activities and programs at the institute. One of which was to provide medication intended to provide better coordination and improve mobility and speech. The next year I saw the great improvements of some of the campers and wanted to participate in the program myself. I had talked to my parents about it many times so they were aware of this program, but could not see any way I could participate in this program as it was in New York City and I lived in Massachusetts. Holly came to my rescue and told me she would ask her mother if she could bring me home so I could be evaluated at the institute. I wasted no time in accepting her generous offer. So for the next seven months I would stay with Holly and her mother in order to go through the program. I was given a battery of tests and evaluations to determine how they could best help me. They were experimenting with the drug Soma at the time. I was put on this medication and supervised very carefully by the institute's nurse. My speech improved somewhat as did my hand coordination.

I had a good time working on the Christmas pageant for the institute. I was the writer and director for the play. It was more work than I had bargained for, but, in the end, it was worth it. It was at this time I realized that I could be a 'leader' and not just a 'follower'. In high school I was pretty much just a 'wall flower'.

While I was staying with Holly in the Bronx, Holly's friend, Fran Gould—who also had cerebral palsy— decided that we should go to Chinatown for dinner one night. She picked us up and drove us there. It was very cold that night. We had to park the car on the Bowery and walk quite a distance to the restaurant. We had a very nice dinner and when we came out we decided to go window shopping before we went back home. It was about 10:00 pm when we got back to the car. We got in the car and the car wouldn't start. We discovered we had a dead battery. Fran and Holly were going to call for help at a pay phone. But I spoke up and said "You are not going to leave me here alone!" So we all went to call for help. By this time it was 11: pm. Holly decided to call her mother and say that we were at Fran's home in Flushing, Long Island, so not to worry about us, that we would be spending the night there. But it was more like 1:30am before we finally got to Fran's house. We did not want her mother to know that we got stuck on the Bowery.

Another incident in New York City was when Holly and I had separate dates. I went to a minstrel show and I don't remember where Holly went. I had to take the subway home from the show. It was about 11 pm. I got in the subway, looked around and, lo and behold, who should I sit next to but Holly. She didn't recognize me because of her poor eyesight until I spoke. Then we had a great laugh and walked home together so we wouldn't have to pay for a taxi.

A group of disabled people went out one Saturday to see an off-Broadway play "Man of LaMancha." After the play about twenty of us went to a Manchurian restaurant for lunch. Each of us ordered a different dish and shared it with the rest of the group. We really had a chance to sample each of the foods. No one ordered the same thing. We had such a marvelous time.

My parents came down to visit me. They stayed at a hotel in Manhattan. My mother had a high school friend in New Jersey whom she wanted to visit. My parents came and got me and we went to the subway. My mother saw the subway train coming and ran to board it, but the door closed before my Dad and I could get on board. We were all supposed to get off at the George Washington Bridge station. We didn't know whether she would just get off at the next station, or go to the George Washington Bridge station. We boarded the next train, thinking mother may have gotten off at the next stop. But she hadn't. My father and I decided we would go back to the hotel and wait for my mother to come back. My mother had gone right to the George Washington Bridge station, where she got off. She found her friend she was going to see and then they waited for the next few trains hoping to find my dad and me. But when she didn't, she and her friend called Holly's mother to see if she had heard from us, which she had. Holly's mother relayed the message that we had gone back to the hotel. Mother had dinner with her friend and then made the trip back to Manhattan alone. I'm sure she was scared to death, so when she got to Manhattan she took a taxi back to the hotel.

I really am so thankful to have had the opportunity to attend the institute. It taught me to be independent of my parents. I will forever be grateful to my friend Holly and her mother for making this possible for me.

Every Saturday another friend of mine from the institute and myself would go out to dinner trying different cuisines. One day we went to a Japanese restaurant. We sat on red cushions on the floor. The food was brought to us and cooked in front of us. They offered us chopsticks. Can't you just picture me trying to work chopsticks?! Holly and I used to shop at Macy's Basement for clothes, but I decided I wanted to try something different so I went to Saks Fifth Avenue where I bought my first expensive dress, $25.00. That was a lot of money back in the 50's. It was a navy blue and white polka dot dress with a bolero jacket. When

I went back home my mother asked me if I was a millionaire! I wore that dress for about twenty years. It more than paid for itself.

That spring before I returned home to my parents, I decided I wanted to see Washington, D.C. I asked Fran Gould to come with me, but for some reason she had to back out. So I decided to go by myself. I bought a round trip bus ticket from New York to Washington knowing that on my return I had to make train connections from New York to Boston. When I got to Boston, I then had to catch the 4:30pm train to Kingston, where my father was scheduled to meet me a few days later. I hadn't told him of this latest adventure, so making connections was a must.

I stayed at the Harrington Hotel because it was inexpensive. Its location didn't really matter much to me then. I was young–23– and foolish. But I had a great four days touring the city, mostly on foot. I went to all the usual government buildings, including the Capitol. When I got there, I was in luck because the Senate was in session and winding down for the day. The security guard asked me who my senator was and I told him John F. Kennedy. "Would it be possible for me to meet him?" I asked, expecting him to tell me the senator was too busy for visitors. But he told me to sit down and wait a few minutes, and he left.

Much to my surprise and delight, he returned with the senator. I stood up and we exchanged greetings. We both sat on the bench and casually chatted for about fifteen minutes. That was so many years ago that I don't recall the whole conversation. But I must have told him that I wanted to become a teacher, but nobody would give me a chance. I remember what he told me. "You will get there by climbing the ladder one rung at a time." And that I did! When I got to Kingston, I was exhausted, but very excited. I couldn't wait until I got to my parents to tell them of my latest adventure. I had been up since 3 am in order to make all my connections. At dinner that evening I talked nonstop for an hour. When I told them I had even got to talk to Senator Kennedy, their mouths fell open. I was only twenty-three at the time and knew very little about politics or even what role a senator played in state and national government.

The following summer I was invited to spend a week with a girl I had met at camp the previous summer. Veronica Byers and I had been pen pals throughout the year. She lived in Montreal, Canada with her parents. My parents, especially my mother, were very reluctant to let me go as it was just too far for me to travel alone. And they weren't about to drive me all the way to Montreal. Finally I told them that I had been saving money all year and I now had enough to cover my air fare and I was going anyway. My father knew there was no stopping me once my mind was made up. He reminded my mother of my trip to Washington, D.C. alone and how I managed just fine.

The plan was that I would fly to Montreal the week before I was to go to camp and Ronnie's parents would drive both of us to camp. Then I would fly home from Albany, NY. My plan worked out well.

I spent a wonderful week with Ronnie and her parents. Ronnie had been attending classes at a day-care center for disabled adults in the city. I spent one day following her around to all of her classes and exploring all of the other activities the center had to offer its clients.

One day Ronnie and her family took me on a tour of the city. We paid a visit to the beautiful Shrine of Saint Joseph's Oratory. It was built on top of Mount Royal and overlooked the whole city. This view was so breathtaking. That was the only time I have been to Montreal, and it is a place I have always wanted to return to some day.

By now I started spending a lot of time with my friend from high school, Diane Snider. She was now married and had two little boys and another baby on the way. She and her husband Johnny were living within walking distance of me so I didn't have to rely on someone with wheels to get there. There was just one problem. One of the families on Soule Avenue had a 'not so friendly' dog. It came at me every time I tried to pass the house and the owner had to call it back to its yard. One late afternoon while I was on my way home, the dog came at me and before its owner could call the dog to the yard, it had a hold of the leg of my slacks and had torn them all the way from the hip to the heel before the lady came to my rescue. The lady brought me to the house and sewed up my slacks well enough to get me home.

My father had had enough of my complaining and he and the chief of police went to have a talk with the family. The family was told to keep the dog tied at all times. I later learned that the dog had been sent to some relatives who had a large farm in New Hampshire where it could roam freely, and therefore so could I.

On nice days I often took one of the boys for a walk in his carriage. We sometimes went back to my house for lunch if I had Rusty, the older of the two boys. He was then two years old. If my mother was home and saw us coming down the back road, she pulled out a few toy trucks and cars I kept in a box in the sun parlor closet for him. My mother enjoyed Rusty as much as I did and played with him while I got lunch. I am in tears as I write this story and you will find out why later.

After Diane moved to Depot Street I still spent a lot of time with her. But since it was a little too far for me to walk either my mother drove me or Diane would come for me. I would help feed, bathe and dress the children. Sometimes Diane needed to run a few errands, and she would put the children down for a nap and make sure they were asleep before she left me with them. After she left I always checked in on them every few minutes to make sure they were OK. I remember one day checking in on them and finding Davie missing. My heart skipped a beat when I called him and he didn't answer me. I had been in the kitchen washing dishes and couldn't see how he could have gotten out without my seeing him. I searched every corner of the house and finally found him way back in the bedroom closet sound asleep with his little blanket covering him. I left him there until Diane came home. She lifted him out of the closet and put him back to bed. If this had happened today, I think I would have panicked knowing about all the kidnappings that are taking place. I enjoyed taking Rusty for walks in the stroller. He behaved so well for me. On day I needed to go to Hall's Corner and I took him with me. I got what I needed in the 5 &10. But before I got to the register, Rusty eyed a big bright red fire truck on the top shelf and he wanted it. I had to think quickly about how I was going to pacify him. Then I remembered that the fire station was just around the corner and my father and the fire chief, Ebon Briggs, were good friends.

I told Rusty I would take him to the fire house and maybe Chief Briggs would let him sit in the driver's seat of a ***real*** fire truck.

When we got to the fire house, Chief Briggs was having lunch. I told him that this little child would like to change places with him. He showed Rusty the fireman's boots and put a fireman's hat on him. The hat was so big it covered Rusty's whole face. We all laughed.

When we got back home, Diane didn't have to ask what took us so long. Rusty was so excited that he got to "drive" a real fire truck.

Years later, when I reminded Diane of this story, she said "Only you could have come up with that one."

At some point, I started to attend some social functions of Cerebral Palsy of Greater Boston, some of which were held at nighttime. On such rare occasions I had to make arrangements to spend the night with someone either from the organization or with my aunt and uncle who lived on a subway line. Many times I spent the night with Edith Schnyder, the director of the organization. She also had cerebral palsy and was married, with two beautiful little girls. We went to night clubs, the Ice Capades, and hockey games at the Boston Gardens, just to mention a few of the things that we did.

It was through this organization that I learned about a program at Emerson College on Beacon Street in Boston. It had a speech and hearing clinic. I never knew whether the clinic was sponsored by the college or in part by the cerebral palsy organization, but it didn't cost me anything to participate in the program. After many months of speech and auditory training, the audiologist in charge of the program and the speech therapist who had been working with me decided that I could benefit from the use of a hearing aid. My teacher worked with me for two or three months training me to use one before I was allowed to use it permanently. Then at last, the day came when the therapist said to me "It's yours to keep". She pinned the little square box to the inside of my clothes, connected the wire to the ear piece, and adjusted the volume to where I could hear her talk in a normal tone of voice. She gave me instructions on how I was to use it for the next week. I was **not** to change the volume and I **was** to wear it from the time I got up in the morning until I went to bed at night. My brain needed time to adjust to all of the new sounds I would be hearing, some for the first time, and others with much amplification.

That afternoon when I left that little cubicle I had been training in for months, I entered a whole new world of sounds. Nothing could have prepared me for that first train ride from the South Station to Kingston. When the whistle blew, it startled me so badly I almost fell off my seat. The hour's ride to Kingston seemed like ten. The roar of the train's engine was almost unbearable. By the time I reached my destination, my head was spinning and I thought I was ready for the nuthouse. I had a headache for two days

I was very jumpy and irritable for about a week. I kept telling my parents to **stop shouting** at me and to turn the TV **down**. Every time my mother closed a kitchen cupboard door or rattled pots and pans,

I was startled by the noise. But after a few days we all adjusted to my hearing aid and things began to return to normal.

When I returned to the therapist the next week, I told her everything that had happened during the week. She was surprised but very pleased that I had carried out her instructions so well.

Some people with hearing impairments, particularly senior citizens, do not do justice to themselves and their hearing aids end up in a drawer unused. I still get lost in a crowd, and I don't like **loud** music. But aside from that, I do pretty well.

My First Teaching Job

I had been attending classes sponsored by Cerebral Palsy of the South Shore Area, Inc. The classes were held one evening a week at the Furnace Brook School. They were for adults with cerebral palsy and other disabilities. The director of the program was a lady by the name of Mrs. Dube, (pronounced Du-bay). She taught a painting class. Also teaching there was Marian Richards, who taught basic reading and math, and Mrs. Dixon who taught rug hooking. I don't remember who taught ceramics but it was one of the classes I enjoyed.

Whenever my work was done for the evening, I would wander over to Mrs. Richards' group and ask her if I could help with one or more of her students. She was very happy to let me assist her. She would tell me to help this one with reading or that one with math.

There was time for a social gathering at the end of the evening after clean up. Sometimes we had refreshments and sometimes we just sat around and chatted and got to know each other.

One day Mrs. Richards telephoned me. I was still living at home with my parents at this time. She said she wanted to come for an afternoon visit. She wanted to talk to me and my mother about something. She wouldn't tell me what she had in mind, but I knew from the tone of her voice that it was very important.

When she arrived the next day, I had afternoon tea ready and we went to the living room. As it turned out, this was to be the most important tea hour of my life.

Mrs. Richards told us that the cerebral palsy organization was going to open a nursery school very soon and she wanted to know if I would be interested in helping out there when it was opened. I didn't have to answer the question. We all knew that I would never turn down this offer.

The project had been on the drawing board for some time. Helen M. Smith, herself a mother of a young boy with cerebral palsy, saw the need for a preschool program. Her son was enrolled in a special education class for children of school age with cerebral palsy. This class was held in the Furnace Brook School where our adult classes were held. She felt that there was a need for a preschool program, since these very young children were being denied the opportunity of an early childhood education, therefore causing further developmental, social and educational delays. Most disabled children were kept at home with little or no contact with other children at all until they reached school age, and then only if the school system could or would accept them. This program would be known as the CP Nursery School to all the communities that supported it, even after it was renamed 'The Helen M. Smith Nursery School', after its founder.

This new program was to be located in the VFW Hall in Quincy. Mrs. Alice Solari was hired as its first teacher. She taught piano from her home and had a private kindergarten. The nursery school opened with eight children, all under age of eight and with varying degrees of mental and physical disabilities. The children were all screened by the staff at the clinic, which was operated by the cerebral palsy organization. The children would receive physical, occupational, and speech therapy once a week, if needed, from the clinic's staff. The children's therapy was then carried over into the school program whenever possible by either Mrs. Solari or me. This was a lot of work and progress was sometimes very slow, even with our carry-over. It meant a lot of extra work on our part, but it would make a big first step toward a better life for the many children who would pass through these doors over the next few years,

The first couple of months of my working in Quincy put a real strain on my mother. It was summertime, and she was taking care of my twin cousins whose mother had passed away unexpectedly just a few weeks prior to my getting this job. She had to drive me to Quincy, a 45 minute drive each way. There was no public transportation from Duxbury to Quincy at that time and I am not sure whether there is any to this day. I had to be at work by 9:00 am, and picked up again at 3:00 pm. She was spending three hours out of each day on the road. The twins were not yet six years of age. When she got home from bringing me to work, she packed a lunch and took the boys to the beach for a couple of hours on sunny days. Then she had to put them back in the car for the trip back to Quincy to pick me up at 3:00 pm. By the time we got home, it was time to start supper. We ate our evening meal when my father got home from work, usually around 5:30.

My job was to keep an eye on the boys until supper time. They were very tired from all the riding and they fought a lot. They also got into things they shouldn't have and did things that were dangerous, like the time they set fire to the woods in our back yard. Mother and I were able to put it out before the firemen got there. The firemen gave the boys a long talking-to.

Getting the boys to bed at night was a real hassle. As long as they were with us, they slept upstairs in my parents' bed and my parents slept on the hide-a-bed in the living room. Sometimes my father had to use harsh words if they got too unruly. He would never have hurt them, but his voice was enough to get them to settle down.

I don't remember just how long the twins were with us. Mother was trying to convince my Uncle Richard to hire a live-in housekeeper so his children could all stay together. There was also a baby girl, age two– my Aunt Mary was caring for her. Aunt Mary had a large family and one more just meant another one to love.

My Uncle Richard had made up his mind to turn all three children over to the State. We were all very upset about this. My Aunt Mary really wanted to adopt the little girl, but my uncle would have no part of this. I never saw any of these children after that summer until they were adults, when I met Ricky and his wife and daughter once when they visited my mother.

Driving me to and from work every day just could not continue indefinitely, and we all knew it. Either I was going to have to find someplace to live where I would be nearer my workplace, or I was going to have to give up my job. I was heartsick. I had a real job and I was going to keep it. I contacted the cerebral palsy office in Quincy and told the director, Mr. Ciampa, about my situation. A few days later, Mr. Ciampa came to see me at work. He had talked to Mrs. Richards and she had an idea she thought I would like. He didn't tell me what it was. I was to phone her when I got home that evening. This was on Friday. At dinner I told my father what Mr. Ciampa had told me that afternoon. He handed me the phone and said "Get with it!" Mrs. Richards and I talked for a long time. My parents were sitting at the kitchen table listening to our conversation. Mrs. Richards would tell me what she had in mind and I would repeat to my parents what she was telling me. Finally, when things were pretty much settled, I handed the phone to my father. He was grinning from ear to ear. When he hung up, he turned to me and said "See, Pet, I told you everything would work out eventually."

The agreement was that I would board with the Richards family during the week. I would occupy the upstairs bedroom, and share the rest of the house. I would have breakfast and supper with the family. All this for fifteen dollars a week!

My parents would drive me to the Richards' home on Sunday afternoon and usually my father would pick me up when he got finished work on Friday. He almost always had jobs in one of the neighboring towns, but when he couldn't my mother would come for me when I got in from work. This was to be my home away from home for the next four or five years.

I no longer had to worry about getting to and from work. The person that transported the children also transported me to and from work.

I began taking on more teaching responsibilities. I hadn't been there very long when I saw the need for individualized instruction. I talked to Mrs. Solari about it and asked her if she minded if I took some of the children and worked with them one on one. She thought that was a good idea. So it was set up so that she would do most of the speech therapy through music and I would start working on a reading readiness program.

Working in the VFW Hall meant the teaching staff would have to set up the room on Monday morning before the children arrived. This meant hauling out tables and chairs, cots for rest period, toys and whatever other teaching materials we had acquired, either through public donations or bought with funds from UCP. Everything would have to be put back in storage on Friday before we left. And if there was some function going on after-hours during the week, everything would have to go back into storage before we left at 3:00 pm, and be dragged out again the next morning. As time went on, we acquired more teaching materials and equipment. Juggling things around in the small storeroom became a real hassle. I hadn't been on the job very long before I saw the need for individualized instruction in activities of daily living skills. It was agreed that I would take one student at a time and get him started on a program that would best meet his needs and capabilities. I began working with Stephen, Ronnie, and Jimmy on number and letter recognition, counting pennies and matching them to the numbers. I bought or made most of my own teaching materials to meet the needs of each child. I acquired an old *Dick and Jane* book and that was what I used to introduce reading to these three little boys. And would you believe it, I still have this book tucked away in a drawer after forty years.

The nursery school began getting a lot of publicity from the local newspapers. It was a pilot project and relied heavily on donations raised through United Fund and the forty-five cities and towns that UCP of the South Shore Area served. It is a known fact that if people can see where their money is going, and especially when it comes to helping young children, they will contribute to the cause more generously.

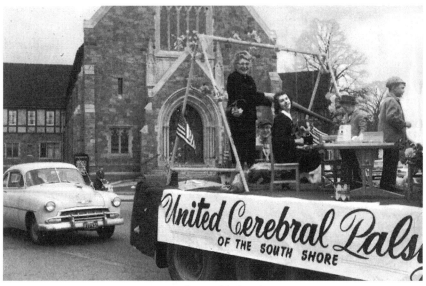

United Cerebral Palsy

During my first year of teaching at the nursery school in Quincy, Alice Solari, my coworker, got permission from our boss Arthur Ciampa to enter a float into one of the community parades. Mrs. Richards, Alice and I spent the whole day before the parade decorating it. We used some of the outdoor play equipment from the nursery school as well as the children's tables and chairs from inside. Mrs. Richards loaned us a small loom from the adult program. We got permission from a couple of the children's parents to let them participate in the event. One of the little boys loved to "conduct" the band at school. He surely showed off his talent to all the parade goers that day.

When Ronnie Chaisson was transferred to Furnace Brook School, where he was integrated into the first grade, I was credited for starting him off on the right foot. He really liked the individualized lessons I had prepared for him daily. I think it made him feel pretty special. I remember how he loved to conduct the band during music sessions. He surely was good at it!

One day Stephen came out of the bathroom with his pants hanging half-off. He asked me to do up the buckle on his pants' belt. I did it for him for the last time. I then called Ronnie over, took both boys into the bathroom, undid both belts and told them to buckle them back up themselves. Ronnie, as I knew, had no trouble doing his, even though, like Stephen, he could use only one hand. I watched carefully. Then it came to me that one of the boys was right-handed and the other one was left-handed, but the belt was put on going in the same direction for both boys. I would just turn the belt around to the girl's side, and after a little practice, Stephen was able to do up his own pants' belt buckle. It was just one more step toward independence.

When Mr. Ciampa applied for state funding for the nursery school, he was denied on the grounds that there was no certified teacher at the school. He knew how well things were going at the moment, but he also knew how expensive this pilot project was becoming. He had no alternative but to find a solution, which meant that he would have to comply with the state's requirements and find a state certified teacher to replace Mrs. Solari. It didn't seem to matter about how good a job she was doing. She didn't have a teaching degree, and he had to let her go.

The teacher who replaced Mrs. Solari had never taught disabled children before now, and was looking to me for assistance. I just pretended not to know anything and continued to work as though she wasn't there. I was very resentful toward her and I think she knew it.

When Mr. Ciampa came in one day, he asked me how things were going. I told him I was there to teach the children, not to train a teacher. He understood what I meant and shook his head.

I don't know whether or not we were asked to leave the VFW Hall. But before the end of that school year he told Elaine Hanson, the other assistant, and me that when we returned to work in the fall, we would be in a new location, and we would be getting a new teacher. He told us that we would be in a church in Weymouth and we would share several Sunday school classrooms and the kitchen. Nothing could have pleased us more.

We were pretty tired of having to pack up all of our equipment and supplies every Friday and haul them out again on Monday and sometimes during the week if there were VFW functions at night. By now we had acquired many supplies. I kept my reading readiness materials in a box and made sure the box got put in the storeroom last so I could get at it. The room was so small and jam-packed that we didn't even know what we had. As usual, that summer I spent time with my parents. I began working on the cerebral palsy fund-raising drive. I covered all of the Island Creek area of Duxbury as well as Tinkertown. We always had an early supper at our house, and I knew that after I had eaten was a good time to catch people at home. Sometimes my mother would drive me to the furthest point and I would work my way home on foot. Some of the people would invite me in for a chat over a cold drink or dessert so I really didn't cover very many houses in one evening. Sometimes it took three evenings just to cover ten houses.

The one lady I always loved to chat with was Mrs. Chase, who was a retired school teacher. When I was a little girl, she would invite all the neighborhood children to watch movies in her big barn. After the movies, she served us hot chocolate and homemade donuts. This was a real treat back in the early 'forties'.

Mrs. Chase also reminded me of how my father would put up her flagpole every spring and take it down every fall until the woodpeckers had taken one too many meals from it.

For me, the cerebral palsy drive wasn't about how much money I collected, as much as it was keeping in touch with the town's people. I loved that!

That summer I spent a lot of time at the beach with my parents. Friends of theirs had a cottage at the far end of Duxbury Beach, known as Saquish Point. It was actually a part of Plymouth, but the only way to get there was a seven-mile ride over the sand dunes from Duxbury Beach in my father's jeep or by boat across the bay. There was no electricity and no telephones. It was just so quaint and restful. My parents and I spent many weekends there with Verna and Charlie Schwab. When we first started going there, there was no running water. It had to be hand pumped and I never got the hang of that. Verna, Mother and sometimes Linda Putnam, Verna's granddaughter, and I would play Bridge on the front porch in the evenings until we could no longer see the numbers on the cards. Eventually Charlie installed a generator, so they were able to have lights and running water. I slept on the front porch, and at high tide I could hear the waves beating up against the stone wall just a few feet from the cottage. I remember one day while riding over the sand dunes, my father hit a pothole. I was riding in the back, and I was sitting on the storage box my father had built for the jeep. When he hit the pothole, I went flying off my seat and landed across my mother's lap. She was seated in the bucket seat next to my father. My father asked if I was OK. I replied "Yeah, but I popped a button on my shorts." We all laughed, and when we got to the cottage, I sewed the button back on my shorts.

In August of that summer, I once again headed for Martha's Vineyard to work at Camp Freedom. You, my readers, will learn more about this camp in a later chapter.

By September of 1961 I was really looking forward to getting back to teaching. Once again I would be boarding with Mr. and Mrs. Richards and their extended family. Mrs. Richards had her elderly brother-in-law and his sister living with us and of course their son Bob, who was also afflicted with cerebral palsy. He could walk but with much difficulty and his speech was sometimes hard to understand. We were one big happy family.

Mrs. Richards had been teaching weaving at the cerebral palsy adult class on Thursday evenings. She had acquired one big floor loom and several table ones. It wasn't long before I was also weaving on all of them. Setting them up with patterns was no easy task. Sometimes it took the two of us a couple of days to do the big one. Weaving became one of my favorite pastimes while I was living there.

We all liked to do jigsaw puzzles, especially the 1,000 piece ones. A card table was set up in the living room and there was always a puzzle on it waiting to be finished. I was hardly ever around to put in the last few pieces. One night I decided to fix this. I put two pieces in my pocket before I went upstairs to bed. The next morning when I came down for breakfast, I headed straight for the puzzle and said, "There, at last, I put the last piece in!" Everyone just laughed.

The nursery school opened on September 11th, in its new location. It would run for forty weeks and would pretty much follow the public school's calendar. I would again ride to work with the driver who picked up the children who lived in my area. Our new location wasn't very far from where I was living, so I was the last one to be picked up in the morning and the first to be dropped off in the afternoon. I really liked this arrangement because I had decided to try my hand at continuing my own education while teaching. I had heard that college was very hard. But how would I know if I didn't try? I don't remember why I selected Lesley College in Cambridge. My first course had to do with teaching mentally disabled children. I would take a bus to Ashmont Station and the subway train to either Central or Harvard Square and walk the rest of the way. My class was from 4 to 7:p.m, one day a week. I got home a little before 10: p.m.

I remember thinking to myself when I looked at my grade, a B+, at the end of the course "Hey! What was so difficult about that?" I think I took two or three more courses there after that.

The Second Universalist Church at 94 Pleasant Street in South Weymouth was like working in heaven when compared to the VFW Hall. I continued to prepare the children's lunches, most of which were made with government surplus food, and they didn't take very long to fix.

My work became so much easier now that we had the use of several small rooms and our supplies were stored on shelves. We no longer had to work out of boxes. Puzzles, toys, books, and other teaching supplies were readily available to the children as well as to the staff.

By this time, Rosalyn Berkowitz, a young lady who also had cerebral palsy, had joined the nursery school team. I was able to give her some of my chores, leaving me with more time for individualized instructions with the children. Roz could play the piano and the children just loved this. She also read to them during rest time. This freed me so I could join Joyce Campbell, the head teacher, and Elaine for a lunch-break. Roz was a big help in getting the children ready to go home, especially in the winter months when they had to wear snow pants, coats, scarves, hats and mittens. She often played a game with them asking them to identify their own clothes. Aside from working with us, she didn't get out very much. Her mother had become disabled and Roz had to care for her while her father tended to his medical practice. One day after work I took her to Boston with me to do some Christmas shopping. Jordan Marsh always decorated its display windows for the holidays. She had never been to Boston before, so this was a real treat. We also walked to the Boston Common to see the beautiful holiday display there. She spent the night with Mrs. Richards and me.

One other time, I took Roz on a weekend bus tour to Old Sturbridge Village. We had a great time seeing and learning what life was like in early New England from 1790 to 1840. The village sits on 200 acres and has many museums and gift shops. We rode in the stagecoach two or three times. We walked through the two covered bridges and saw all three authentic water-powered mills.

I don't think we missed anything. We both learned a lot and had a splendid time. We were both thankful to be living in the twentieth century.

By the end of that school year we had seen a lot of progress in the children. Some were ready to move on to other programs. Others we would have for another year or two.

In early May I received a letter from the Institute for the Crippled and Disabled informing me that I was one of the two to be chosen to receive the Will and Way Fellowship Award. I had been unaware that the Institute had been following my teaching career ever since I graduated from their program in 1958. I was lucky I got the letter at all because the Institute didn't even have my address and sent it to my friend Holly, who was still a client there.

It didn't take long for the news to travel. My story was written up in all the local newspapers. Mrs. Irene Sherwood, my high school English teacher, wrote one of the most inspiring articles for the *Duxbury Clipper*. It reads as follows:

"High Honor for Arlene Sollis"

Arlene Sollis, Daughter of Mr. and Mrs. George Sollis of Island Creek, has been notified that she has been named as one of two recipients of the achievement awards given annually by the Institute for the Crippled and Disabled of New York City. Each Year the Institute selects from its graduates, two young people who have been notably successful in their careers. The other award this year goes to a young man who is now a psychologist at the Institute.

INSPIRING STORY

The Institute has been following Arlene's career since she attended it in 1957-58 after graduating from Duxbury High School. She has also taken courses at Emerson College and at Lesley College. At present, she teaches at the United Cerebral Palsy Nursery School in Quincy where she has full charge of the kindergarten class.

Arlene finds time, even with her teaching, to pursue her hobbies of sewing, reading, and ceramics. She stays in Weymouth to be near her school but comes home to Duxbury frequently for weekends.

This summer she plans to continue her studies at Lesley or Boston University."

The Award Ceremony took place on Thursday, May 24, 1962. It was held at the new Rehabilitation Research and Education Building at 140 East 24th Street (In New York City) in conjunction with the dedication of the new building. I needed to be there by 2:00 pm.

I took the 7:00 am train from South Station in Boston and arrived at Grand Central Station in New York around 11:30 am. When I got there, I headed straight for the subway and my destination. When I got to the institute, I was very surprised when someone handed me an orchid corsage and a note. Tears welled up in my eyes as I read the names on the card, Mrs. Hendricks and Mrs. Sherwood, two of my high school teachers. I brought it home and pressed it in my scrapbook for safe keeping. I spent three nights with Holly before returning home on Sunday.

At the close of this school year Mr. Ciampa came to me one day and told me that he couldn't find anyone to head up the fund-raising drive for Duxbury. He wanted to know if I knew of anyone. I told him I had no idea at the moment, but I knew one thing, it was a job 'I' didn't want. It was more responsibility than I wanted to take on. When I got home, I told my mother about it. Much to my surprise, she said "Well, Arlene, a little money is better than no money at all. Let me give it a try." Neither of us thought we would be able to do much with it. One evening we sat down and mapped out the town, then about three thousand people. Who do we know in this area? Who do we know in that area, jotting down names as we went along. I think we spent a whole week on the phone. Mother wasn't very happy, because she didn't know anyone on Standish Shore or Powder Point. And she knew she needed someone there if the drive was going to be successful.

Out of desperation, she asked one of her best friends, Blanche White, if she knew of anyone on Standish Shore who had a little time to spare, and who could organize this section of town. At this time Blanche was doing private duty nursing for Katie Franke, who had had surgery to remove a brain tumor. Katie needed something to do with her free time.

So mother called Katie, who was very excited about having something useful to do.

A couple of days later, Katie called back to tell mother she had organized the whole area. Katie then wanted to know if there was something else she could do. Mother did not have Powder Point or Washington Street covered yet. Maybe Katie could find someone to do them. Katie did them herself, of course.

For someone who knew almost nothing about fund raising, Mother managed to pull it off very well. Katie would head up the drive for the next couple of years and do much more than that.

Mrs. Patrick hosted a coffee hour to get the crew of workers together. Mr. Ciampa would come to talk to them about cerebral palsy and inform them of the work the organization was doing and the many programs being offered to his cerebral palsy clients. I suggested that we bring along a couple of the children from the nursery to show the fund-raisers just where the money was going. He thought that was a splendid idea. He left it up to me to choose who I thought would be the best ones for the occasion. He would then send out letters to their parents requesting permission to take them out of school for the morning.

The head teacher and I talked it over and together we decided that Stephen Jordan and Danielle Crevier would be the best.

They were both very friendly and very well behaved. Neither one could walk at that time, but with continued physical therapy they were on their way. The nursery school made a big difference in their lives. But so did they make a big difference in the nursery schoool.

Me and Nursery School Children, Danielle and Stephen

Shortly after the fund-raising drive was over, Katie organized a women's group to raise money for much needed equipment for the nursery school. They called themselves "The Duxbury Friends of the CP Nursery School".

One of the first pieces of equipment the school acquired through 'The Friends' was a much needed tape recorder. It was donated by Sweetzer's General Store on Washington Street. My mother, Katie, Mr. Ciampa and I were on hand to receive this generous gift. Our picture was published in the *Duxbury Clipper*, the local newspaper, along with the story. That was the summer of 1964. I decided I wanted to try something new. I had applied for a job at a camp for the mentally disabled in Vermont the summer before but was turned down because the positions were filled. But I reapplied in January of this year. And, lo and behold, my application was accepted. It was volunteer work, but I didn't care. I would get five dollars a week and room and board. I was told that if I wanted the job, I had to report to the camp by June 22, for a three day training seminar. I could stay the full season or choose the number of weeks I wanted to work. Since I was already committed to work at Camp Freedom again for the month of August, I could only stay for the first four weeks. Camp Silver Towers was located in a very small town called Brookfield in the Green Mountains of Vermont. It served about five hundred mentally disabled children throughout the state, many of whom were from state institutions, and camp was their only chance for a change of scenery.

I took a bus from Boston to Northfield, VT. That was so long ago that I don't recall whether I had to change buses anywhere along the way. I was met by W. Earle Forman, executive director of the Vermont Association for Retarded Children, Inc. The camp served one hundred girls during the month of July and the same number of boys during the month of August.

I was assigned to the youngest group of children and I also worked in arts and crafts. Other programs included swimming in the camp's large pool, archery, horseback riding, hiking, and weekly cookouts at Allis State Park.

On my day off I rode into Montpelier with the maintenance man when he went into the city for supplies, so I could get away from the camp for a couple of hours, and have a change from camp cooking.

I learned that the main house where I slept was left to the state and the Elks Club bought it and the six acres of land to build this camp. They were hoping to buy more land so they could expand it and accommodate more campers.

I returned to the camp the next summer for the full season, once again I was assigned to the youngest group. But this time I was given more responsibilities. I slept in the cabin with them. I had to be sure that they got to their assigned activities and meals on time. I also assisted with the arts and crafts program again. When I had time to spare, I volunteered to work with the camp's director, Mr. Hugh Haggerty, on the camp's newspaper. This paper would be sent to the members of the Elks Club. I think it was used for publicity purposes in their fund-raising efforts.

While I was working during the boys' session I heard that one of the older campers bit one of the younger ones on the arm. At first I didn't pay it any mind. But that night while the children were getting ready for bed, I noticed a bright red streak running down one of the boy's arms. I asked if he was the one who had gotten bitten a few hours earlier. When he said he was, I wasted no time. I called one of the other counselors to finish putting the rest of the boys to bed and rushed him, pajamas and all, to the nurse's station. The little boy spent most of the week in the hospital on antibiotics for blood poisoning. That was not the way he wanted to spend a week away from the state school. We had a very rainy week and all of the boys were getting very restless and unruly. On about the fourth day, Mr. Haggerty decided to organize a rain hike. I wasn't very happy about this until Mr. Haggerty came to me and asked me if I would mind staying back with one of the campers. He said he didn't think Jimmy, who had cerebral palsy, could keep up with the rest of the campers, and he needed one of the counselors to stay back with him. Of course, I was very pleased to accept this assignment. I gathered up some craft supplies and board games and the two of us had a very enjoyable morning.

I am most grateful to have had the opportunity work at Camp Silver Towers. I enjoyed the children and learned a lot from them.

I was always on the move. In September of 1964, the CP Nursery School would have to start a new school year without me. I would join the staff two weeks late.

On September 8, Johnny April and I, along with twenty-five others from the Boston area, flew into Montreal International Airport. We were joined by another disabled group from New York. We were making a pilgrimage to the Shrine of Our Lady of the Cape in Quebec. We spent five wonderful days at Madonna House of Three Rivers. For me, the trip was a much needed vacation as well as meeting my spiritual needs. I was very tired after a hectic summer of working at two camps and I took every opportunity to be 'waited on' for a change.

The shrine is located about half way between Montreal and Quebec City. Oftentimes pilgrims access it by taking a cruise on the St. Lawrence River. However, we were taken by bus from the airport.

Our Lady of the Cape Shrine is the first shrine to Our Lady in North America and the oldest church still in existence in Canada, dating back to 1714. In the winter of 1879, work had begun on the construction of a new church to accommodate the growing population. There was just one problem– the stone needed to complete the construction had to be transported from across the river, and there was no bridge. It had been unseasonably warm for March and all the ice had melted on the river so there was no way to get the stones they needed to complete the construction of the new church until the next winter when the river froze over again. The churchgoers prayed to Our Lady for help. Then another cold snap came and lasted long enough to freeze the section of the river needed to fetch the stones. This later became known as *the miracle of the ice bridge.* A statue of Our Lady was the placed in the original church and became known as Our Lady of the Cape. It was recorded that on the night the new church was dedicated, on June 22, 1888, that the statue opened her eyes to the river. This was witnessed by Father Lue Desilets and two others. These two stories left a lasting impression on my mind and I thought they deserved a place in my book. When I returned to work in September, I was busier than ever. Katie Franke had organized the Duxbury Friends of the CP Nursery School, and the wonderful ladies had been hard at work raising money for supplies and equipment that the CP organization could not give us. I would meet with her to discuss how these funds should be spent. Here is some of what Katie wrote for the *Duxbury Clipper,* the local weekly newspaper.

Duxbury Clipper, October 8, 1964. **CP NEWS,** by Katie Franke

"Arlene told me first about the wonderful tricycle donated by Nancy Fisher. One little girl, her legs encased in ankle braces extending part way

up her legs, has had the time of her life riding the trike. After the child's feet were placed on the pedals in the proper position, her knees are pressed down alternately by hand until the brain understands the entire process. Now the girl wants to take the trike home to show her mother and eight brothers and sisters that she can ride it.

Not only were Arlene's choices at the Arrowsmiths, a local toy shop, excellent for teaching coordination and perception, but she is now using her ingenuity to make toys even more appealing to youngsters. One purchase, a wooden house with knobbed doors, is a favorite with the children. Arlene has developed a system whereby she places pictures behind each door to surprise the children and to provide an incentive for them to better their manual dexterity by grasping the knobs between their thumb and forefinger, one day, say, the pictures are all of farm animals and tools, the next day the pictures may be of a fire station.

The Friends are lucky to have a consultant like Arlene, and isn't the Nursery School fortunate?

Lately, the Duxbury Friends of the CP Nursery School have been having the fun of spending some of the money raised last summer.

With both the entertainment of and therapy for the kiddos in mind as suggested by Arlene Sollis, a teacher at the school for the past five years, we thumbed through several catalogs to compile the following order: two large rag dolls, a sister with a brother; two sets each of interlocking floor trains and tug boats; a child-sized doll carriage; a clown punching bag; a clay work kit; a tricycle; and a set of 100 pop-it beads.

In addition, we sent Arlene, herself, with a certain amount of money to spend, to pick out needed items at the Arrowsmith's fabulous toy shop. Teacher Sollis had a "field day", since the A's, bless them, discounted many of the items, thereby s-st- t-r-r-r-retching the original sum considerably! Thank you both for your generosity!

Arlene's masterful choices filled a good-sized carton, and the Friends feel as though we have been doing some Christmas shopping early."

In November, Troop #663 of the Junior Girl Scouts decided to make gifts for other children for Christmas. Under the supervision of Mrs. William Bumpus and her administrative assistant, her daughter Tina, the thirty girls in the troop stitched, sewed and stuffed soft Humpty-Dumpty pillows for the children at the CP Nursery School, who were entertained at a special Christmas Party given by the residents of the

Old Sailors' Home, of Snug Harbor, on December 10th. When Katie and I got together for coffee on a Saturday morning, she mentioned the gifts to me. She told me that the Girl Scout Troop #663 was making pillows for the nursery school as a project. I was delighted to know that other children were doing things for those less fortunate than themselves.

Katie wrote individual letters to each one of the parents of the children in the nursery school inviting them to a Christmas Party in Duxbury. It was necessary to get the parents' written permission to take the children out of school for the event. The parents all responded with enthusiasm to the invitations. In the invitations Katie explained the details of the party. Lunch and refreshments would be provided for all before the appearance of Old Saint Nick with his bag of gifts carefully selected for each child by Joyce Campbell and me. The Duxbury Girl Scouts added their hand made Humpty-Dumpty pillows. It was a wonderful experience for the children to have a Christmas Party at the Old Sailors Home of Powder Point. The residents of the Home really enjoyed the laughter and play of the children, and the refreshments.

It was a custom at the Nursery School that when a child had a birthday the staff would give them a little party to celebrate the occasion. But, on January 13, when Leslie Claflin of Hingham celebrated her fifth birthday, and again on January 15, when Kimberly Drew of Weymouth celebrated her fourth birthday, this custom was changed somewhat. The parents of each of the two children felt that their child should have a party at home and invite all the children from their class. Since this would not have been possible, the parents decided to bring the parties to the Nursery School.

One mother, herself unable to be present, sent in by way of the taxi all of the refreshments, birthday napkins, plates and some party favors.

The other party was celebrated in pretty much the same manner, except we had some unexpected guests to make it even more exciting. This mother brought her little girl's playmate and the mother and brother of one of the other youngsters who attend the nursery, along to share the fun.

One beautiful spring day in May, one full of fun and excitement, the happy little children from CP Nursery School were looking forward to their outing at King's Castle Land, a small family-run amusement park in Whitman. This outing was again sponsored by the Duxbury Friends. Since this was to be a family outing, including parents, sisters and brothers of the children, it meant that additional transportation would be needed. So once again the Duxbury Friends came to our rescue with three volunteer drivers, Jean Krahmer, Carol Marshall and Martha Wyllie, who picked up several youngsters and parents before reaching the nursery school where the buses and a station wagon of children, parents and staff were anxiously waiting a horn toot signal to parade down Route 18 to the land of nursery rhymes and fairy tales. It was arranged that the gates would be opened especially for our group, with reduced rates for the whole group. At first, the children, some in strollers and some on foot, were shown about the grounds, identifying and singing the rhymes and listening to the stories that each child-size play house represented. Since most of the houses were ground-level even the children in strollers were able to join in the fun.

The interiors and the exteriors of some of the houses, such as *Red Riding Hood*, the *Three Little Pigs,* and *Simple Simon*, were colorfully painted to illustrate their stories. *Noah's Ark, The Old Lady in the Shoe, The Little Red School House, and Peter's Pumpkin Shell* seemed to be the children's favorites.

Old King Cole called for *his Fiddlers Three,* who played their merry tunes throughout the morning.

Some of the children played in and around the play area on swings and canopy-covered sand boxes while the adults took time out for rest and to chat.

There was a very nice picnic area with tables and benches carefully selected for our comfort and convenience. Each of us brought his own lunch, excluding the drinks which were purchased at the snack bar by Duxbury Friends.

A few of the children were so fascinated with the dragon, which ejected fire from its mouth every few minutes, and by the giant which stood at least 25 feet from the ground, that they had to be reminded to eat their lunch.

This wonderful outing ended with a ride through the paths in a circus cage pulled by a tractor. The youngsters were let off just outside the gate where Mr. Joseph Walsh and "Don" were waiting to retrace their morning route back home.

Most of the children from the nursery school were not old enough to sit through a three-ring circus at the Boston Garden, but Betty McDermott, Flint Craig and Ricky Tirrell were among the 150 or more CP children and adults who attended this wonderful outing. It was sponsored by the Taleb Grotto, which chartered three Eastern MA buses, bought tickets for the best seats in the Garden, and supplied refreshments of ice cream and Cracker-Jacks. We all had a wonderful time.

The Savastanos of Duxbury contributed a large sum of money to the Duxbury Friends in memory of their son who had cerebral palsy, but who had passed away at the age of 2 ½ years. It was with a portion of this money that we purchased our most recent addition, something that the children are really enjoying now that the warm weather is here, the outdoor gym set. It had two swings and a glider with a jungle gym. Besides being a source of enjoyment, it is a great aid in developing and strengthening those larger muscles needed for walking and pushing and pulling.

Mr. White, from whom the Friends purchased this gym set, took special care in seeing that it met the requirements of the children by equipping the swings with rubber seats for safety and comfort.

Most of the time when a child was ready to move on to other programs or schools, I knew I probably would not see them again. Not so for one little boy. One morning I was very busy in one of the smaller rooms. The door was closed to avoid distractions from the other children playing in the hall. I heard a faint knock on the door. At first I paid it no mind until it opened. Joyce called to me and the child I was working with to come to the big room. Before I got there, I heard the voice of a child say "Miss Arlene, I came to show you that I can walk now."

It was little Tony Nocera. With tears welled up in my eyes, and a smile, I bent down and gave him a big hug and said "I knew you could do it."

Tony had spent nearly a year at Kennedy Memorial Hospital where he underwent numerous operations, followed by many long and painful hours of physical therapy. He wore long leg braces and used crutches. But he *was* walking, and he wanted his mother to bring him by to show me. This was in the days before Public Law #94-142 (The Education of all Disabled Children) was passed, and there were very few opportunities for educating the mentally bright children with physical disabilities in the public school system. Their parents were left with very few options. Either they could send their child away to a boarding school at their own expense as my parents did, or have the child home-schooled. One such child was Wayne Hadley. He could walk but he was very unsteady on his feet. He was being home-schooled. He had spent two years at the CP Nursery School. I had worked extensively with him in a reading readiness program. His mother wrote our staff and sent along a sample of Wayne's work. She said that it was attributed to the "fine preparation he received at the nursery school." Once when I was working with Wayne, Mr. Ciampa came in with a photographer from one of the local newspapers to do a story on the nursery school. Lo and behold, the next day, a large picture appeared in the paper showing me working with Wayne on writing the letters of the alphabet on the chalkboard. I kept the picture all these years. That was 1964. I wonder what Wayne is doing today!

At some point I had to find new living arrangements. Mr. and Mrs. Richards wanted to retire and do a little traveling.

The CP office secretary knew a very nice lady in Quincy who took in boarders. She had a room available and she would let me have it for the same price as I was paying at Mrs. Richards'. This sounded like a very good deal. So I set up an appointment to see her the next day. I knew what I had for the past six or seven years could not be duplicated but I needed a place to hang my hat during the week, so I took the room. The lady asked me if I minded pets. I told her "not at all. I love animals if they like me." She showed me to my new room. It was very small and dingy, but clean. It had a bed, an old worn out over-stuffed chair and a small chest of drawers and no curtains at the window, just a worn out pull shade. Hey! I wasn't going to be here very much, so what difference did it make where I slept? The lady told me I could watch television any time I felt like it. When I told my mother about it, she wasn't too happy about it, but I had no choice at the moment, and the price was ok. There was one other boarder, an elderly man. He ate breakfast with me most of the time. Then he left and I didn't see him again for the rest of the day. For breakfast we had cold cereal, which most of the time was stale. I don't think our landlady ever took the boxes off the table until they were emptied. The canned juices were served warm if they had just been opened that morning. It is a good thing I don't like coffee because what she served smelled so strong that it almost made me gag if she put the pot in front of me. When I got to work, I fixed a cup of tea and sipped it while I prepared the children's lunches.

The evening meal was equally as bad as the breakfast. The lady never served fresh vegetables. Everything came from a can, including potatoes. She served fried chicken a lot. I had to peel all of the skin off to avoid eating all that grease and fat from the skin. The hamburger meat before it was cooked was light pink, almost white, and full of fat. I didn't touch that. I told her I was allergic to beef. I often ate what I fixed for the children at school and, when suppertime came, I told the lady I had eaten at work and wasn't hungry. The weekend couldn't come soon enough. I looked forward to getting home and filling up on my mother's **good** cooking.

The best thing about that experience was the dog. It was part husky and part German shepherd. He followed me everywhere like he was protecting me. If I started up the stairs, he waited at the bottom until I reached the top before he came up. He slept in my room on the floor by the door and blocked it every time the other roomer passed it. I often took him for walks in the afternoon and played with him a lot.

I hadn't been there very long when I started checking the local papers for rooms for rent, but when I would check them out, I discovered that they were no better than what I already had. Then one day after about three months of searching, Elaine handed me a small clipping she had cut from a Quincy paper and said "Arlene, I think this is what you are looking for. I had Charlie drive me by yesterday to check it out and I talked to the landlady, who said she would hold the room until you came by this afternoon." I called to tell the landlady I would be there as soon as I got off work. I had the driver drop me off at 98 Bigelow Street, just two blocks from Quincy Square in one direction, and two blocks from the CP office in the other. Mrs. Wein was waiting for me when I arrived. She and her husband lived on the third floor. I liked her right from the moment we met. She was very businesslike and to the point. She reminded me that she ran a rooming house and not a boarding house. I told her I was more than ready for that. We chatted for another ten minutes before she took me down one flight of stairs and showed me the room I was to have and the rest of the house. The room was small but clean and neat with a bed, a chair and a chest of drawers, all that I needed.

The two full sized bathrooms were clean and had no foul odor. She said that each of the roomers was responsible for cleaning up the kitchen after herself immediately after using it. There was no food left out and no dirty dishes or pots and pans in the sink. There were two refrigerators, and each lady was assigned a half a shelf, and four ladies shared one freezer. She then led me down the back stairs to the cellar where the laundry room was. At the far end of the large room there was a coin operated washing machine with clotheslines strung from one end of the room to the other. I was so excited, and I could hardly wait to move in. We went back up stairs and I gave Mrs. Wein four weeks rent and she handed me the keys to my room and all of the outside doors. Oh, one other thing, there was a pay phone on each floor. I telephoned my mother and told her to have my father pick me up at 98 Bigelow Street the next day for the week end. As it happened he was working in Wollaston and it was not out of his way.

I took a taxi back to my old room. There was nobody home. I was very pleased about that. I went upstairs and packed my clothes, came back down, sat at the kitchen table to write a note to the landlady that I wouldn't be returning, said good bye to the dog, and left.

By the time I got back to my room with my belongings, I was exhausted and hungry, and I knew I had to go out again for something to eat. The nearest place was Montillio's Restaurant and Bakery. I ordered a sandwich and a cold drink for supper and some Italian pastry for breakfast the next morning then I headed back to my new room again, this time for the night. Mrs. Wien lent me a set of sheets and a blanket for the night. By then, it was 6:30 and all the women were in from work and the floor came alive. Everybody was friendly, but I was too tired to talk much and just wanted to be left alone.

I almost couldn't believe what I had just done. The afternoon seemed like a daydream, a fairytale. I never questioned my decision. I just wondered what my mother was going to say when I got home the next day. I really didn't much care. I knew I had to get out of where I was before I got sick from not getting enough good food to eat.

After I had eaten and before I settled in for the night, I phoned Elaine to have the driver pick me up at 98 Bigelow Street.

She said "WOW! That was a quick move."

That night, as tired as I was, I couldn't get to sleep. I heard somebody come in around 1:00 am. During the next week I would learn the names of all the women on my floor and their routines, but for now, they were all strangers to me.

I was sitting outside on the front steps when my father came to pick me up the next afternoon. When I got into the car and he pulled away, he asked me if I was visiting somebody. I said "No, Dad. This is where you will be picking me up from now on. I couldn't say anything yesterday when I called because, well, you know how Mother is. She worries too much." I told him why I had to move and all about my new home away from home, and all the changes I was making.

I asked him if he thought Mother would be angry with me. He said "No, not angry, just a little confused. You know how she is when you try anything new."

I said, "Yeah, I know. She always thinks of a million reasons why I shouldn't. And if I took her advice all the time where would I be today? I take chances. If things work out, all well and good. If they don't, I just try something else. That's just the way it is. Two steps forward and one back." We talked all the way home.

Mother greeted us at the kitchen door and asked me where my dirty clothes were. I replied "I didn't bring any home, because, from now on, I will be doing all my own laundry from now on. I will explain at supper." I didn't give her a chance to comment.

That weekend I was very busy collecting things I needed for my new way of living. At the moment, I needed the bare necessities, including bedding, a few dishes, tableware, a couple of pots and pans, and of course, something to make tea in. I still couldn't carry a cup of liquid without spilling it, so I needed something small and non-breakable and with a cover on it.

Mother and I went to the back cellar where she stored a lot of things that she no longer needed and probably should have discarded ages ago. I filled a good sized carton with enough kitchen supplies to get me started. I felt like I was at a yard sale, only minus the price tags. I guess my mother hardly ever threw anything half usable away. I had a really good time shopping in our cellar's back room and closet. I had the weirdest collection of dishes and cooking utensils. Nothing matched, but I didn't care. They were usable, and that was all that mattered.

We went back upstairs. She threw a couple of towels and washcloths on the top of the carton and said "There, that should tide you over for a while". I knew that if I needed anything else, I could probably find it in

The Bargain Center in Quincy at a later date, as it was within walking distance of my new "home".

I told her I could go shopping for food when we got to Quincy and got my things put away there. She agreed to that. I expected her to give me a hard time, but, to my surprise, she didn't. My father was very pleased with how smoothly things were going between my mother and me. If my mother was upset, she didn't let on to me. I was waiting for her negative comments, but, much to my surprise, there were none the whole weekend.

Shopping for groceries was a little tricky because we had limited space in the refrigerator and four of us had to share one freezer, which, back then, wasn't very big and it did not freeze ice cream very well. It took several weeks for me to shop for just what I needed. At first, it seemed like I always needed something I didn't have. I really had to sit down with pencil and paper and figure out exactly what I needed and how to keep my cooking very simple. I loved to cook and I was good at it. But now I had to limit my time in the kitchen I shared with seven other ladies, most of whom had different work schedules than mine. It didn't take long before everything fell into place and I was just another roomer with my own schedule. Those who didn't work soon learned and respected mine. They left the kitchen free for me when I got home around 3:30 most afternoons. I, on the other hand, was long out of the kitchen by the time the others got home later.

There was very little storage space in the kitchen for cooking supplies and non-perishable items, and what there was, was out of my reach. At first, I had to keep everything in the small closet in my room. But when I saw a space in the entryway to the back stairs I had an idea. I went to talk to Mrs. Wien about buying a small metal storage cabinet to put there to store my kitchen supplies. She said that was ok with her. That solved this problem easily and with very little expense.

She also lowered one of the clotheslines so I could reach it better. There was no way I could carry a clothes basket down a flight of very steep stairs. So I bought a canvas laundry bag.

Thus I could throw it from the top of the stairs and fetch it when I got to the bottom. As long as it worked, who cared how it worked. Coming up the stairs was no problem. I set the bag on the steps in front of me and moved it up as I went along.

All and all, I adjusted to my new living situation in no time and was very happy.

It was like one big family. I made friends with all the ladies very quickly. Most of us never bothered to lock our doors when we went out. One of the ladies had a big black and white cat named Muffins. Everybody loved him. Most of the time, he had the run of the floor. His owner never knew where she was going to find him. He spent a lot of time in my room. I gave him a lot of attention when I was home. He liked high places and one of his favorite spots was on top of the refrigerator. One time I had just wrapped Christmas presents and placed them on my bed. I went out for a few minutes. And when I got back, Muffins was sleeping in the middle of them. He would have made a very pretty Christmas card. Mr. Wien was a very short, heavy set man, I think in his seventies. He was a retired chemist. He had a small lab in the back room of the cellar and he spent a lot of time there during the day. I was doing laundry one afternoon and I had a bad cold. He called me into the back room and handed me two small bottles and said "Here's a cure for that cough. Take one for Laura, she has a bad cough also. But don't let my wife catch you with it." I put them one in each of my jacket pockets and said "Thank you. I sure won't." When I got to Laura's room, I handed her one of the bottles and told her what Mr. Wien had said. She offered me a seat and closed the door. There was enough whisky for two drinks apiece. I had one with Laura and saved the other for bedtime. I mixed it with lemon juice and honey. It tasted terrible. But it did work.

When Patty got married and moved out, I requested her room. It was a little smaller than the one I had occupied for the past year, but it was by far more convenient. It was off the kitchen and next to one of the two bathrooms. The bed had no headboard, and I really liked that. I bought some gold and black corduroy fabric at the Bargain Center, enough to make a cover for my bed and cover the two bolster pillows. My parents bought me a small maple rocking chair. My friend Jeanne came down from Stoneham one Saturday and painted the walls light beige. They had been white. My room was pretty livable in no time.

Mr. Wien often used my room for a rest stop on his way from the cellar to the third floor. Sometimes he'd be all out of breath and stay for quite a while and chat with me. He found my rocking chair very comfortable

Sometimes after the Wiens had a party the night before we would find goodies on our kitchen table with a note which read something like this "You girls finish this. My husband doesn't need it, he's too fat." There might be half a rum cake, or a couple of pies minus a piece or two.

I began spending more time in Quincy and less time in Duxbury with my parents. Jeanne was an RN and she had every other week end off. She often came for me on Friday afternoon. We would head for the Cape or the White Mountains of New Hampshire. Back then, we could get a motel room for around ten or twelve dollars a night and we packed a cooler full of food and drinks and bought our main meal at noontime to avoid paying dinnertime prices. We had a good time on twenty dollars apiece for the whole week end. One time during the summer Jeanne and I rented a trailer for a week. We camped in Maine, Nova Scotia, and Prince Edward Island. We spent two or three days in the beautiful Bay of Fundy National Park.

One other time we drove to Niagara Falls. We crossed the border several times without incident, but one time we had forgotten about the strawberries we had bought at a roadside stand earlier that day. Later, when we got to the border, the inspector opened the cooler and found them. He said we were not permitted to take fresh produce across with us. I had the perfect solution. I said to Jeanne, "If we eat them now, we will no longer have them." We set the box of berries between us and had a feast. When we had finished them, the inspector was satisfied and he let us go across.

Jeanne had a miniature dachshund that traveled with us. One very hot summer night we were camping out somewhere near Corning, New York. We requested a campsite away from the other campers because we didn't want the dog to be distracted by them every time someone walked past our site. We were given a corner lot with wire fencing on two sides. It was a perfect site for the dog and for us. Jeanne walked the dog. Then she attached the leash to the leg of her cot and we both settled in for a good night's sleep, or so we thought. We were awakened a short time later by the dog's loud growl. At first we thought it was some camper passing by our site, so we tried to ignore it. But when he didn't let up, our curiosity got the better of us. We got up and took our flashlights and followed the dog to see what was disturbing him. He led us to the fence, but before we got very far we heard the sound of cows mooing.

When we shined our flashlights in their direction, we saw four cows hanging their heads over the fence.

Once when I was spending a few days at her house, Jeanne phoned me from the hospital to tell she had to do a double shift and would be home around midnight. I got something to eat, fed the dog and settled in the back bedroom with a book, as I often did when she had to work late. Around 9 pm the dog started to growl. I knew it wasn't time for Jeanne so I tried to ignore him, but this time the growl was one I hadn't ever heard before. So I got up and followed the dog to the kitchen. His growl got even stranger. He went to the living room door. I opened it and let him out. It was summertime and all the neighbors had their windows opened as did I. By now the dog was really barking and a trash barrel was rolling down the hill and down the street. The whole neighborhood was lit up when the people heard the commotion. Someone saw a man trip and knock over a trash barrel trying to escape from the dog. Jeanne's house had been broken into a few weeks earlier and some antique glassware was stolen. On this night, whoever it was didn't see her car in the garage, and no lights were on, so he must have assumed nobody was home. I got the dog back into the house and gave him a big treat. One of the neighbors called the police to report the incident. Two policemen came by to talk to me a few minutes later. I told them what had happened, and when they were satisfied with my story, they left.

Every time I went to Jeanne's after that and she had to work late, I made sure the house was well lit up after dark.

My parents had gone to England in the summer of 1967. When they got home, they told me all about their experiences and how they met and stayed with relatives near Liverpool.

That winter I started making my own plans to take a similar trip. I contacted Mother's cousin in Runcon, England. She wrote me back and said I could stay with her for a week in July. That was all I needed to hear. By the end of May, I knew pretty much what I wanted to see and do. I would spend one week with Alma and two weeks of free travel with the last few days in London so I could make my flight back to New York.

My parents drove me to Logan Airport. Mother was giving me all kinds of advice all the way, but, as usual, I wasn't paying much attention to her. I was too excited and just wanted to get to England. I had not flown on an overnight flight before. The flight from New York to London was uneventful, except for the fact that I did not sleep at all even with those blue blinders to cover my eyes. My mind was too busy thinking about all the things I wanted to see and do for the next three weeks. Aside from the time I would spend with Alma, I had an open itinerary. I was headed for Edinburgh, Scotland and London. Alma met me in Liverpool that afternoon and we had dinner with some other relatives before we headed home. She knew I must be tired from the long trip and said she would let me sleep as late as I wanted in the morning. I told her I was an early riser and left it at that. I had no intentions of spending my holiday sleeping.

The next morning I was up at 7 am and ready for whatever Alma had planned for the day. At breakfast she asked me what I knew about the area. I told her that I knew it had a Roman history. With this information she knew where we would spend our first full day together. But what she didn't know was that I had a lot of inexhaustible energy.

During the morning she showed me around Liverpool, Manchester, and Runcon. We had lunch in one of the pubs before driving to Chester, where she wanted to show me the Roman Wall. When the town was founded in 79 AD, it was given the name of Deva Vitrix, translated to mean *The Legion on the River Dee*. I not only wanted to admire this ancient structure, but when I learned that it was possible for me to walk it, I wanted to do that too.

So it was, that Alma and I took the two mile walk on the wall around the city. She was an excellent tour guide for me. She pointed to St. Peter's Church. It is the oldest church in Chester, and was founded in AD 907. It was constructed from local sandstone. Even though the exterior has been restored several times, the interior still remains as it was back in Roman times. This church was built on the site where the old Roman headquarters once stood. Another very old church is St. John the Baptist. It was built in 1075. It is said to be best example of 11th and 12th century architecture in Cheshire County. A solid oak coffin with the words "Dust to Dust" painted on it was found when the church was undergoing repairs in 1813. This is an example of medieval craftsmanship.

The beautiful clock above the Eastgate was funded by the people of Chester to celebrate Queen Victoria's sixty years on the British throne. Alma told me that Chester is the only city in the county where the streets have retained their Roman names along with their British ones.

We later browsed through the many gift shops on the side streets and strolled through the nearby gardens before having supper in one of the pubs.

The next day we drove through the beautiful countryside to Stratford upon Avon. I had studied Shakespeare in high school and I wanted to see his birthplace even though I really didn't care much for his writings and still don't. I prefer the early Greek plays over Shakespeare's.

Alma and I found a tour and joined it. It took us through the Royal Shakespeare Theatre. Even though we didn't get to see a play, we did get to meet some of the performers. They were sitting on the banks of the Avon having lunch. A couple of them were altering or mending their costumes.

I also got to see some of the beautiful gardens and stately homes along the tour route. I also visited Anne Hathaway's Cottage. Twelve rooms doesn't fit my definition of a cottage, however. She lived here until her marriage to William Shakespeare at the age of twenty-six. He was eighteen at the time and she was pregnant with his child. She lived with him in Stratford. She did not travel to London with him where he spent much time working on his plays and writing sonnets.

Alma and I spent the night in a guest house just a few miles from Stratford. That evening after dinner Alma asked me if I had ever been on a ghost walk. I told her I hadn't, but I heard they were fun and a *little* scary. I wasn't prepared for just how good a storyteller our guide was. When we got back to our room, I remember looking under my bed and in the closet to be sure there were no unexpected visitors.

The next morning before we left for Warwick, we took a very enjoyable boat ride on the Avon. This was my first glimpse of the magnificent mediaeval castle from the boat. Alma and I would spend the remainder of our day touring Warwick Castle. (I am not going into details about this building as I could not do justice to it here. There is enough history here to fill the pages of a book by itself.). We got home very late that evening. We were both pretty tired and went to bed after we gave her cat Toby some much demanded attention.

The next day the weather was so very nice. We met some other relatives for a picnic at Tatton Park. I had never seen any gardens so beautiful as these Elizabethan gardens at the park. I spent the afternoon strolling through the Park and admiring the magnificent stately homes on the property. I strolled off to see the farm animals as well.

That evening Alma and I were invited for tea at the relatives. I am sorry that I don't recall their names. It was over forty years ago and I only met them that one time. The English cakes, biscuits (cookies), and pastries were so delicious that I wanted to sample everything, but of course I didn't.

Two weeks before my trip, I decided to practice holding a tea cup the proper way, a task I find very difficult even to this day. I tried first with no water in the cup. I was all thumbs. I was used to using two hands on the cup, much like the Chinese, or using a mug with a big handle. Most of the time, I ate alone. So it didn't really matter much about using proper table manners. But I knew I would be invited to formal teas when I got to England and I didn't want anyone to think I wasn't taught proper etiquette. All things considered, I think I did pretty well.

The day before I was to leave Runcon, Alma took me to a travel agent so I could plan out the rest of my trip and be in London at least four days before returning home. I bought my ticket for Edinburgh, Scotland. I would need to take an early morning train from Liverpool to Glasgow, where I had a two-hour layover before heading for Edinburgh. This settled, the travel agent went to work to find a short tour that fitted into my schedule and still allowed ample time in London. He found a three-day bus tour down the east coast to London. I think it cost £35. It included two meals a day, hotels and transportation. Everything fell so perfectly into place.

When I arrived in Edinburgh the next night, it was late. Alma had told me to ask a taxi driver to find me a bed and breakfast somewhere near Princess Street for the night. I did just that. The people at the bed and breakfast were so nice. I stayed there the whole time I was in Edinburgh. I remember them very well. The couple was in their fifties. They had a son who was studying music at the conservatory. Every evening after dinner he would practice his pieces for about two hours. When the couple discovered I liked classical music, I was invited to their son's study to listen to him play the piano. I never heard anybody play as well as he did. He made the piano talk and dance so beautifully. I wanted to stay with these lovely people forever. I took a one day bus tour to the beautiful sea resort town of Oban. It is on the west coast of Scotland. I met a family on the tour and when I told them I was traveling alone they invited me to join them for lunch at one of the restaurants overlooking the harbor. After lunch I took a tour of the distillery and wandered into St. Columbus' Cathedral. On the way back to the bus, I met up with a group of bagpipers parading down the main street. I heard them from a distance and followed them to the dock. I had never seen or heard bagpipes before. I remember thinking how nice they sounded off in the distance, but how morbid they sounded close by.

It was late when I got back to Edinburgh. I hailed a taxi to take me back to my room. A lady got in before I could get to it and the driver sped off. This happened two more times. Three boys in their late teens were standing nearby taking in the scene. One of them came up to me and said "It won't happen again." He hailed a driver and handed him a £5 note and told him to take me where I needed to go. The trip would have been around £2.

Of course, I had to visit Edinburgh Castle where Mary Queen of Scots was imprisoned for many years, and was later beheaded in England at the orders of Queen Elizabeth I. The castle sits high on a hill. I remember walking the full mile to the top to reach it. I expected the interior to be similar to that of Warwick Castle in England. But I would soon learn that all castles do not serve the same functions.

I had afternoon tea in one of the many tearooms on Princess Street. There were no vacant tables that I could see. The host ushered me to a table with four other ladies and pulled out a chair for me to sit down. At first I hesitated thinking I was intruding on the others at the table. I soon learned that nobody knew one-another before that afternoon. It was such a wonderful experience chatting with these strangers. In a few minutes the conversation flowed as freely as though we had known each other for years. Two of them were local Scots, one was from New Zealand, and one was from Iceland. I remember how we joked about one and others English. We all spoke the same language and yet we didn't. The Scots had a great sense of humor. It was a great way to end my Scottish holiday.

I don't recall where our tour spent our first night on the way to London. But it could have been Lincoln. I remember going through the beautiful cathedral, and also Lincoln Castle. It housed one of the original copies of the Magna Carta.

I know we spent the second night in Cambridge. I spent hours strolling the grounds of the many old buildings of the university. The architecture of many of them are just so magnificent.

One of the first things I did when I got to London was to take a guided tour of the city to find out just where I wanted to spend my time. I only had four days and I had to make every minute count. There was just so much to see and do here. That afternoon after I finished the tour, I went back to the Tower of London to explore it on my own time.

I was very curious about the ravens living at The Tower. A warder told me that ravens had roosted there for centuries. Legend has it, that if the ravens leave The Tower, the kingdom will fall. The birds' wings have been clipped to prevent them from flying away, otherwise they are free. They are well cared for by the warders (beefeaters).

The Tower is also home to the Crown Jewels. They have been here since 1303 when most of them were recovered after having been stolen from Westminster Abby. Attempts have been made to steal them from here also. It has been said that the only time they were moved from here was during World War II when they were taken to Warwick Castle to safeguard them from the bombings of London. Since they can never be taken out of the country, this was the most likely place to take them for safekeeping. They contain the world's largest diamonds along with many other priceless gems, are still used during coronation ceremonies. The Tower was for centuries a prison as well as a palace. This is where King Henry had three of his wives beheaded for not producing an heir to the throne.

I spent almost an entire day at Westminster Abby. It was originally the Collegiate Church of St. Peter. Construction was started in 1050, with work continuing until around 1745. It is the final resting place for many of Great Britain's poets, statesmen, actors, and nobility. One of the sections of the Abby is known as Poets' Corner. I spent a lot of time here. I was surprised to see just how many names I recognized from my high school English literature class. Mrs. Sherwood surely taught me well. King Henry VIII was the first monarch to be buried here. However, many of them are buried at Windsor Castle and elsewhere. Nowadays, only a person's ashes can be buried at the Abby.

Most of Great Britain's coronation ceremonies have taken place here since 1066. They are performed by the Archbishop of Canterbury. The coronation chair is presently stored at Edinburgh Castle in Scotland.

One morning I browsed through the Old Curiosity Shop made famous by Charles Dickens and found my way to Samuel Johnson's House. I remember, I had a hard time finding that. It was tucked away on a side street and the map wasn't much help. I found a bobby on horseback and he led the way. That afternoon I took a relaxing boat ride on the River Thames. I passed under London Bridge, which has since been dismantled and is now in Lake Havasu City in Arizona, and the Tower Bridge. I passed by the House of Parliament and the Tower of London. I remember thinking how everything seemed so massive and so old here.

I had one last place I had to see before I left London to return home and that was Piccadilly Circus. I had no idea what was there or why I had to go there. All I knew was I just had to see Piccadilly Circus, circus meaning circle in Latin. I learned later that the street was named for a tailor by the name of Robert Baker, who made all kinds of collars known as piccadills or piccadillies. I found the area to be much like that of Times Square in New York City with its theatre, restaurants, and night life. I decided to live it up. I bought a ticket to a play and had dinner in one of the nicer restaurants. I had been eating in pubs much of my stay here, but this was a special time and I didn't know if I would ever get back here. I got back to my room at 2:30am, in time to for a catnap before leaving for the airport and New York. This trip was quite a great experience for me. After that I always enjoyed traveling alone and doing my own thing in my own time. Company is nice, but until recently it was not a necessity.

Sometime in the mid '60s my right leg started giving me trouble. I began walking on my toes. I could not get my heel to touch the ground and the muscle spasms were terribly painful at times. I went to see the CP clinic's doctor. He had no idea why this was occurring so late in life since I was very active and on my feet a lot. I was not born with the problem and it was a big puzzle to him.

He decided to try bracing the foot using a drop foot brace for a while to see if it would correct the problem and put the hip in proper alignment. At first the brace seemed to working ok. I was walking better and the spasms were less frequent. But I began to notice that I was having a real struggle getting the brace on in the morning. The Achilles tendon in the back of the leg was just so tight.

Dr. Woll was a physiatrist, a doctor of physical medicine and rehabilitation, at Lemuel Shattuck Hospital in Jamaica Plain. He sent me to see an orthopedic specialist at the hospital. The specialist said he hadn't seen anything quite like this before. But he said in cases of children with this problem surgery sometimes works.

The longer I thought about this, I thought "the worst that can happen is that I will have to go back into the brace if it doesn't work. What do I have to lose?"

I spent ten weeks in the hospital only because the doctor wanted to make sure I didn't develop an infection from the foot rubbing against the cast. The cast was changed weekly and I had no problems with infections. I had the surgery in June, and I was back to work in September, without the brace and without the pain from the muscle spasms. I would need to have the other foot done a few years later. Once again, the nursery school was moved to a new location, and a new head teacher was employed and a few new students were added to replace those who had moved on to other programs. Many of the changes were for the better, of course. We were becoming pretty cramped with all the new and larger pieces of equipment the Duxbury Friends were purchasing for the children. We were very fortunate to be housed in Trinity Episcopal Church in Weymouth. We were to occupy the big hall and have use of a small room for individualized instruction. Mrs. Phyllis Fazzio was the new teacher.

That year I was assigned to work extensively with one of the new students, Tommy Rymut. He was seven and soon would be eight, old enough to be in some other program. The family had just moved to the area from Long Island, New York. Tommy was a very bright child but also one of the most severely disabled that I have ever worked with. He was braced from head to toe, literally. He was fitted to a Milwaukee brace to support his neck and back, and long leg hip lock braces to support the rest of his body. Without the braces Tommy could not sit or stand unaided, and had to be placed on a floor mat. He had no usable speech either. Most communication was done with his eyes or very limited hand gestures. He was a very happy child in spite of his severe disabilities and he was a great pleasure to work with.

I remember one time working with him before he got the neck brace. He had been put in the standing table. Mrs. Fazzio decided the children would do finger painting that day. I had gone beach combing with my father a few weeks before and found half a dozen men's old shirts that had been thrown over the Gurnet cliff. I knew right away what I was going to do with them, cut the sleeves off and use them for coveralls for the kids when they painted. I put one on Tommy back side to and buttoned it at the neck so it wouldn't fall off. I took all the jars of paint to him so he could choose the colors he wanted. I was very surprised when he pointed to black, and none other. So black it was. I played games with him by writing numbers and words in the paint and I asked him to identify them. He loved these little games. He had very little control of his hand and when he tried to erase what I had written the paint went everywhere. We were both a mess by the end of the session. I told him he looked like *Little Black Sambo*. Then I went and got the big mirror so he could see for himself. We both laughed so hard we had tears streaming down our cheeks. I then had the not-so-fun job of cleaning him up. But it wasn't all that hard as we discovered the magic of mixing a little shaving cream with the finger paint. I worked with him a lot without his braces on. I would sit him up Indian style on the mat during circle time and other group activities so he wouldn't be left out. I fed him snacks.

Mr. Rymut, Tommy's father, worked at Logan Airport in Boston. He arranged for all the children from the nursery school to visit the airport and have lunch aboard one of the big planes. We talked to the children a lot about the airport, how some people checked bags outside while others carried them on board. We told them about the loud noise the planes made on takeoff.

When we got to the airport, Mr. Rymut had arranged for a stewardess to greet the children and show each child to his or her seat. Each child was given a "ticket" with a seat number on it to show to the stewardess. We had the children practice this all week. Once the children were all seated, the stewardess came around with sandwiches and drinks provided by the airline. This day made Tommy feel very special.

I had begun to work more closely with Trudy Babbit, the occupational therapist. She told me of a two-year college program offering an associate degree in that field. She advised me to look into it. My career was at a standstill at the nursery school. I saw myself being gradually pushed out with more state control over the way the school was run.

I knew I did not have enough money to continue my education as a teacher even though that was what I really wanted. But just maybe I could convince the state's Department of Rehabilitative Services to pay for a two-year program.

After much red tape, I finally managed to get DRS to sponsor me. When the dust finally settled in December of 1969, arrangements were made for me to attend Manchester Community College in September of the next year and live at the YWCA in Hartford, Connecticut for the two years of my studies. I really wanted a four year program in special education, but I would take this opportunity and worry about the rest later. I was advised to take a couple of courses in Boston while I was still working at the nursery school, so that I would not have such a heavy study load when I got to MCC. DRS would pay for me to taxi all the way to Boston. I thought that was crazy when there was a junior college practically in my back yard and the courses I needed could be taken there. I argued that it would be cheaper to taxi me there. DRS told me that they could not taxi any students to and from a college within the town where a student was living. This did not make any sense to me. I pointed out that the cost of sending me all the way to Boston would have cost fifty dollars a round trip against five dollars for transporting me within Quincy. I finally won my point, and I registered to take two English classes at Quincy Junior College.

Working full time and going to college two nights left me very little time for much else. I was pretty tired by the time the weekend rolled around and I just wanted to stay put. I saw very little of my parents after the Christmas holidays that year. I knew I had to make good grades or I would not be able to continue with my studies the next fall. I had the opportunity I had been waiting for and I wasn't about to blow it now. I knew I was going to have to close the doors to the nursery school pretty soon, but I knew others would be opened to me. I was ready for a change, whatever it was and wherever it would take me.

Camp Freedom

During the summer of 1960, the nursery would be on vacation. I would be spending much of my time with my parents and working on the door-to-door fund-raising drive for UCP. The organization sponsored a one-day trip to Martha's Vineyard Island and, of course, I went along. I don't remember where we all met. But most likely it was Woods Hole, where we would board the ferry for Oak Bluffs, cars and all. Mr. William Pinney, a prominent businessman from the island would meet us at the ferry and give us a sightseeing tour. He would take us to Gay Head, an Indian reservation and a very picturesque sight. Those of us who could, got out of the cars so we could get a better view of the magnificent breathtaking clay cliffs, and also wander into the gift shop. This shop sold Indian jewelry, hand-made from sea shells. There were also many other items, such as pottery made from the beautiful multi-colored clay taken from the cliff nearby.

On our way back to the ferry Mr. Pinney made one more stop. He had been telling Mr. and Mrs. Smith, the founders of the nursery school, about a 4H camp that had been occupied by some cerebral palsy children during the month of July and was vacant in August. He was offering it to UCP for adults from our area with cerebral palsy and other disabilities. The clubhouse was visible from the street and the cabins were set back in a pine grove– very rustic. Everyone on the trip that day was very much in favor of the idea. We all knew that it wouldn't take much to convince the board of directors to take advantage of this unique opportunity.

Needless to say, I was one of the first to request a position at the camp the following August and I would be there for four weeks of the most enjoyable work experiences of my career. I was hired to assist the cook, Mrs. Grace Murphy. She was a very sweet, elderly lady and a neighbor of the director of the camp. Together we would plan and prepare all the meals according to the day's activities. On nice days, when the campers would be off to the beach, we would pack peanut butter and jelly sandwiches, cold punch, and some homemade cookies from one of the local church groups. If we were going to be gone all day, we prepared the main meal in the morning so that, if we unexpectedly spent more time away from camp, we wouldn't be eating supper at midnight. The camp qualified for government surplus food: powdered milk, canned vegetables and fruits. I would have to whip up the milk in the morning for the campers to drink during the day. To make it drinkable I had to doctor it up with chocolate syrup. If it was cold, that milk really wasn't too bad. On Sunday mornings everyone was loaded onto the camp bus and driven to the church of his choice. For many, this was the first time they were able to attend church in many years. As Johnny April of Duxbury wrote in the camp paper– *Vineyard Views*– in 1964:

"At Camp Freedom, Sunday is the best day of the week because it gives me the opportunity to go to church which I normally can't do at home. Enjoying the privilege of summer's luxury, I am enriched spiritually and gain strength in my faith by not only entering the Holy Sacrifice of Jesus, but also, in receiving the Lord into my heart through Holy Communion, sustaining me indefinitely.

For this I am grateful, not only to Camp Freedom, but also to good priests at Our Lady of the Star of the Sea Church and to the people of the parish who so patiently and graciously assist in getting me into the church in my wheelchair."

The campers would attend every community event on the island, and take part in them whenever possible. And, of course, all the staff was needed to lend a helping hand wherever it was needed. There were wheelchairs to push and mouths to feed. So I got to go wherever the campers went and do whatever they did.

There was one very unique area in Oak Bluffs. It had several streets with gingerbread cottages on them. It was a tradition that every summer the people who owned them would decorate their porches with beautiful Japanese lanterns. I think each would try to outdo the other, and on certain nights that they called "Illumination Nights", they would light them for the whole island. It was always a spectacular sight. There was a band on the Methodist Tabernacle Camp Grounds that played on far into the night. The campers and staff would have a night out that many of us would never forget.

One morning Mrs. Murphy and I were busy making our *famous* peanut butter and jelly sandwiches to take with us on the ferry to

Nantucket. It would be a very long day. It was a three-hour trip and we would feed the campers on the ferry so they would have the rest of the day to explore the island. I was really looking forward to this trip as much as any one of the campers. It meant that I would be able to come and go pretty much as I pleased as long as I made it back to the ferry before it left.

The campers decided that if they were going to do the island justice, they would take the tour bus as I had done a few years earlier. Our driver was very knowledgeable. As we rode along he would stop at a number of houses and give a little history of each the house and its owner. Many of the houses were owned by famous sea captains back in the days when whaling was the main industry of the island. We passed many beautiful old homes with widows' walks on the roofs where wives would await the return of their husbands' ships. Of course, many of these ships were lost in the rough waters of the North Atlantic, never to return. Following the three-hour tour, we wandered through the old cobblestone streets and in and out of gift shops. May of the most interesting items found in the shops were carved from whalebones and were rather expensive. Many of the tourists got around on bicycles that they rented at the dock. At the time I saw very few cars there.

On our return trip aboard the ferry **Nantucket** the campers and staff were given the use of the ship's beautiful stateroom and lounge. We were entertained by one of the crewmen who played the guitar as we sang along to many of the popular tunes. When we got to the Vineyard, the crewmen were most helpful with getting the campers off the ship safely.

Our last part of the trip back to camp was most unusual, and I'm sure the most talked about for days, not only by the campers but also by the residents of Oak Bluffs as well. One of the councilors was sent ahead to fetch the bus to have it waiting to take the campers back to Camp Freedom as soon as they got off the ferry. When he got back to camp and tried to start the bus, the engine wouldn't even turn over. He was unable to get the bus started. He came back to the dock to inform us of the bad news.

Here we were, twenty-one tired, disabled campers and staff, stranded at the ferry's dock late at night, and no way to get back to camp. But in a few minutes our fears turned into joy when we saw some Tisbury police cars pulling into the parking lot. The policemen loaded most of the campers into their cars. With their sirens blasting and blue lights flashing they paraded through the streets of Oak Bluffs and got the campers safely home. The rest of us rode back in the camp's station wagon. What a way to end a day!

It was quite late by the time we got back to camp that night and most of us headed straight for our cabins for a good night's sleep.

One afternoon I took a stroll with a couple of the campers down New York Avenue in Oak Bluffs. We passed a stand where a young boy and girl were selling lemonade. They asked us if we wouldn't like a drink. It was a warm day so we said "Sure!" When we went to pay for them, they would not take any money. They said "All you CP campers will get your drinks free today." This was the kind of generosity we experienced throughout our month on the island.

One day three of the campers decided they wanted to try their hand at bowling. This is their story as told by Jane Augustine:

"Bowling, Rolling Away"

"On Monday Eugenia, Manny and I went bowling in Vineyard Haven. This is the first time that I ever tried this sport. The bowling alley is managed by Mr. and Mrs. Brickman. It is a combination bowling alley, poolroom and a lovely restaurant. There are many lanes with candlepins being used. The bowling balls are the small size, so this makes it easy for me to handle.

Eugenie has invented a special "bowling chute" to enable the wheelchair folks like myself to enjoy this popular sport.

Manny and I took turns using this device with assistance of Eugenia. Manny has been bowling with his Newport, MA C.P. adult group for some time. However, this has been my first time, and it may be that "beginners luck" was with me as I ended with a score of 101 with a spare to my credit.

After we were through with this wonderful game, we wanted to pay for our strings. Not only was this "gratis" from Mr. Brickman and his lovely wife, but also, we were served delicious frappes on the house. Mrs. Brickman sat and chatted with us and helped us with our drinks. As we chatted with her, she made us feel very comfortable because she was so patient and attentive to our fumbling speech and awkward movements of our hands.

Let us end here by saying, "Blessed are you who take the time to listen to a cerebral palsied's speech and blessed are you who give us comfort in and your attention. We need time rather than sympathy to prove that we can do 'the impossible', which surprises you and us."

One morning when I was helping Mrs. Murphy to clean up the kitchen after breakfast one of the campers, George Fox, came to the kitchen door and said "Arlene, something stinks in my cabin! Would you please come down and see if you can find the culprit?" I followed him to the cabin. Before I got to the door, I could smell *"the complaint"*. I entered the cabin and traced the odor to a suitcase under one of the bunk beds. When I pulled it out and opened it, there I found a dead fish. I asked George whose suitcase it was. He said he didn't know. I then asked him who went fishing with him yesterday. He told me the names of all who went with him. I knew right away which one it was and called him to the cabin and inquired about the dead fish in his suitcase. His reply was "I'm going to take it home for my mother to cook for supper." I will just mention here that this camper was mentally as well as physically handicapped. I was thankful for the camp counselor who took the clothes from the suitcase to the Laundromat and ran them through three or four washings. The suitcase was discarded, as was the fish!

I really don't remember whose idea it was to be a part of the Martha's Vineyard Society Live Stock Show and Fair. For most of the campers, just to get to go to the Fair was a big treat. But when they were told that they would have

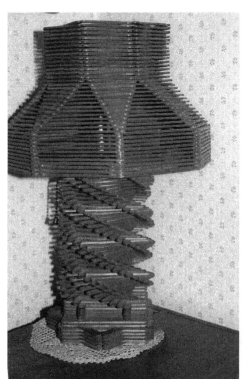

Johnny April's Popsicle Stick Lamp
Paul April

a display table there, every spare moment they had was devoted to their hand made arts and crafts.

George Fox was busy making leather goods. Johnny April was hard at work putting the finishing touches on his lamp made from popsicle sticks. I had introduced him to that craft the first summer he was at camp. Johnny did not have manual dexterity in his hands and therefore had to use his teeth to squeeze the glue from the container to the popsicle sticks. He then had to use his teeth to apply the sticks to the lamp he was building.

Another camper, Eugenia Faryniarz, was working on stained glass paintings. She would go on to win a ribbon for "best design".

Another camper was working on tooling copper pictures. Making jewelry and stuffing toys were among the favorite items of the female campers. George and Eugenia were nominated by the campers to set up the campers' exhibits at the Fair. They did a superior job and, thanks to them, our display took first prize and a Blue ribbon. Johnny's lamp attracted a lot of attention, comments and questions. It was the talk of the whole Fair. This was a very rewarding and exciting time for campers and staff of Camp Freedom.

I have often said that C.P. not only stands for "cerebral palsy", but also, *"capable people"*. And these campers certainly showed proof of this.

I remember one year when the whole camp was invited to spend the day at Mr. Pinney's home on Chappaquiddick Island. We would drive over "that infamous steep wooden bridge" where Ted Kennedy later had the accident that took the life of the lady who was riding with him

Johnny April at Chappaquiddick Beach

on that fateful night. The Pinneys owned a beautiful waterfront home. We spent the afternoon bathing and relaxing on the white sandy beach.

Later on, I looked up one of my grade school teachers who had retired to the island. We had afternoon tea together. We set aside time for our visit each summer that I worked at the camp.

For the most part, the whole staff was on call for the full four week of camp, we all pitched in to help wherever and whenever we were needed.

When I had some time to myself, which was very seldom, I would take a stroll down the road to the Flying Horses Carousel. This is the largest merry-go-round on the East Coast.

Eleanor Marnock and Johnny April at Mr. Pinney's Picnic

I had volunteered to round up new campers who lived on the mainland and assist them onto the ferry on Sunday afternoons. I also accompanied them on their return to the mainland on Saturdays to meet the drivers who would take them home. I never encountered any problems, but I was well prepared for any traffic tie-ups at the Sagamore Bridge and on the Route 3. Cape Cod traffic is terrible during the summer months. The drivers could have been delayed for an hour or more, and the campers would have been worried that they may have been forgotten. The steamship company was very cooperative and helpful in getting all the campers on and off the boat safely. And, best of all, they permitted me to ride free. I would look forward to the Saturday ride back after dropping the campers off and the Sunday ride over to meet the new ones. It was one of those times when I had an hour of the peace and solitude that I so much needed to get me through the long week ahead. If the weather was rainy, the campers found plenty of things to do to occupy their minds and keep busy. A group would congregate in a corner of the dining room to tell stories of their camping experiences and jot them down for the camp's paper. For those campers not able to write, someone would volunteer to be his secretary so he would not feel left out. This paper was a great success due in part to the generosity of one of the local residents, Mrs. Albert Silvia. She loaned the camp a mimeograph machine which made it possible for the campers to print the *Vineyard View* for all to enjoy. I kept a copy of these papers in a scrapbook and they are the main source of reference for this chapter. 1964 would be my last summer working at the camp on the Vineyard. For the next two summers I would be working at Camp Silver Towers. It was a camp for the mentally handicapped in Brookfield, Vermont.

Spain and Portugal

One winter in the mid '60s my parents were planning a trip to Florida to visit their friends Blanche and Norman White. They asked me if I would like to go along with them. At first I thought this was a grand idea. I loved to travel and see new places. Since I was working at the time, I knew this would have to be during the Christmas break and I would need to return before they did.

The more I thought about it, the less I wanted to go with them. But before I said anything to my parents, I decided to check out some other options to see if there wasn't something that I would like to do better. Just before Christmas I went to a travel agency in Quincy and started poring over some brochures. I found just the perfect vacation for me. I phoned me parents and told them not to book my flight to Florida until I got home and could show them what I had in mind instead of going with them.

That Friday evening after supper, while they were still seated around the kitchen table, I showed them my brochure and said "This is where I am going, to spend a week, in Spain and Portugal." I didn't give my mother a chance to dream up reasons why I shouldn't. I told them that I could have a ten-day holiday for only one hundred dollars more than the cost of the airfare to Florida. And since they were going to pay for that trip anyway, all I needed to come up with was the hundred dollars, and that was no problem. My father just shook his head and said "Leave it to you to find something like that." I think he was a little bit envious of me. Knowing how my father loved to travel, I think he would have liked to have come along with me.

This would be the first time I would be traveling in a country where I didn't speak its native tongue. Although I would be traveling on a group tour and be with it for most of the time, there was going to be some free time where I would want to venture off and do and see some things on my own as I had done in Great Britain a few years earlier. While some tourists use their free time to catch up on lost sleep, I knew I wouldn't do that. The week before I left, I took a good look at my itinerary for this tour and decided what I wanted to do in my free time during the day, so I would be back with the tour in time for dinner and the evening's planned activities. All my planning really paid off. When I got to Lisbon, I was met at the airport by my tour guide, who was rounding up her group to take us to our hotel. I asked to meet with her to go over the itinerary with me to make sure nothing had been changed. She told me one of the hotels on the itinerary was filled, and– we would be staying at another one. I took out a pack of 3x5 note cards I had prepared with the things I wanted to see and do, and asked her to print out the exact address of each place. This was to be used as a means of communicating with the taxi drivers to get me to places I wanted to go to, and also back to my hotel, since I did not speak the language. I could show the driver where I wanted to go and hopefully he would get me to my destination with no trouble. I found this technique very useful for me and I would use it again for a future trip.

Fortunately I have no trouble converting money from one currency to another, and I can use the local currency with reasonable accuracy once I have it. Before I left the hotel, I would figure out about how much money I was going to need for the day since the hotels gave a higher exchange rate than most other places did. This also saved time and confusion on the part of the proprietor when purchasing things. I learned that messing with traveler's checks can be a real hassle when dealing with the general public as I had experienced when I was in England.

I spent that first afternoon in Lisbon wandering through the waterfront area. In the harbor I came upon a beautiful white carving of a ship's bow with the twelve apostles standing guard over the harbor. Unfortunately, I have not been able to find any history of this beautiful piece of artwork.

I was very surprised to see just how new much of Lisbon was. I expected to see many old castles, palaces, forts, and cathedrals as I did during my trip to Great Britain. I soon learned of the Great Earthquake of 1755 that struck and destroyed most of the city. And what wasn't destroyed by the quake itself was destroyed by the fires that broke out throughout the city after the quake and the tsunami that followed. The entire city had to be rebuilt. I was very excited that this tour included a day trip to Fatima. I had read the story about the three shepherd children who were visited by the Blessed Virgin Mary on the 13th of May, 1917, and on the same day of each of the next five months. I had also seen the movie when it first came out in 1952. Now I was going to visit where this event took place. It was a 90 minute bus ride from Lisbon and I would get to see some of the country side of Portugal before heading for Spain. The Blessed Virgin Mary's predictions and secrets as told to the children are much too detailed for me try to condense for my readers. Your mouse can lead you to their story on your computer.

Before we left Portugal for Madrid, our tour guide warned us that we needed to change currencies. I was already aware of this and had very little Portuguese money left and what I did have, I packed in my suitcase the night before so I wouldn't get the two currencies mixed up since they are very similar.

Dinner hour in Madrid begins at 9 pm and lasts far into the night. Following dinner our group met in the hotel for a nightclub tour. We would do three nightclubs in one night spending about two hours in each one. Wine and food were served in all three of them along with great entertainment. At my table there were some college students on Christmas break and I had a great time chatting and joking with them. The first two clubs we were taken to we watched gypsy dancers. They came to our table several times and the young guys had a good time flirting with the dancers. I remember that the wine was very potent and I could only manage to sip on one drink throughout the entire show. The third nightclub was very formal, much like the Lido in Paris, the food and wine was so much better here than the other two. It was good that the tour saved the best for the last. By the time we got back to our hotel it was 6:30am. I didn't feel at all tired, but I knew I had to get a little catnap. Maybe a couple of hours would do. Anyway, I was on vacation and wasn't about to spend it sleeping.

During one of my strolls through the streets of Madrid, I came upon a man with a donkey cart. I soon discovered that he could understand and speak English pretty fluently. He asked me if I wanted to take his tour of the city. I had never ridden in a donkey cart before and I was all for trying new adventures, so I paid my fare, something like a dollar in American money. He said the tour would take about an hour and would end where it started. I thought this would be a good way to get to know the city so I wouldn't waste time deciding what to do next. I think he took me though every street and alleyway in the city. The one hour tour lasted two and a half hours. The poor donkey must have been exhausted. The man dropped me of at my hotel and told me to enjoy the rest of my stay in Spain. I gave him a big tip and thanked him for showing me the city.

At dinner that evening my travel companions asked if I had a good sleep as they hadn't seen me all day. I told them that I had a catnap and was out touring the city and spent the better part of the afternoon in the Prado Museum. I also told them of the donkey cart tour and how much I enjoyed it. I learned that most of them slept until two or three that afternoon. I think the college students slept off their hangover from all the wine that they had consumed the night before.

The tour included a visit to Toledo. It is noted for its steel industry and manufacturing of swords and knives.

Toledo is where El Greco the painter and architect spent most of his later years. I had seen many of his works of art in museums.

The next stop was in the province of Granada in the southern part of the country. The highlight of this tour was a visit to the Alhambra. I learned that this word means "the red fortress" in Arabic. It was built in the mid-14th century when the Muslims ruled this part of Spain.

In 1527 Charles V, the Holy Roman Emperor, built his palace within the Alhambra. There have been many changes to this beautiful complex of palaces, gardens and fountains over the centuries. But it still remains one of the finest examples of Moorish architecture in all of Europe.

The first afternoon I was in Cordoba I decided to do some shopping. I strolled down a couple of streets only to find them deserted. I went back to my hotel and asked the clerk at the desk if this was some sort of Spanish holiday that we Americans didn't celebrate. He looked at me puzzled at my question and said "No, Madam. It's just another day here."

"Then how come all the shops are closed here?"

He told me that most businesses and shops are closed every day at this time– the Siesta. They close at 13:30 (1:30) and reopen at 17:30 (5:30).

I spent a very enjoyable afternoon at the Patio de los Naranjos (Orange Tree Courtyard). It is said to be the oldest living garden in all of Europe and was started on the grounds of the Great Mosque in the year 784. It is an enclosed area with three separate parts and in the center of each section of the garden is a Renaissance style fountain. I strolled through the orange trees that were planted sometime in the 1700's or earlier.

Toward evening I headed out to do a little shopping. I wandered in and out of the small shops. When I went to pay for my gifts in one of the stores, I was told I would find the same item cheaper four doors down. I thanked the store owner kindly, but decided I would pay him for what I had selected. I did go on to the shop four doors down to see for myself and I did find the same item for about a dollar less. I had never had this experience before.

I don't recall where we stayed next, but it was some small town on the Mediterranean Sea. It was Sunday and I decided I wanted to go to church. The hotel clerk wrote out the address, and said it was a short distance away, about five minutes by cab. In those days the Catholic service was said in Latin so I knew I would have no trouble following the Mass. It was great. I could go anywhere in the world, drop into a Catholic Church and not feel like a stranger. This is not true today, however, because priests no longer use Latin in their church services.

It was a beautiful day and the beach was just a few blocks from the church and I had nothing planned for the afternoon, nothing until dinner time that evening. Our tour guide told us that Sunday was also a day of rest for the tour. A day on the beach was just what I needed, the peace and solitude, along with being away from the hustle and bustle of city life and the tour for a few hours. When I got to the water's edge I took my shoes and socks off and put them in my over-the-shoulder bag which was a little smaller than a backpack and contained several small zipper compartments. The two in the back were where I kept my passport and money. The bigger one in the front served as a catch-all and a shopping bag and was deep enough to hold a pair of shoes even though I hadn't planned for this when I bought the bag. I never left my room without it. I still have this bag and I have used it several times since this tour.

I met a man walking his dog along the water's edge. He spoke very fluent English but I didn't recognize his accent. He told me he grew up in New Zealand but had moved to Spain to attend a university. We chatted for some time. His dog was very friendly and playful. I would throw a stick into the water and he would fetch it and drop it at our feet, shaking the water from his coat each time he returned with the stick. Needless to say, my clothes got a little wet. But I was having fun and I could have cared less. I would just lie on the beach while the hot Mediterranean sun dried them in no time. It was a perfect way to end my Spanish holiday before the long bus ride back to Lisbon and the flight home.

Hartford, Connecticut

Since Manchester Community College did not have dormitories on campus, it meant that I had to find a place to live while I was attending classes. My friend Jeanne and I spent several weekends that summer in and around Manchester checking out places on the housing list given to me by the college. Most of the rooming houses were too far from the college and there was no public transportation within walking distance. Finally, out of desperation, Jeanne said, "Arlene, there must be a YWCA somewhere near here where young working girls can live. Not everyone has a car, you know. Maybe we ought to try and see if there is one near the college." That afternoon we drove back to the college and talked to the lady in charge of housing for out of town students. She told us that the nearest YWCA was in Hartford, the nearest big city to here, and only about a twenty minute drive. She told us there was bus service from Hartford to the college. I told Jeanne, "This sounds more like it to me. Let's go check it out".

When Jeanne and I got to the YWCA, it was around 3 pm on a Friday. The director showed us to her office. Her name was Miss Bartlett. She spoke with an English accent and very businesslike. I told her I had been accepted at Manchester Community College and I was looking for a place to live and study for the next two years. I told her that I was being sponsored by the Department of Rehabilitative Services (DRS) while I was at college. I told her that I would give this information to DRS, but I thought this would work out for me. She said that there was a cafeteria that is open five days a week but closed on weekends and a laundry room and vending machines in the basement.

As soon as I left work, I had reapplied for Social Security Disability and I knew this money would cover my living expenses here. With DRS paying a dollar a meal, I could make ends meet okay. I left Miss Bartlett's office in a much better frame of mind than when Jeanne and I started out earlier that morning, knowing that our search had failed to come up with anything for four week ends in a row.

I spent the next two weeks with my parents relaxing on the beach when the weather permitted.

I tried to spend as much time as I could spare with my best friend Diane and the children. At this time she was living just up the street from me. She was going through a very difficult time. Her second son David had passed away from complications from having his appendix out. He had been given an overdose of anesthesia at Jordan Hospital in Plymouth, Massachusetts and never made it home. By the time he was transferred to Children's Hospital in Boston, it was too late. The damage to his brain had already been done.

On top of this, Diane's oldest boy Rusty had been doing poorly in school. I told her I thought he might have a learning disability and advised her to have him tested at Massachusetts General Hospital's Speech and Language Clinic. I had learned about the clinic through a very dear friend of mine, Ruth Gardner, who taught remedial reading and also trained under the director of the clinic. At this time, the mid 1960s, not much was being done to educate these children. Many of them were labeled (mentally retarded) or they fell between the cracks of the educational system because teachers were not trained to work with them. This happened to be the case with Rusty. Once the diagnosis was made, nobody knew how to teach him.

Today, there are programs and even schools to help these children. But, even so, many are not being given the opportunity to reach their full potentials. Rusty surely wasn't. I worked with him when I was home, but this was not enough and I knew he needed more help than I had time for. Diane was very concerned about him and I knew it.

I need to tell you about my friend Ruth Gardner. We met one summer at Camp Jened in the Catskill Mountains Ruth was a paraplegic. She lived at the Boston Home for the Incurables. The name doesn't do the home justice, and was later changed to The Boston Home. She taught from her wheelchair. The Home had given her the use of a beautiful sunroom to use as a schoolroom. She kept all of her books and teaching supplies there. She had a large blackboard and a table and chairs to fit her very young pupils. She tutored one on one. Most of her pupils came to her from private schools like Thayer Academy or from well-to-do parents who could afford to pay to have their children tutored.

Ruth was a graduate of Radcliff College and taught for many years before she became ill with a cyst that had interwoven with her spine and had left her paralyzed from the waist down. She was one of the most inspiring persons I have ever met.

I had talked about Ruth often with my parents. Finally my father's curiosity got the better of him. He wanted to put a face to the person I had so admired. He said, "Why don't you invite her to have dinner with us some Sunday." I was delighted with the suggestion, but I knew it meant he would have to drive all the way to Dorchester to pick her up. And I knew how much my father hated driving to Boston. It meant four hours on the road, two round trips in one day. But since he was the one who mentioned it, not me, I guessed it was ok.

I visited with Ruth shortly after that and told her what my father had suggested. At first, she thought like I did, that it was putting too much of a burden on my father. But I told her that it was his idea in the first place and I thought he would be very disappointed if she declined. We set the date.

And when the day finally came, everything went so perfectly. I went with my father to get Ruth, while mother stayed at home to prepare a roast beef dinner. I think I talked about her all the way up. I had told my dad that Ruth wore long leg braces and that she needed no help getting in and out of the car. She was used to traveling by taxi whenever she had to go anyplace. My Dad had cleaned out the trunk the night before to make room for her wheelchair. Our house had one step onto the back porch and this was no big problem.

I had to ride in the back seat on the way home so Ruth could have the front one. My father and she talked all the way home. I couldn't get a word in edgewise. My father was the type of person who never knew a stranger, so I had expected that. That afternoon after dinner, we all went for a ride around town. We showed Ruth the 'Miles Standish Monument'. It was known to be "the tallest monument in the world, 225 feet tall with 'Miles' on top of it!" We showed her where I went to high school, and I pointed out my church. We sat at the yacht club for a while and watched all the boats come and go. We took her over the old wooden bridge to Duxbury Beach where the boards rattle with each passing car and where workmen can be seen each summer replacing a board or two, but never really making much of any improvements.

This was such a perfect day and I hated to see it come to a close.

She passed away not long after this visit, but the inspiration she showed me lives with me forever.

The move to Hartford took quite a lot of planning. I knew that once I got there I wouldn't get home again until the Christmas break. By now, I had been used to living in one room, but if I forgot something, it was no big deal. I could wait until I got home in a week or so and take it back with me. This time it would be four months before I could get home.

I decided I had better make a list of the things I needed to take and things that could wait until I got settled in and could buy locally. At the top of the list were things I needed for college, my electric typewriter, the tape recorder and a large box of tapes, enough to tape all of my lectures for a full year. DRS had bought the recorder and the tapes so I wouldn't have to rely on other students' notes since my own handwriting is so poor and I cannot hear all that well. The one thing I can't live without is a good dictionary, and of course notebooks and plenty of paper and pens.

I needed clothes enough for all four seasons and I knew space was very limited at the YWCA, so I really had to plan my wardrobe very carefully. Mother and I were the same size and we often shared our clothes. I tended to lean a little more toward the casual look than she did, and the more conservative colors. I figured that anything green, purple or yellow was hers and anything blue, red or brown was mine. She never complained. So I guess I must have left her with enough of the right things. This was to be the last time we would share one another's clothes.

The week before I left, I phoned my friend Jeanne and asked her if she would drive me to Hartford. I knew only too well that my dad did not like driving long distances, especially on unfamiliar roads. She could come down from work the day before and have dinner with us. We would use my parents' car, and they would be riding with us. My dad was delighted with this arrangement. He had ridden with her one summer when they picked me up from camp in the Catskill Mountains, and we all had a very enjoyable week end.

I really didn't like riding with my dad. He would never stop to ask directions and would drive for miles not knowing where he was going. Jeanne and I had done the trip many times over the past few weeks. By now, I think she knew every back road and short cut there was from Duxbury to Hartford.

My dad packed my things into the trunk of the car and we were on our way. I rode in the front seat with Jeanne and my parents settled themselves in the back seat. Jeanne and I had found a really nice restaurant a couple of weeks before, where they served home style meals, and I knew my parents would like it. Besides good food, it was also a most unusual Christmas gift shop. I can't remember whether it was on Rte. 44 or Rte. 63. In any case, it was in Connecticut half-way between Providence and Hartford.

We drove through Manchester so I could show my parents where I would be going to school for the next two years. They were quite pleased that it was a small college.

They were disappointed that I couldn't find a room nearer the college. I said that if I didn't have to rely on public transportation, it wouldn't have been a problem. Besides that, the Y appeared to be very well run and the commute wouldn't be all that bad. I had no early classes and no night ones either. My earliest was at 9:30 am, and my latest one ended at 3:30 pm. This put me back at the Y in time for the evening meal. At least I wouldn't be riding subway trains at nine o'clock at night like I had in Boston some years earlier. I knew my parents were happy about this. All my parents wanted to do now was to get me settled in, so they could get home before dark. The first semester was perhaps the hardest for me. I was taking four classes and all were very demanding. The one class I had the most trouble with was philosophy. The professor taught it like his students were all graduate students, not undergraduates. He knew his subject too well to be teaching a freshman class. I think most of us in this class felt the same way. All I wanted was a passing grade so I wouldn't have to take it again. And that is exactly what I got.

I took the history of fine arts for two semesters. This was one of my favorite classes. One of the girls I met at the Y, Rita Goff and I spent many Saturday afternoons at the Wardsworth Atheneum in Hartford where I could see first-hand what I was studying. This was a big help to me, plus the fact that I had been to Europe and had seen much of the old architecture and grew to appreciate it.

My sociology professor was very good. But he had a very bad habit of wandering up and down the aisles as he lectured making it very hard for me to catch everything he was talking about because of my hearing loss. He also had a German accent which added to the problem.

One day I had had enough of his aisle walking. I got to class early and rearranged all the chairs so there were no aisles, just rows of seats like in a theater. I did this several times. There was no more aisle walking. I think the rest of the class knew what I had done, but nobody ever said anything.

I had plenty of free time to devote to my studies. I was taking four classes. Two were on the same day, so I only had to go into Manchester three days a week and I really liked that. If for some reason I had to use the college library, I would plan on spending an extra two or three hours there after a morning class and be back at the "Y" before the rush hour. The main bus stop on Constitution Avenue was sometimes worse than New York's Grand Central Station in early morning and late afternoon. People were like a pack of wild dogs fighting for their prey. People pushed and shoved and even used language that I never heard before. I remember once getting pushed against the side of the bus so hard that two of my fingers on my left hand were broken. The college nurse splinted them and sent me on my way. I was warned by the director of the "Y" never to carry a purse. And I took her advice seriously after I saw what I was confronted with at the bus stop. I wore slacks with deep front pockets most of the time and I didn't carry much more money than what I needed for the bus and a snack from the vending machines at college if I had to stay to use the library.

I met two very nice young ladies at the "Y", Rita and Kathy. They were keypunch operators. They both worked in the same office in Weathersfield, a small town just outside of Hartford. We usually ate breakfast and supper together during the week and on Saturday afternoons we met for a little recreation and lunch after we cleaned up our rooms. Sometimes we would spend the afternoon just window shopping. Rita and I were about the same size and we had the same style haircuts, short and straight. We also had similar tastes when it came to clothes. I remember a couple of times when we were shopping we came home with the same outfits and dressed alike. The director, Miss Bartlett, would say "There go the Bobbsey Twins." I am very petite and enjoyed shopping in the children's department for things like pajamas, socks and under pants, not only because they were cheaper than adult sizes, but because Connecticut had no sales tax on children's clothes at that time.

Rita, Kathy and I often attended Sunday Mass at Saint Joseph's Cathedral on Farmington Avenue, just a couple of blocks from the "Y". This cathedral was first opened in 1962. It replaced the old gothic cathedral which burned beyond repair in 1956. The new cathedral has some of the most spectacular stained-glass windows that I have ever seen. I learned that they were crafted and imported from Paris. I also learned that the ceramic tile mural behind the main altar is the largest of its kind in the world. Some of the organ's pipes, 8000 in all, are so long (32 feet) that they had to be lifted into place with a crane before the roof could be put into place. The cross on the steeple is made of stainless steel and stretches 25 feet toward Heaven.

I often came back to the "Y" from church and prepared my lessons. I knew I had to do well in all my studies if I wanted to remain in the program. Since I am a very slow reader, I had to spend much more time on my homework than most of my classmates. If I had a paper due during the week, I locked myself in my room until it was finished. Typing is still very tedious work for me. But, thanks to modern technology, I have fewer typographical errors now than I did then. If I had a really long paper to write, it took double time because I knew I had to pay someone to retype it for me. A few times I was able to use the same research paper for two classes, changing some of the details a little. I never studied beyond midnight. This was a ***golden rule*** for me. And I stuck to it throughout all my studies and even when working on this book. If I needed more time, I just got up a little early the next morning and began on a well-rested brain. When I was finished with all the demanding book learning of the course, I was more than ready for the next stage of the two year program. I would be spending my next ten weeks in training at Cedarcrest Hospital, a psychiatric hospital. I would have to live in one of the staff dormitories for the ten weeks training.

On the first day of our training we were given a walking tour of all of the buildings and introduced to many of the daytime staff and saw some of the patients we would be working with in the coming weeks. I don't recall how many buildings there were in all, but each building was identified with a number as opposed to a name. I think this made it easier for the staff in the event of an emergency when outside help was needed. There were times when the alarm would go off in the middle of the night. If the students listened carefully, we knew which building signaled the alarm simply by the number of beats between intervals. Of course, we never knew which patient was in need of help until the next morning when we gathered for a briefing and were given our assignment for the day. I remember one such incident when a man had set his night clothes on fire. Once I had been working with a lady during the morning and when I went back to get her for a group session that afternoon, the nurse on her floor said she had choked to death on a piece of meat at lunchtime. I did hear the alarm go off a short time earlier, but I was too busy to pay it much mind.

I remember working with a fourteen year old girl who was there because she had stabbed and killed her brother with a kitchen table knife. She said they had been fighting and they both picked up something and threw it at each other. Her drawings were always in black crayons and showed a lot of people at a grave with a casket on top of the grave. I wanted to cry every time I saw what she had drawn. Once she asked me if anyone would ever forgive her. I told her God always forgives, even when people don't. We talked about this often. This young girl stayed in the back of my mind long after my training was over.

I don't recall just where I did my next training, but it was a very big hospital in Hartford and again I lived in a dorm. This time it was for nursing students. I bought most meals in the hospital's cafeteria, and did much of my studying in my supervisor's office where it was quiet and where I had access to her teaching materials. Most of my weekend evenings were spent here.

My training session went very well here when I finally got to work with the patients. Being that I lived in the dorm, I often went to the patients' rooms to assist them with bathing, dressing and eating, activities of daily living skills (ADL). I remember one of my patients. He had been in a motorcycle accident. He was pretty banged up. He was in a body cast and not able to move much. I think his spinal cord was badly damaged. I doubted very much that he would ever walk again. All he kept talking about was the day when he would get out of the hospital so he could get back on his motorcycle again and join his racing buddies. I guess he hadn't learned anything from the accident.

I worked a lot with stroke patients. Most of them had good communication skills but they were hemiplegic and had to learn to do a lot of things one-handed. This can be very frustrating for the patient, particularly if the dominant hand has been badly affected from the stroke, and he had to learn to write and feed himself with the other one.

Working with children who are born hemiplegic is so much different than working with adults who acquire this condition later on in life. You train a child to use what he has, while you have to retrain an adult and it is much more difficult. Children have never known any different, so they are much easier to work with. Their attitudes are so much more positive and they are more accepting of their condition. They often don't even realize that they are different. They just fit in and go along with the flow. Adults get very frustrated and angry at the time it takes for retraining. They are generally very impatient, or they just give up altogether. They often think they have to accept the way they have become as an end to who they really are.

YWCA Tour of Western Europe

Long before my training session ended, I had decided to go to Europe with a YWCA tour. Little did I know that this trip would interfere with my graduation date from college. My heart was in having some fun in Europe, and nothing was going to change that. The college would just have to mail me my diploma. I earned it and nobody could take it away from me. I don't know if my parents were disappointed with my decision, or not. But if they were nothing was ever said. I was very happy to leave Hartford and the college behind.

I had a most wonderful two weeks of sightseeing. Our hotels weren't the best, but this didn't really matter to me. I spent very little time in them anyway. In Paris the hotel was on the River Seine and within walking distance of Notre Dame Cathedral. I bought two pictures, one of The Crucifixion which I still have hanging over my bed, and the other of 'The Agency in the Garden' which I gave to my friend Rita. She still has hers too. My Dad made the frames for both of them. I took a boat ride at night. The cathedral is such a spectacular sight from the river. I went to the top of the Eiffel Tower, and walked under the Arc de Triomphe. I spent an afternoon in the Louvre. I just had to see Leonardo De Vinci's painting of the Mona Lisa. Of course, nobody in his right mind would visit Paris without doing a nightclub tour and ending up at the Lido. I guess I wasn't out of my mind; I did that too.

Our next city was Amsterdam. We spent two days here. Of course I wasted no time. As soon as we got our room assignments, I was off to see about a city tour so I would know where I wanted to spend my valuable time. My number one place was the house where Ann Frank and her family spent their last two years in hiding from the Germans during World War II before they were captured and sent to a concentration camp. I was told by the tour guide that if I wanted to go inside, it would have to be on my own time as the house was too small for group tours. I skipped dinner that evening so I could get in without waiting in the long lines earlier in the day.

I had read *The Diary of Ann Frank* earlier that year and when I saw this house, I couldn't see how the whole family survived for two years in such a small space. It brought tears to my eyes. When I saw the play a few years later, I had a better idea of just how little room the Franks really had. It wasn't even as much as the stage on which the play was performed.

I just had to see some of the Dutch paintings. This meant a trip to the Rijksmuseum. I especially wanted to see some of Rembrandt's, Van Gogh's and Van Dyke's paintings. The museum is just too large to take in everything and I learned how to select what I was interested in and forget the rest. I don't know what the rest of the people on my tour did in the evening. But I took a canal tour and enjoyed it so much that I took the same tour twice more before I went back to my hotel for a good night's sleep. In Brussels I took the city's tour to see where things were located. I don't know whether the tour guide spoke Dutch or French, but it didn't matter much to me. I just wanted to be able to find the best shopping area and a museum or two. We only had an overnight stay here and I wanted to make the most of my time. Belgium is noted for its beautiful lace, and I had told my mother I would bring her something special from here. I found the perfect gift, a beautiful bureau scarf. It was about 5 feet in length. I don't think Mother ever took it off the bureau except maybe to launder it. When our tour got to Lucerne, Switzerland, for some unexplained reason, our hotel reservations were messed up and we were sent to the Benedictine Abbey in Einsiedeln. Most of the other tourists were disappointed, but not me! It was one of the most memorable experiences of this trip. After we got settled in and met for dinner in the abbey's beautiful dining room everyone had decided to make the best of the situation. That evening, a few of us gathered to chat with some of the nuns. They spoke German but understood far more English than any of us did German. Nonetheless we seemed to be able to converse pretty well. The next morning I was up very early and decided I would wander through the courtyards and gardens of this beautiful abbey at sunrise. From my window I could see snow on the mountain peaks of the Swiss Alps even though it was summertime and quite warm where I was staying.

As I started past the church I heard the organ playing and decided it wasn't too early to pay a visit and explore the inside. I had studied art history in college the year before, but nothing could have prepared me for what I was about to see here. I had been in many beautiful gothic churches over the past few years but never had I seen anything more magnificent than this baroque structure of pastel blue and gold. It was so breathtaking. As I entered the church, the first thing I noticed was the beautiful main altar of black marble against the gold and pastel background.

I learned that in 835 a monk had left a monastery to live the remainder of his life as a hermit on the site of this beautiful church. Meinrad brought with him a crow and a Black Madonna. After twenty-six years he was murdered. The statue was found and a small cloister was built on the site to house it. According to legend, the crow followed the two bandits responsible for this murder, hovering over them making strange loud noises until they were captured some thirty miles from the site.

Nothing remains of the original building including the Black Madonna. Everything was destroyed by fire and was rebuilt over the centuries. The Black Madonna I saw over the altar was carved before 1466.

Our tour would travel through the beautiful mountain sides of Austria and Liechtenstein before returning home. We spent two nights in a mountain town in Austria. It was probably a very busy ski resort in winter. It had many very nice gift shops. Some of us enjoyed an afternoon of hiking. I have never regretted taking this tour over graduation exercises. I got my diploma and that was all that mattered to me.

Norfolk, Virginia

When I first moved to Norfolk, I took a room at the YWCA. It was located on the top floor of the Jefferson Hotel, one block from downtown.

After I finished my schooling at Manchester Community College, I went home to my parents' for the summer and began a long search for a job as a certified occupational assistant (COTA). I answered an ad in the Occupational Therapy Journal that was looking for a COTA at Tidewater Rehabilitation Institute in Norfolk, Virginia. I had no idea where Norfolk, Virginia was, only that it was somewhere on the coast of Virginia. I knew it had the largest Navy base in the world. I looked it up on the map and told my parents that I had answered the ad. The head of the department of occupational therapy called me one afternoon to tell me that she had accepted my application for employment. I was delighted with this and told my parents that I was going to try it out. I had no place to stay and knew no one in Norfolk, so I decided to call the YWCA once again. They told me they had rooms and asked what days I needed. I told them I wanted a permanent residence, so I packed my suitcase once again and was off to a new adventure.

My parents drove me to Logan Airport in Boston, Massachusetts and I bought a 'one-way' ticket to Norfolk, Virginia. I didn't know it at the time, but I would never call Duxbury, Massachusetts my 'home' again. I would be standing on my own two feet from now on.

Upon arrival at the Norfolk International Airport I took a taxi and gave the driver an address on Busch Street. I didn't know that the YWCA was the same address as the Jefferson Hotel and I was kind of confused. Before I let the driver leave I went into the hotel to make sure I was at the correct address. The hotel clerk said that I was. She told me that the YWCA occupied the top floor of our hotel. I went out and paid the driver and told him he could leave now, since I was at the right location.

I arrived at the YWCA on a Friday night and had to start work on the following Monday morning. I was shown to my room. It was quite a large room. I was told that I would have a roommate.

This was 'news' to me. My experience with my first roommate was a disaster. I found money missing from my drawer. She used personal items without my permission. She just helped herself to all my things. I could not deal with this so I reported her to the YWCA director. She took her out of my room. She replaced her the thief with another lady. We became long-time friends. She worked at the Chrysler Museum and was the Educational Program Coordinator for the museum. Her name is Ann Vaughn. When I started teaching, I would make arrangements with Ann to take my group to the museum. She would always ask me what age group I was bringing because, in the beginning, I had young children along with adults. So she had to put them into two separate tours to meet the needs of the group. She made the tours so interesting, regardless of the age group. She was just so wonderful with the groups. We often met at parties and social gatherings and it was so great to see each other once again. She always made a point to sit down and chat with me for a while. I will forever be grateful for her friendship.

On Monday morning I started my new job at Tidewater Rehabilitation Institute (TRI). The institute was an outpatient treatment center affiliated with Norfolk General Hospital. It was a separate building from the hospital, and across the street. When I arrived I was introduced to the rest of the staff by the director of occupational therapy. My new working area was a very large, sunny room and was very well equipped.

I really did not want to work in occupational therapy. I wanted to be a teacher. But, unfortunately, in order to continue my education I took what the Department of Rehabilitative Services offered me. I was not very happy working at TRI because my heart was in teaching, not in occupational therapy. I did not last too long there. I don't remember if I quit or was fired.

After leaving TRI I went to a program for mentally retarded children at a Catholic Church on Government Avenue. Many educational programs for physically and mentally disabled children were located in churches because the cities and towns would not accept the responsibility for their education. They were privately sponsored by other organizations. I wasn't there very long when they referred me to the United Cerebral Palsy Organization.

UCP in turn referred me to a program that was located in the Bayside Presbyterian Church in Virginia Beach. I left the Catholic Church program and started working for the UCP program located in the Presbyterian

Church. There were two groups in this one program. One was for very young children and the other for adults, all with cerebral palsy. The mentally handicapped young children had been rejected from the public school system. The adults with cerebral palsy had no other programs to attend. Some of these adults were very bright. I felt such a bond with them. We could relate to one another and I felt at home with them.

We had three drivers to drive the vans to pick up the clients. Some of the clients lived in Hampton and Newport News. They had a very long ride to and from the church every day. They had to go through the Hampton Roads Tunnel to transport the clients. Sometimes the traffic tie-ups at the tunnel were unbelievable, especially in the mornings during rush-hour traffic. Sometimes the trips would last three hours one way. The children were very cranky before they even got to school and then they had the return trip in the afternoon. My heart went out to the very, very faithful and patient drivers.

Lunch time was a busy time at the center. One day another worker and I discovered our wallets were missing from our purses. She called the police immediately. They found our wallets in a ditch by the side of the road not too far from the church, with the money missing, but all our identification papers were intact. I had learned to carry only as much money as I thought I would need for the day, so I didn't lose much. And I was delighted to get all my ID paperwork back. We never did find the thief. But only God knows who he was!

I worked for UCP for a couple of years until the funds dried up and the organization could no longer afford to pay its staff. The program was then taken over by the Virginia Beach Community Services Board. At first, Norfolk residents were allowed to remain in the program. And things seemed to be going along quite smoothly. But, when Virginia Beach residents applied for the program, space was limited and there wasn't enough room for everyone to participate. So the Norfolk residents were put out of the program.

I often worked with the younger children while Diana, as the head teacher, worked with the older folks. We had two volunteers. One of our volunteers was Sylvia Roughten, whose husband owned Roughten Pontiac. The other was Connie Zudima. She later became a special education teacher. She was an elementary school teacher who later on got her master's degree in special education. Both ladies were members of the church. There were others, but these two became my good friends. Connie took over the program when Diana left to get married. Connie and I worked together very well.

When the "Y" closed its doors a year later, a few of us stayed on as residents of the hotel. There was no dining room in the hotel and we had to eat most of our meals elsewhere. I was given permission to buy a small refrigerator and a hot plate for heating food and water. I used to have to buy meat that was already cooked, and mostly canned vegetables, which I hated.

I decided it was high time I started looking for a furnished apartment. I checked the newspapers daily until I finally found something that sounded reasonably priced. I had no idea where Ocean View was, but decided to check out the apartment anyway. It was quite a long distance from downtown on the bus. It was on the waterfront. I thought this can't be too bad. I went to the landlord and checked the apartment out. There was a gentleman sitting outside on the bench. I asked him if there was police protection here. He told me "Oh yes Ma'am. We have 24 hour police protection here." I thanked him for the information, but knew right then and there that I didn't want to live there because I knew it was a rough neighborhood.

My search for an apartment was still ongoing. I found another apartment. This one was off Colley Avenue, on 51st Street. I decided to check it out the next day. I took the bus to 51st Street and strolled down the street. It looked like a pretty good neighborhood, very residential. And the houses were well kept. I saw a lady sitting on her porch and went up to her and asked her if the area was police patrolled. And she said "Oh no Ma'am...this is a residential neighborhood. We have no need for police patrol here at all."

I said "Thank you very much." I saw the outside of the house that the apartment was in. I liked what I saw, and when I got back to the 'Y' I called the landlord and asked him if I could see the apartment that he had for rent. He and I made an arrangement to meet the next afternoon at the apartment. I had made up my mind beforehand that I would take the apartment anyway as it looked like it was in a good neighborhood, and it was on a bus line. The next day he showed me the apartment. It had two rooms, a big kitchen and a living room/bedroom combination. I gave him a deposit and told him I would move in the next weekend. He gave me the key right then and there and said "It's all yours." I thanked him very much and almost 'danced' out the door.

A few days later my girlfriend, Diana, one of my co-workers and I shopped and got $13.00 worth of cleaning supplies and went to the apartment. She started at the top in the kitchen, pulling open the cupboards and finding rotten food in some of them. We had a few laughs before we got serious about cleaning it out. It was a lot of work but we managed to get the place livable. She put shelf paper in the cupboards and the drawers. The table in the kitchen was a drop-leaf with two chairs, one of which was broken. In the living room was an old-fashioned, double-sized brass bed. There were no closets in the living room, but there was an old-fashioned wardrobe with double doors and a drawer underneath. There was a sofa in this room that had two pillows on the seat. When I lifted the pillows up I found two big holes underneath. We managed to get everything cleaned up so it looked presentable. There was a three-piece bath, but no tub, just a metal shower. The shower was rusted on the outside.

This was my first apartment. I had to make many changes in it to make it more livable. The first thing I did was to get rid of the kitchen set and get a new one, bright yellow and white. There was the table and two chairs. Shortly after that I bought a hutch to match the kitchen table and chairs. The kitchen really looked pretty nice at this point, except for the badly worn out linoleum. I had my own refrigerator so the landlord took his out. By now my apartment was really 'coming together'.

There was a cat that kept coming to me and I inquired about it to Edie, one of the neighbors, and she said that the previous tenant of my apartment had gone off and left it. I finally let it in and fed it. I wasn't supposed to have any pets so I had to make sure it was out when I went to work. One morning, when I went to go to work, I couldn't find him. I thought he was out. While I was waiting for my ride to work, I glanced up at my apartment and saw the cat 'sitting pretty' in the window behind the curtains. I had to go in and let him out. I said "You sneaky thing!" So from then on he was called "Sneaky". The previous tenant came back two months later looking for 'her' cat. Edie told her the cat had a 'good home' now. I had Sneaky for about fifteen years.

Edie knew I was alone. She told Barbara, who lived in back of her, that I would like some company and suggested that she come and visit me. Barbara said she wouldn't go alone so Edie introduced us. And, it wasn't long before Barbara and I became best friends. We discovered that we liked to read the same kind of books. We read a lot of historical novels and biographies. We also liked classical and easy-listening music. I soon learned that she was a home-body, while I liked to be on the move. We both loved Scrabble and we played it by the hour. We both had good vocabularies which made for interesting games. We were not bothered by time and we didn't care how long it took to finish a game.

One day Barbara and I were playing Scrabble and her dog, a Chinese pug named Susie Wong, got hold of two tiles from the game that had fallen on the floor. Barbara caught her chewing on them and took them away, but not before she had left her teeth marks on them. One of the letters was an 'A' and the other was a 'U'. After that, when we played Scrabble, we never took the chewed tiles until one of us got the 'Q' so we could play the 'U' with the 'Q'. I guess this was cheating, but what the heck, we had fun anyway.

I remember one time I bought Barbara a Scrabble dictionary for Christmas and she was *so* excited when she opened it. Her husband Lee was so angry because she liked my gift better than what he bought her. I would buy Barbara books for Christmas and her birthday, but would always read them first to make sure they were well written. If they were not well written, she didn't get the books. I think she did the same for me. I would tell her about something in the book and she would tell me she already knew about that. That is how I knew she read the book before she gave it to me. It didn't matter whether the books were new or not. We had our favorite secondhand bookstore. We got to know the owners pretty well, so they would let us put books on lay-away. Sometimes one or the other of us would go in to pick up a book that was on layaway and it wouldn't be there. We knew immediately what had happened. We would just have to wait for that next special occasion to roll around.

Barbara seldom went out of her home. She always had the excuse that she had to 'clean something' in the home. Edie drove when we went out. She invited Barbara and me to go shopping at the most **exclusive** shops in town. Barbara had expensive taste so that sounded like fun to her. Edie took us to Salvation Army, Goodwill and a thrift shop where they hired help with mental disabilities. Barbara said "That's one you pulled over on me!" And then she laughed so hard she had tears running down her cheeks. Edie and Barbara were so much fun to be with. I never knew what was going to come out of their mouths.

I hadn't lived here very long, when my parents decided to pay me a visit. They flew down from Boston and rented a car when they got here. I guess they were curious to see what I was up to now. My father wanted to paint the living room walls to brighten them up. They were so drab and dirty looking. My mother wanted to paint the shower. My father asked me if I knew the neighbor next door so he could borrow a ladder. I told him I did. "A very nice lady across the street, and her name is Edie" After supper that first night, he said he was going to see if she had a stepladder he could borrow for a couple of days. I said to my mother "He is gone for the night!" Mother asked what I meant by that. I told her that Edie will have met her match when she meets my father, since they were both good talkers. Sure enough, my father came back three hours later without the ladder. I thought maybe he forgot to ask for it, or maybe she just forgot to give it to him. The next morning the ladder was at the back door. That day we went shopping for paint and other supplies. By the time my parents left a few days later, my apartment looked so nice. My mother had painted the shower white, but then took a sponge and dabbed it in yellow paint and spotted the walls of the shower and also painted the rest of the bathroom to match it. The yellow paint matched my kitchen set. Soon after my parents left, I got rid of the old brass bed and in its place I got a captain's bed with drawers underneath for my linens and towels. There was an old, worn-out oriental rug on the living room floor. I replaced that with a new, bright-colored carpet. These changes really livened up that place.

One day when I was in the living room I heard a crash. I went to the kitchen to see what had happened. I thought the cat had gotten into something. To my horror, I found a big chunk of the ceiling had fallen down. I cleaned up the mess and called the landlord and told him that a part of the ceiling in the kitchen had fallen down. He did nothing about it. I reminded him the next week, but still he did nothing about it. A month later it was still the same, so I decided to call the Norfolk Health Department.

When the health department inspector came over a day later, she said "The ceiling has to be fixed and the landlord will have to put in new linoleum on the kitchen floor. He will also need to replace those outside steps going into this apartment." Otherwise the apartment would be condemned. The Norfolk Health Department contacted my landlord with this information.

To my surprise, everything was done within a reasonable time frame. Rather than rebuilding the stairs, he built a platform and a ramp with a railing along the side. I got some green paint and painted the railing. I got some indoor/outdoor carpeting to put on the ramp so it wouldn't be slippery when it got wet from the rain. I lived here until 1978 when I found a much nicer apartment on 47th Street and Colley Avenue. It was a little nearer to Old Dominion where I was taking courses.

I was living on 47th Street at the time my father passed away in January of 1979. Mother was staying with Edie on 51st Street for the winter. I spent a lot of my spare time at Edie's particularly on weekends. Barbara would often join us for a game of bridge in the afternoon. Sometimes when Edie would go off for the day, Mother and I would play Scrabble.

The next year Mother came down before Thanksgiving and stayed until the end of March. I was still living on 47th Street, but things were about to change once again. Barbara's aunt Mildred, who lived in the same apartment house as Barbara, had passed away. Barbara talked to her landlord, who happened to be my landlord also. She asked him if I could have Mildred's apartment and he agreed. I was delighted with this. At last, I would have a **real** apartment. I would no longer have to eat and sleep in the same room. I would have a bedroom and a dining room separate from my living room. Each apartment (there were four, two up and two down) had its own screened-in porch. Another nice thing about this was that Edie's house and my apartment were back to back with a low fence separating the two yards. Edie put cement blocks on both sides of the fence so we could visit each other without having to walk around the block. We just climbed over the fence. For about a week before I got moved, Edie, my mother and I began taking some of my things to my new apartment on 52nd Street. Then Sylvia Roughton and one of her boys came with her station wagon to move the few heavy pieces of furniture I had, the hutch, the captain's bed, and an over-stuffed chair, and the kitchen table. She had to make two trips. While she and her sons were loading the station wagon for the second trip, it started to snow.

This was the beginning of a three-day blizzard, so rare for the Tidewater area. Norfolk literally shut down for nearly two weeks. The city did not have adequate snow removal equipment to handle such a large amount of snow. The equipment it did have was barely able to plow the main streets, and the side streets just had to wait until the temperature got above freezing and the sun came out during the day to melt the snow.

    I was in my senior year at Old Dominion University and my final semester before graduation in June. I was student teaching at Lakewood School. At that time this school was divided into two sections to accommodate mentally retarded children at one end of the building and the physically disabled who could not attend classes in neighborhood schools in the other end. I was very fortunate to have been assigned to this school for both sessions of my student teaching. Each of us had to teach a certain number of hours in order to graduate in June. When the big snowstorm came and all the schools in the area were closed for more than a week, it made us very uneasy as we knew it would be difficult to make up for lost time. Unlike the other classes where there are extra-curricular activities for student teachers to participate in, special education classes did not have any. Our lost hours had to be made up somewhere and we all knew it. We sat down with paper and pencils and figured out how many hours we would have to make up. We figured out that if we arrived an hour early and stayed an hour later each day, by the end of the session we would accumulate enough hours to meet the graduate requirements. While I enjoyed this experience very much, I was relieved to put it behind me. Mother came down in May of 1980 for my graduation. My dad would have been *so* proud of me. I lived on 52nd Street until 1986. Because I wasn't near a shopping area, I had to depend on Lee or Edie to take me grocery shopping. Helen Wolff was living in Granby House, one of the two senior citizen apartment complexes at the time in the Ward's Corner area which was the oldest shopping center in Norfolk. Even though I was not yet a senior citizen, I qualified to live there because of my disability and low income. I talked it over with my mother and she thought it was a good idea. Since my rent would be based on my income, we both knew I would have a roof over my head. I would have to be put on a waiting list and wait my turn but this didn't really matter to me.

    One evening while I was at my mother's following her stroke in the summer of 1986, I received a call from Helen informing me that the manager had been trying to reach me to find out if I was still interested in living at Granby House. If I was, there was an apartment available on the first floor across the hall from Sarah Smith, a young lady also with cerebral palsy. The manager thought we would be good company for each other. I phoned the next morning and told the manager I definitely wanted the apartment. I explained my situation and told her that I could be back in Norfolk to fill out the paperwork in a couple of days so I could get moved in as soon as possible. Mother's condition had improved enough so that I could leave her long enough to return to get moved. I stayed in Norfolk for about three weeks before returning to Plymouth to be with Mother until she passed away in late August.

I really was not ready for senior citizen housing. I was only in my early fifties at the time and most of my neighbors were in their seventies and eighties. I had a very difficult time relating to them and felt very out of place. I was disabled, but I was not **old**. The only good thing about living there was that it was affordable since the rent was based on my income and I knew that I would have enough money to keep a roof over my head and food on the table. Before now, if I needed anything mother saw to it that those needs were met. One time when she came for a visit and had to sleep on my old second-hand studio couch in my living room, she said "Arlene, I think this has seen its better days. I will ask Edie to take us to a good furniture store so you can pick out a nice hide-a-bed and a comfortable chair." Another time she knew I was looking for a hutch for my dining room. All the ones I looked at in the stores were much too big for the space I had. I had just about given up on the idea until one day when I was at craft show in Downtown Norfolk where I met a man who made furniture. I told him what I was looking for and asked him if he could make a hutch. He said he would be delighted with the challenge. When he came to my apartment to measure the space where the hutch was to go I was very surprised when he told me how much he would charge to build it. I was expecting it to be a lot more. Before he left I phoned Mother to tell her the good news. She knew where it was to go and said the room would not look nice with a blank wall. I told her that I had intended to have a second one built, maybe in a year or so, after I had saved up enough money to pay for it. She told me to ask him how much he would charge to build two. I old her I only had enough money for one and the second hutch would have to wait. She told me to consider it a birthday present. I think she enjoyed spoiling me a little.

I knew now that if I needed or wanted anything, I would have to think twice before buying it. I was always careful about spending money and tried to live by my father's advice to me when I was a teenager and asked him if I could ***borrow*** some money. His reply was "Arlene, if you don't have it today, what makes you think you will have it tomorrow?" I was disappointed at the time, but I knew he was right. I have always lived up to his rule and have never been in any financial trouble.

I knew now that Mother was no longer here, I would have to be extra careful with what little money I did get to live on from Social Security. I knew I could manage as long as I was living in government subsidized housing and took advantage of the government medical programs offered to people with disabilities and senior citizens. I realized that working for pay was no longer feasible. I would have to be satisfied with doing volunteer work in the community. And the Tidewater area provided me with many opportunities for that. In 1975 the "Education for All Handicapped Children Act" was passed by Congress that stated that ***all*** handicapped children under twenty-two had to be educated in the least restricted environment which meant, for the most part, children had to be placed in special education classes in their community. This included the children in our program. As a result we no longer had children in our program. It became a program for adults with cerebral palsy. This meant that we no longer had to transport people from Hampton and Newport News as they were included in the special education programs in their own home towns.

One spring we planned a field trip to Washington, DC. The brother of one of the ladies in the program worked for Trailways Bus Company. When we were planning our trip, we called the bus company to see what the charge would be for the day. We knew it was expensive so we sold raffle tickets to cover the cost of the bus trip. We contacted our congressman at that time, Bill Whitehurst, to let him know that we would be in Washington on a certain date. He arranged to meet our group in the Capitol Building and we all had our picture taken with him outside on the Capitol steps. We were shown around the Capitol. I am a history buff so I really enjoyed myself very much.

Mr. Davis, the bus driver, picked us up at 5:00 am. That was a very early morning for all of us. We drove through the Chesapeake Bay Bridge Tunnel at dawn's early light and saw the sun come up over the bay. This was my first time through the tunnel and probably the first time for the others as well.

We ordered submarine sandwiches from the sub shop in Norfolk and had them for lunch on the bus. As I recall, we ate half of them at noontime and had the other half of our sandwiches on the bus on our return trip. Sometimes you just do what you have to do. We were all exhausted from getting up at 3:00 a.m. Most of us slept all the way home. The next year our group planned a bus trip to Philadelphia. We used the same bus company and even the same driver. We had to have a second driver to bring us home as Mr. Davis was only allowed to drive a certain number of hours in one day and the trip to Philadelphia would have exceeded the limits. The trip was five hours each way from Norfolk to Philadelphia but the bus drivers were not allowed to drive more than eight hours in one day.

During this time, I had been knitting and typing a lot and my hand started tingling. I went to the doctor's and he did some nerve tests and discovered I had carpal tunnel syndrome in both wrists. The doctor told me that the only way I could get rid of it was to have surgery to relieve the pressure. He told me he was going to do one at a time in order to let one heal before he did the other one. I told him "Nothing doing! I want them both done at once or not at all." To my surprise, he did both hands on the same day. There were two doctors, each one working on separate hands. I was in the hospital over Fourth of July weekend. When the doctor came to discharge me, he told me not to get my hands wet. I asked him how I was going do dishes without getting my hands wet. He pulled a pair of rubber gloves out of his coat pocket, handed them to me and said "Here, now go home!"

My mother came down to help me the first week I was home from the hospital. One night I decided to have my new friends Barbara and Lee come for supper. I decided to have spaghetti because I knew Barbara and Lee liked it. My mother did the cooking that afternoon. I bought the groceries and Mom put it together. And in the process of putting it together she said "I am making enough for an army!" I said "But they are an army!" There were no spaghetti leftovers that night.

At this time I was still working in the adult program in Virginia Beach. My co-worker, Connie, decided to go back to school. She got her master's degree in special education and decided to go to work in the public school system. She really enjoyed working with the children, and the pay was much better.

After Connie left, the Community Service Board hired a very nice lady, Clissie Sheatler, to head up the program. The program had changed dramatically. It was no longer an educational program but rather a social and recreational one for physically handicapped adults. Clissie and I worked well together. The program was cut back from five days a week to three days a week and became a community-oriented program.

We began taking short day trips and attending the special community events such as the Strawberry Festival in Pungo. We also took day trips, one of which was to Kitty Hawk, North Carolina where the Wright Brothers made their inaugural flight. We took trips to the Chrysler Museum. We went to the Greek Festival in Norfolk. It is held annually the first full weekend in May and runs Thursday through Sunday. We enjoyed the Greek food and entertainment. We also went to the Azalea International Festival. This Festival had an air show with the Blue Angels. The entertainment shows in the Azalea Festival were outstanding.

I no longer got picked up at my apartment so I would meet Clissie either at the office or somewhere along the route as she picked up the clients. Sometimes we met in unusual places. One time we met behind Krispy Kreme Donut Shop. Another time we met behind the Patriot Ledger Office Building. A couple of times I even spent the night with Clissie if we had to get an early start the next morning.

The Norfolk Therapeutic Recreation Program

The Community Service Board paid me for the hours I worked, but were cutting my hours back. When they cut my hours too much, I just quit. And that is when I decided to do something for the Norfolk residents who had been eliminated from the Virginia Beach Program. I got the cerebral palsy residents together and we decided to do a program similar to the one in Virginia Beach. Transportation was a big issue. Virginia Beach had its own van. The residents of Norfolk would have to use public transportation to take advantage of the program. This was very expensive and we had to find ways to raise money for transportation for the program. I was responsible for the fund-raising. This was when my friend, Silvia Roughton, donated $600 to the transportation fund. This money did not last very long and I knew I could not be solely responsible for the transportation much longer. I decided to go to the City of Norfolk Parks and Recreation Director. I told her I had *the program*, I had *the people*, but I needed a place to house the program, and transportation for the clients. This is how the Therapeutic Recreation Program of Norfolk was started.

At that time I met Fran Merchant who was on the Norfolk Mayor's Commission for People with Disabilities. Unbeknownst to me, she had been trying to get recreation for the disabled in Norfolk for many years. When I came along and she heard about my program, she was overjoyed because at last she had someone to work with her.

She was a blind lady who was very active in working with disability issues in the community. We paired up and began working together. Parks and Recreation said we could use the Norfolk Arena for our meeting place and in the next few weeks Parks and Recreation hired a therapeutic recreation specialist. One day he asked us to write down what we wanted to do in the program. I wrote across the top of my paper "other possibilities". He came by and saw what I had written on my paper and he said "That is what we will call your group, 'The Other Possibilities Club'." And that is what it was called for many years.

At some point I was appointed to serve on the Norfolk Mayor's Commission for People with Disabilities. I was also appointed to serve on the Norfolk Transportation Board. The Mayor's Commission was a group of people, made up of both disabled and able-bodied people. The purpose of the commission was to inform the city council of the needs of the people with disabilities that live in the city of Norfolk. And don't think Fran and I didn't let the mayor know just what we needed. When Fran and I realized we needed another van for transporting the participants to and from the programs and to improve and embellish the recreation programs, we would go down to city council and submit our requests, whether it was a van or other equipment we needed. The participants in the program thought we were "nuts" and were just wasting our time. But to their surprise, a month or two later, when we got word that we were going to get what we requested, including the van, they were all quite pleased that our efforts finally paid off.

One day Fran and I headed out for city council. We sat in the front row because Fran had a seeing-eye dog and it was easier for her to get up to the podium. We had been to city council several times before and by now the mayor was used to seeing us there.

At one such meeting Fran and I took our seats, as usual.

We always got there early partly because of transportation arrangements. Most of the time we were picked up in the same van and encountered no problems but when we arrived separately, we met in the lobby at the back entrance to the building. When the mayor came out with the city councilmen, he looked around the room, spotted the two of us and looked at us as if to say, "Oh no, not you two again...what do you want now?" I could almost read his mind. I started laughing. Fran nudged me and asked what is so funny. Because she is blind, she couldn't see the mayor's expression that I was laughing at. I couldn't say anything then, so I told her I would tell her later. This is how Norfolk got the wonderful therapeutic recreation program that the disabled citizens enjoyed so much.

We not only had programs for the physically disabled but the therapeutic recreation staff developed programs specifically for the mentally disabled as well. Fran and I had a lot of difficulty with combining the two groups as the mentally disabled would often act up when we went out in public and it put a stigma on everyone there. As a result, we advised the therapeutic recreation staff to separate the two groups, the physically and the mentally handicapped, for most of the activities. They finally took our suggestions and it worked out much better, especially with regard to field trips.

Norfolk had a large population of disabled children and adults. When the children reached adulthood and were no longer eligible for education programs there were no programs for them, so they had to just stay at home. They lost all contact with their peers. Most of the time they were home with their parents until the parents got too old to care for them any longer, and then they were put into nursing homes. The therapeutic recreation program brought them back together so they could socialize again amongst their own peers. It also helped them to get out and mingle with the community.

Fran and I worked well together in the community to make a better life for many hundreds of participants who went through the program. We had our disagreements at times, but always put the welfare of the disabled above our own feelings.

The city of Norfolk eventually gave us our own center. It was previously the Mary Calcott Center on East Evans Street. The city had to remodel the building to meet the needs of the disabled but I guess that was cheaper than building a whole new building. When we weren't going on field trips, the therapeutic recreation staff held classes in ceramics and acrylic painting which I enjoyed very much. The program included swimming and aquatic exercise classes at one of the city's public pools. The pool we used most was built with a ramp at the shallow end for easy and safe access for people with mobility impairments. Door to door transportation was provided by the recreation staff to all who needed it, which was most of us. The participants paid a small fee to attend most of the activities. But the benefits they received outweighed the cost one hundred times over.

Norfolk Continued

A lot was going on in my life at this time. My father had been diagnosed with skin cancer. He came down to see me one time and he had to wear long-sleeve shirts. He had lesions all over his arms and face and could not be out in the sun at all. It was so hard to see my awesome Dad like this. While he was visiting with me, we were given tickets to the Norfolk International Azalea Festival. This Festival is sponsored by NATO, and each year the Festival selects one NATO country member as the Most Honored Nation, and a young woman from this country is crowned Queen Azalea.

One part of this Festival is the coronation of Queen Azalea, along with the accompanying military concert. The coronation and concert are usually outside events, but because of the rainy weather they were held inside the Chrysler Hall that year. My Dad totally enjoyed this. We got wonderful third-row seats so we could see and hear everything. This was one time we were all thankful that it was raining. It was much better than sitting outside on the hard bleachers for more than two hours.

It wasn't long after that visit that my father had to undergo chemotherapy. The treatments made him very, very sick. He was sick for two and a half years.

In the mean time I had decided to go back to school for a teaching degree in special education. I had been working on my education for three or four years, taking courses part-time at Old Dominion University and working at the same time.

It was during the Christmas break that I was called home. I had to take my final exam in math before I left for home. I don't know how I ever passed the math course. A lot of the credit goes to my professor who helped and encouraged me. Because my writing is so poor due to my disability, my professor had to write my answers as I dictated them to him. He would keep encouraging me by saying "What comes next, Arlene?"

It was Christmas time and I told my Mom that we needed to get a real Christmas tree this year and not use that artificial one.

I remembered when I was a little girl, how my Dad and I would go out in the woods at Christmas time. He would send me out to find a tree. I would come home all excited and say "Dad, I found the *perfect* tree!" He would then follow me out in the woods until we came to the tree. I pointed to a big white pine and said "Daddy, it's this one right here." He took a look at it and said "I think we need a hotel lobby to put that one in!" We both laughed, and then together we would tree-hunt until we could agree on a perfect one for our home. Dad and I found the tree and he chopped it down and I dragged it home. Mom did the decorating. I never cared much for decorating a tree as I was all **thumbs** when I tried to put the ornaments on the branches. I remained in the background and more or less supervised while Mother did the work. Dad would set it in its stand so it balanced just right. Then he would put the strings of lights on the tree, and would leave the rest to us. My parents were living in a mobile home in Plymouth Mobile Estates at this time. When I came home that year and walked in the door, the pine scent was overwhelming and brought back a lot of good memories. This would be my Dad's last Christmas and I think we all knew it. He was very sick, but somehow managed to drive to Hyannis to pick me and my cat Sneaky up at the airport. He wasn't up to driving into Logan Airport in Boston. I stayed with my parents until mid-January when I would return to college. We made the most of a sad situation.

The following year I went home for Christmas, but it was not 'Christmas' at all. My Dad was in the hospital and not expected to live more than a few weeks. When I got home my Uncle Philip was there. Mother just couldn't take me to see my father as he had lost so much weight and looked really bad. She asked Uncle Philip to take me to see him, which he did. I had planned to be home two weeks but I stayed there for an additional three weeks so I could be with Mother so she wouldn't be alone during my father's final days. We visited him every day in the nursing home. Towards the end, I prayed that God would take him home so he would not suffer any longer. We got the call from the doctor at 4:00 am. to tell us he was gone. Because of the snow and ice we had an indoor service. ***I am who I am today, thanks to my Dad and his allowing 'me to be me'***. He always encouraged me to be all that I could be. He really encouraged me to finish my education, which I did. He told me "Arlene, nobody can ever take that away from you." He surely was right about that! He would have been so proud of me when I finally completed my studies and received my B.S. Degree in special education the following year.

I was living on the corner of 47th Street and Colley Avenue at this time. I had moved there a few months earlier from 51st Street. I had a second floor efficiency apartment. It was small, but it was all that I needed for now. The kitchen was very small and my hutch just did not fit in it. There was a big walk-in closet off the living area and this was where I had to put it.

The year before my Dad passed away, Edie's husband (everybody thought they were married and so did I for a long time) had passed away a few months earlier, so she invited my mother to come and spend a few weeks with her following my Father's passing. I was delighted with this arrangement. I knew I didn't have the room and I didn't want Mother to have to be alone after I'd returned to Norfolk. Edie had the extra bedroom and I thought they would be good company for each other. This worked so well that she stayed for the rest of the winter. Edie worked for the American Red Cross and invited Mother to go in with her. She was sure her boss could find plenty of volunteer work for Mother to do. This was so perfect for all of us.

Mother and Edie got along so well that she would be invited back to spend the winter months with Edie every year from that time on until Mother passed away during the summer of 1986. She would come down just before Thanksgiving and return to Plymouth at the end of March. All the neighbors in Norfolk loved her and they looked forward to her visits each year as much as I did.

It was during this time that Mother and I developed a new kind of bond between us. For the first time, we became ***friends***. The mother-daughter relationship that I knew so well, and sometimes hated, was now changing. She was listening to me more and I think she realized for the first time I was no longer a child who needed to be told what to do and when and how to do it.

I became involved with the cerebral palsy organization once again when Adell Campbell became its new director. I was still working with Connie in the adult program in Virginia Beach at the time. Adell came in to get acquainted with our program and to meet some of her new clients. I told her that I had served on the cerebral palsy board in Quincy, Massachusetts for a number of years before moving to Norfolk. At this time her office was in her home in Virginia Beach. She told me that she had a very nice volunteer secretary, Helen Wolff, working in her office while she was out in the community. It wasn't long before the three of us became good friends. I spent a lot of my weekends with the two of them. Whenever Adell had to make a business trip, she often invited me along for company. One such trip took us to the Eastern Shore, a narrow strip of land on the Chesapeake Bay known as the Delmarva Peninsula. The only access to this area from Norfolk is through the twenty-three mile long Chesapeake Bay Bridge Tunnel. The area is very quaint. Many of the residents still earn their living from the Bay or from farming. Blue crabs, clams and oysters are still quite plentiful here. Adell and I had no trouble finding a good seafood restaurant for lunch.

 I never knew what sort of fund-raising events we would be involved with. Once I was asked to work on the Cerebral Palsy Telethon. Adell gave me a list of time slots that needed to be filled and I had to find the clients who I felt could best fill them. Another time she had me selling roses at the Military Circle Shopping Mall on Mother's Day weekend. I remember one time we even manned a beer concession stand at Waterside, the waterfront area of Norfolk, during one of its many special events. I don't mind fund raising for an organization or a church, but I disapprove of any disabled people standing on a street corner with a cup in their hands begging for money for themselves. This is not the way disabled people should "***earn***" a living. I not only consider this degrading to the disabled community but also very dangerous in this day and time.

 Adell and I remain good friends to this day. She lives in Arlington, Texas and has a radio talk show. I have visited with her a couple of times after she moved to Texas. One time Helen and I paid her a visit. She took us to the State Fair where we had a very enjoyable day. She took us into Fort Worth where I enjoyed a tour of the Stockyards. I learned that these stockyards are the only ones still standing in the United States today. The area has been a historical district since 1976. I also visited with Adell one Christmas. She had been volunteering as tour guide at the DeGolyer House which is located on the grounds of the Dallas Arboretum and Botanical Gardens. The house was built around 1940 by Everett DeGolyer who was in the oil business. The beautiful mansion has 17 rooms and it contains many 16th and 17th century antiques and artworks. At Christmas time many of these rooms are elaborately decorated to represent the customs of many European countries.

The day after Christmas she took me shopping at Dillards. I had a hay day'. Everything was half price or better. I spent $74 on clothes. When we got home that evening, we took out the sales tickets and added up the original prices of all the items I bought. And to my surprise, the total we came up with was more than double what I paid. I love bargains and seldom pay full price for clothes or anything else for that matter.

One day while I was visiting, we got an early start and headed for Austin. I had wanted to pay a visit to the LBJ Presidential Library and Museum. It is located on the campus of the University of Texas. I was very surprised when I we got to the main entrance and just walked in. I learned later that this is the only presidential library with *no admission fee.* Of course, I wanted to see and read everything. It took me back in time to the beginning of the space program and the race to put a man on the moon, and President Johnson's War on Poverty. I remember thinking how stupid it was to waste so much money on sending a man to the moon when so many people were living in substandard conditions and didn't even have a place to live or enough food to eat. So this was the way the president was fighting the *war on poverty?* I don't think so. My thinking on this matter has not changed to this day.

My Brother

In the spring of 1986 I received a call from my mother's neighbor, Lou McKenzie, telling me that my mother was in the hospital. She had had a stroke and was in serious condition. Lou advised me to come home immediately. I told Edie, who was working in the back yard, that my Mother had had a stroke and I had to go home right away. I asked her if she could take me to the airport after I made the reservations.

When I called the reservation desk, I told them that I had an emergency in Boston. And they gave me the next flight out which was a connecting flight from Norfolk, VA to Pittsburgh, PA and then to Boston. I called my friend Diane and asked her to meet me in Plymouth. I would take the bus from Boston to Plymouth. Diane took me to visit with my Mother even before I went to my Mother's home. Every day thereafter Diane would call me early in the morning and ask me if I needed her for that day. She was such a faithful, awesome friend. Some times I would tell her I needed her to take me to visit with my Mother but some times I would find my own ride. Other times I would need Diane to take me to the grocery store.

John Morgan, Minerva, and Kathy

My Mother's stroke was pretty severe with paralysis on one side. When she got well enough they transferred her from Jordan Hospital to Lakeville Hospital for rehabilitation. Mr. Burgess, a longtime friend of my Mother's, would take me to see her sometimes in the evening. He stopped by late one afternoon and I asked him to stay for supper. We ordered a pizza. We had a friendly chat and out of the blue he made the statement "Wouldn't it be nice if you had a brother right now?" At first I didn't think anything about it, but then I said "Yah...I guess it would." I thought he was referring to the baby who died before I was born. Then he said to me "You do." With that statement my mouth fell open. I said "What do you mean that I have a brother! Where is he?"

He then said "He lives in Maine. He was born before your Mother met your Father." I asked him how I could get in touch with him. He told me he didn't know. I asked him if Mother was in touch with him all these years. He said she was. I told him that I bet the address and phone number must be in her address book that she kept for many years. I found the address book and went through all the pages and found nothing to indicate that she had put his name and phone number in the book. She really ***didn't*** want me to find it. So I asked Mr. Burgess "What do I do now?"

He said "I guess you will have to wait until you can talk to your mother this evening and see how she wants you to handle this situation".

That evening when we got to the hospital, Mr. Burgess told my mother about our talk at supper. I think my mother was quite relieved that this life-long secret was finally out.

I asked her if anyone else in the family knew. She told me that my uncle Philip did. He had to know.

I told her that I wanted to meet my brother, or at least talk to him to let him know that I at last was told about him and his family.

Later that evening when I got back to my mother's home I was able to get in touch with my brother by telephone. We talked for a long time. I did find the phone number on the back page her address book but with a false name.

I told him that Mother's health wasn't very good. She had had a massive stroke, and that she had congestive heart and kidney failure and wasn't going to be with us much longer. I invited my brother and his family to come and spend a few days with me so I could meet them and together we could spend a little time with our mother. This was in mid August. Looking back, one evening the previous May, just after I had returned to be with my mother, the telephone had rung. A man whose voice I did not recognize came on the line. I asked him who it was. He said "John". I said "John who?" If he said "John Morgan", I did not catch it, most likely due to my hearing loss. I don't really remember what he told me. But I think I told him that Mother was not at home right now...

she was in the hospital. I believe he had called to wish Mother a Happy Mothers' Day. I wouldn't know that it was my brother that I had been talking with that night for another couple of months. He told me after we had met that he thought he had **let the cat out of the bag** that night.

When the story was finally out, my brother John, his wife Minerva and their daughter Kathy came down to Plymouth and spent several days with me. When he got out of the car, I had no trouble identifying him because he looked just like our Grandfather Morgan. And my niece Kathy looked just like our Mother, her Grandmother. It was at this point that I learned why I never knew I had a brother.

Back in the 1920's a baby born out of wedlock was not acceptable. My Grandfather Morgan sent Mother, who was pregnant with John, to a home for unwed mothers until after the baby was born. I don't think Mother ever got to see the baby after he was taken from her. My grandfather sent him to a family in Maine who already had two children, a boy and a girl a little older than John, and they raised him as their own. They did not legally adopt him. Therefore, John was able to maintain the family name of Morgan. Mother was living with her father who was a very domineering man. While she was living under his roof, she did as she was told....no questions asked. So when he told her she was going to a home for unwed mothers...she went, no questions asked. And when he told her that she would not be bringing the baby home, she had to consent, whether she wanted to or not.

When my mother and father got married, my father knew about John. When I was two years old, my Mother had written the family in Maine saying that it was John's tenth birthday and she was sorry she couldn't be with him but she was having trouble with me. I wasn't yet walking. She knew she had her hands full with me and John was better off staying where he was with the only family he had known. After John had been married, my Mother and Father took a trip to Maine to visit with them. My Father bought Kathy her first tricycle. I believe she was two or three at the time.

John and I kept in touch by phone. In August of 2009 I phoned to wish my brother a Happy Birthday. This is when I learned that he was seriously ill. When I had talked to him a few months earlier to ask the family's permission to write this story, I knew he wasn't feeling well. He told me he was tired and sleeping later than he used to. But I don't think anyone had any idea at this time just how ill he really was. He passed away a week after I talked to Minerva in August.

I had sent a copy of what I wrote to him as soon as I had written it, for him to review and make any changes, before I wrote the final draft. I learned from Minerva in August that I had to make a few minor corrections. I am sorry my brother won't get to read my story. I am so grateful that I got to know him and his family. I still treasure the week I spent with them shortly after Mother passed away. We got to know each other and put the pieces of the puzzle together. Every family has its soap opera stories and this is mine.

I was so pleased to learn that Kathy is a reader like me. She went on to earn her Master's Degree in Library Science. She is now assistant director at the Norway Memorial Library in Maine. I expect that she will one day be its director. I learned also that she likes to travel, as do I. I understand she is a fighter and a go-getter just like her Aunt Arlene.

Sarah and Me in Great Britain

In 1986, the year my mother passed away, I decided that I didn't want to be home over the Christmas holiday and planned to be out of town. I didn't know where, just out of town somewhere, anywhere. One evening that fall, I had a group of friends in for supper, among them was my neighbor Sarah Smith Irvine. She was going through a hard time as her boyfriend had broken off their plans to get married. Out of the clear blue sky, I asked her if she would like to come with me to England for the holiday. I think I took everybody by surprise, but most of my friends knew that when I made a statement like that, I meant it. They all told Sarah she would be missing out on a chance of a lifetime if she turned down my offer.

Sarah was a bright young lady with cerebral palsy. Like me, she could get around quite well. And like me, her gait was a little awkward. But I thought she could handle this trip quite well. She was used to using local public transportation so I knew getting on and off buses and trains would not be a problem for her.

After she got her family's approval, we started making plans for a month long vacation to Great Britain. My friend Connie had been living in Dublin for about a year and I wrote her and asked if Sarah and I could come and spend a few days with her. Sarah wrote to some friends she knew through her church who lived somewhere in England and asked if we could spend a few days with them on our way from Edinburgh, Scotland. I thought it would be nice if we could take a guided tour of the English countryside before we ventured out on our own and she agreed with me. Everything just seemed to fall in place so well. We would end our trip in London where we started from.

By the end of November, everything was shaping up very nicely. The tour for our first leg of the trip meant that we didn't have to worry about where we would sleep and many of our meals were taken care of also. When we got to London, we would be met at the airport by our tour guide and taken to our hotel where we would join the rest of the tour for dinner that first evening.

Since we had taken an overnight flight, it was noon by the time we got settled in. This meant that we had the whole afternoon free. I had no idea what was in the area of the Kensington Hotel but it didn't take me long to find out. The Victoria and Albert Museum was just a few blocks away. I had not been there before and I thought this would be a good place to spend out first afternoon, and Sarah agreed to it.

The next day was Sunday. Sarah had jet lag and slept late. I knew she was very tired, so I let her sleep while I went to get some tourist information, mainly maps of the subway system, the Tube as the Londoners call it, and bus routes. I knew she wanted to see the Crown Jewels and they are in the Tower of London. I showed her the map and told her we could take the Tube to the Tower. A taxi would just be too much money from where we were staying.

Sarah and the Yeoman at the Tower of London

After we toured the Tower we went to St Paul's Cathedral. A Sunday service was about to begin, so Sarah decided we should stay for it. The service was quite long and much like a High Mass of the Catholic Church. I enjoyed it very much. I told Sarah I thought this was the Anglican Church of England. She said "It sure wasn't Baptist." I just laughed at her remark.

After the church service we headed back to our hotel and rode a double decker bus through Piccadilly Circus. We could have walked in the time it took for the bus to get through the traffic there, even on a bleak Sunday afternoon. Our first full day in London was quite an adventure for both of us. We both slept well that night and had overcome our jet lag. The next day we joined our group for a guided tour of the city and an evening at the theater.

Before we left London, Sarah wanted to pay a visit to the cerebral palsy office. We also went to a thrift shop which was run by the cerebral palsy organization. I bought two sweaters from there.

Our group would leave London for a four-day tour taking us to Oxford University, Blenheim Castle, Stratford upon the Avon, Stonehenge and Windsor Castle before we headed for Dublin.

Stonehenge
Arlene Sollis

Sarah and I were very fortunate to have had the opportunity to visit Stonehenge when we did. This prehistoric circular burial site dates back to around 2500 BC. When we were there, we were able to walk amongst this stone formation and get close-up photographs of it from all angles and I took a whole roll of film while we were there. It is now roped off and these photos would no longer be possible to get today. The above photograph is one that I took and should not be mistaken for a professional photographer's picture.

We also spent a day touring the Roman Bath in Bath, England. Sarah really enjoyed this. She went to see if the water was really warm coming from the springs and she said it was.

Just before we left our tour, Sarah and I were very surprised when our tour guide handed each of us a postcard signed by some of our tour companions. I guess they thought we were pretty special.

When we finished our tour, we were on our own. Our tour guide made sure we got to the train station to continue on with our plans to Holyhead(pronounced Hollyhead) in Wales where we would take the ferry across the Irish Sea to Dublin. We had to spend the night at a bed and breakfast in Holyhead and take the ferry the next afternoon. It was a nice train ride through the countryside of England and Wales. We would use our 30-day British rail passes for the first time. We put them on the back of the seat in front of us for the conductor to stamp the date on them. At the end of our trip we put them back in our purses and forgot about them until we returned to Holyhead a week later and had to use them for the rest of our trip. When we got to Holyhead we hailed a taxi and asked the driver where there was a place to stay for the night. He asked if we wanted a hotel or a B&B. I knew a B&B would be less expensive than a hotel, so I told him a friendly B&B would be just fine, and it was.

We were shown to our room and got settled in. We hadn't eaten since breakfast and we were both very hungry and tired from the long day. We found a fast food place within walking distance and brought the food back to our room. That evening we were invited to the sitting room for a friendly chat with the owners.

The next morning at breakfast, Sarah mentioned that she would like to go to church. The owner asked what denomination. Sarah said "Baptist." The owner said jokingly "Welsh Baptist or English Baptist?" He then said he would take us and pick us up when the service was over.

So we got to ride in his old, beat-up VW van. It had two bucket seats in front. Sarah rode in the front seat next to our 'chauffeur' and I climbed in the back and sat on a wooden box. I think he kept tools in it.

When we got to the church, the minister was standing outside greeting his congregation as they entered the church. Sarah and I were introduced to him by our 'chauffeur' before we went inside to take our seats. Much to our surprise, during the sermon, the minister introduced us to the whole congregation as "some very special Americans."

When our driver came back for us, I thought we would be taken back to our room to wait until it was time to catch the ferry for Dublin. But he had a different plan. He gave us a very nice tour of the

Me, Connie, and Sarah feeding Ring-Tail monkeys at Dublin Zoo

area we would not have otherwise seen. I left a nice tip on the dresser before we left. He drove us to the ferry.

It was quite late by the time we got to Dublin. Connie would not drive to meet us at the ferry because, unlike in America, the Irish and British drive on the left-hand side of the road and she thought it would be too risky. So we had to take a taxi from the ferry. I gave the driver the paper with the address and phone number on it. After a few minutes he said he didn't know where the street was. He stopped to ask another cabby, but he didn't know either. Our driver finally called Connie to get directions. I thought "These taxi drivers ought to take a few lessons from London's cabbies." They were trained on horseback and knew every street and alley way before they were permitted to drive a taxi.

Sarah and Me at the Zoo

Connie showed us a really good time. It was the Christmas season and the city was decorated and very busy with shoppers. I really enjoyed our tour of Dublin Castle and the Dublin Zoo. I got a real surprise when Connie said we would have lunch at the zoo. I thought it would be hot dogs and hamburgers, not a first-class restaurant as this one turned out to be. The food was excellent.

I also liked the way the animals were being sponsored and cared for. Most of the larger ones were sponsored by big corporations like Mobile or Exxon while the smaller ones were the responsibility of the community, a school or a class in a school, i.e., a fourth grade class might raise funds to feed a rabbit for a year.

When we left Connie's we took the ferry back to Holyhead, and boarded a train and were on our way to Edinburgh. We took our tickets out and placed them on the back of the seat in front of us as we did before, only to notice that they hadn't yet been stamped and dated. This meant that we still had thirty days in which to use them. I was delighted with this as it meant that they wouldn't expire before the end of our trip. I am sure it was an oversight on the part of the previous conductor as this time they were stamped and dated.

When we got to Edinburgh, it was quite late. We hailed a taxi and asked the driver to find a B&B. The first place he stopped at, Sarah went in to check it out. When she came back, she shook her head "NO". She knew neither of us could manage the narrow spiral staircase we would have had to climb to get to our room on the second floor. The driver continued up the road to the next one which was where we stayed for the first few nights of our visit to Edinburgh. We had planned to leave the day after Christmas and head south to spend a few days with Sarah's friends in England before heading to Canterbury.

The first couple of nights in Edinburgh we stayed with a very nice family, the Dickie's. They told us that they were having a house full for the holidays but that they would phone around to see if anyone had room for us for the remainder of our stay in the city. I was delighted when the Dickeys' informed us that they had found another place for us. They even drove us to our new B&B.

The Cowan's were a lovely couple. The man was a school psychologist and his wife was a teacher of the blind. They really went all out to make us feel at home. The day Sarah and I went to the Highlands, Mr. Cowan drove us to the train and picked us up in the evening when we returned. Mrs. Cowan even had a delicious dinner waiting for us. I think we paid five dollars for our evening meals, but they were well worth the price. Everything was fresh and cooked to perfection.

That Sunday we attended a service in one of the small local churches. People were so friendly here. When they saw that Sarah and I were strangers, they invited us back to join them for their Christmas party at the church that evening... We had a very nice time. We seemed to fit in as though we were members of the group. After the party, two young fellows offered to drive us back to our room. They told us they wanted to show us some of the city's decorations before they took us back to our room. All and all, it was a most enjoyable and memorable evening.

We had planned to leave Scotland the day after Christmas. But when I went to pay for our room we were told we would have to stay another day as there would be no train service that day since it was a holiday. We learned that the British celebrate Boxing Day on December 26th and everything would be closed.

Boxing Day dates back to the Middle Ages when the well-to do would give gifts to their servants or the less fortunate people of the lower social class. Boxes were filled with food and other staples and presented to them the day after Christmas.

In churches, donations from the collection box of Christmas were given to the poor in the community the day after Christmas.

In England a clay collection box was placed in shops for anyone passing though the shop to leave any amount of money he wished. This box was broken open the day after Christmas. This money was divided among the employees as bonuses. The breaking of the Christmas box lends its name to Boxing Day.

I really don't remember what we did on Boxing Day but I do know we were well taken care of by the Cowan's. They prepared our evening meal as usual.

The next morning they drove Sarah and me to the train station and saw us safely off to England where we would spend a few days with Sarah's friends before heading south to Canterbury.

About two weeks before Sarah and I left for our trip once again I decided I needed to practice holding a tea cup properly just in case Sarah and I were invited to High Tea. When I was a teenager, Mother tried to teach me this. But I could never master it to perfection, and to this day I haven't. My efforts paid off as I didn't have any embarrassing moments.

Sarah's friends did have an afternoon tea with oh so many different kinds of tea biscuits (cookies). I wanted to sample all of them, but of course I didn't. I put good manners first.

These folks sure were good cooks! And there was just so much food! They served two of my favorite desserts, plum pudding and trifle. The English are noted for their trifle. It is made with lady fingers or sponge cake usually layered with fruit or raspberry jam and light custard and topped with whipped cream. I have tried to make it at home, but it never turns out as tasty as when the English make it.

When we left Sarah's friends, we headed for the last leg of our trip. We took the train to London. I suggested that we book a room for our last night in London before we headed for Canterbury where we would spend a few days. I wanted to be sure we had a room not far from the airport. This was the only reservation we made during our whole trip.

When we got to Canterbury, we took a room within walking distance of the cathedral and the center of the city. We found a small restaurant near our room. It served home style meals at very reasonable prices. One day when we were doing a walking tour of the historical area of the city, Sarah eyed a sign that read "Fish and Chips". She pointed to the sign and said, "That's what I want for supper tonight, I am so tired of formal meals." I told her she could have her fish and chips but I wanted my formal meal. This was the only time we went our separate ways during the five weeks we traveled together.

The day before we left Canterbury, we went to Dover. I wanted to see the "White Cliffs of Dover" and explore Dover Castle. It was a very cold day. I had to put the zip-out lining in my London Fog coat for the first time since leaving Edinburgh. It was a long walk from the train to the castle and an up-hill climb. When we reached the pay booth outside and took out our money to pay the lady, she told us to put it away and ushered us to the door. We spent a very enjoyable afternoon climbing through the many tunnels. During World War II the castle served as an air raid shelter and an underground military hospital. A military telephone command center was also established here at that time.

One evening not long before we were to return home, Sarah was reorganizing her suitcase for about the hundredth time.

I picked up her pocketbook to move it to a chair. It weighed a ton. I asked her what she had in it that could go in the suitcase. I didn't give her a chance to reply. I turned the contents out onto her bed. I knew right away what she was doing and told her to count all those coins she had been collecting for the past month, the equivalent of $73 in British money. I told her she could not use any more paper money to buy anything until most of these coins were used up. They would be worthless once we left the country. We both had a good laugh over this.

The trip did us both the world of good. Sarah and her boyfriend had a fresh start and they were married shortly thereafter. And I was able to pick up the pieces and get more involved with disability issues throughout the community.

After Sarah moved out of Granby House the next year to get married, I got a new neighbor. I was delighted to see that she was a little younger than I. We were introduced by the director of Granby House even before she moved in. Granby House was a senior citizen residence which at that time accepted a certain number of disabled people under the age of 55. Debbie Ungar had been on the waiting list for some time, so as soon as Sarah's apartment became available, Debbie was notified. I think she could have gotten in earlier, but the director waited until Sarah moved out so I would have a younger neighbor. I was 52 at the time and most of the other residents were in their seventies and eighties.

Debbie and I became good friends. She had a cat and I had two. We sometimes left our doors open so the cats could visit back and forth. Our neighbors never complained if we got a little rowdy at times. Debbie was a good cook and she liked to party. Often we would share the food and I would house her guests for dinner, supper or Sunday brunch. She was the life of the party and could tell jokes better than anyone I ever knew. Nobody ever knew what was coming next. We liked the same TV programs and sometimes after supper, I would go to her apartment and watch them with her.

Suzanne Kinney was another good friend even before she moved to Granby House. She was a retired gym teacher. She had arthritis and had to have hip replacement surgery and could no longer teach gym. She loved children and often babysat in her apartment to earn a little extra money. She loved music and often played the piano when a group would gather for supper, either at my place or hers. She learned to play *bridge* shortly after she came to live at Granby House. This is one of my favorite card games. Barbara, Lee, Suzanne and I played it often. It is an easy game to learn, but a difficult one to master. Even though I knew how to keep score, I don't think we ever did. I think we just played each hand as a game and changed partners often. When I play Bridge on line, I really have to pay attention to the scoreboard or I wouldn't last two minutes.

Teaching at the Endependence Center

I finally earned my Bachelor of Science Degree in Special Education from Old Dominion University in Norfolk in 1980. I began teaching in a literacy program at the Endependence Center, also located in Norfolk. That is not a typo error, Endependence means "end dependence". I worked with the physically disabled adults, most of whom fell between the cracks of special education classes. Some had severe speech impairments, and, I think because of this, the public schoolteachers either labeled them mentally retarded, or they just did not have the time to devote to these students. To me, it really didn't matter how severely disabled my students were or at what level. I would find a way to work with each one individually, usually for an hour a session

I remember one young man. He was severely brain injured as a result of a gunshot wound. I had to start him at a kindergarten level. I saw early on that teaching him to print just was not working and I switched him to cursive writing so there was less of a chance for him to reverse letters. Eventually his penmanship was far better than mine, and if I needed something written out, I gave the job to him to write it out for me.

For most of my students repetition was a must, and the lesson planning took a lot of my time. Teaching supplies were very limited and the ones that were available did not meet the interests of my physically disabled students. I spent more time adjusting and rewriting the lessons than I did teaching them. One of my students was visually impaired, and he needed all of his lessons to be copied and magnified two hundred percent or more.

One of my other students, Orrick Toliver, wanted to read *Uncle Tom's Cabin*. The print in the book was a little too small. I took the time to copy the whole book so he could read it without having to use a magnifying glass. This was the first full-length book Orrick had ever read. He was working toward his GED through the city's Literacy Council but needed a little extra help. After we started working together his grade level increased by two or three grades in a very short time. He enjoyed a vocabulary program using the computer. He didn't care how long it took him to master a lesson and neither did I.

One young lady with cerebral palsy was non-verbal. She was a real challenge for me. I had worked with her in other programs and I knew she understood what was being said. I also knew how frustrated we both got when she tried to tell me something and I failed to make out what she was telling me. I knew I had to find a way to improve her communication skills. I knew her reading level was very low, but this didn't matter to me. I had to find a way for her to get across to others what she wanted to tell them.

After working with her for about three years, I began to compile all of her sight vocabulary, and together we began to make categorical lists. At first I typed out each list on a separate sheet of paper. This did not work too well because the print was just too small and the words were too close together, and when she tried to finger point to a word, it was too difficult to make out what word she really meant. After many tries, I finally came up with something both of us were happy with. Spacing the words and magnifying each page really did the trick. I bought a loose-leaf notebook and put each page between clear plastic to protect the printed pages. I was careful to leave enough space on each page for adding more words as needed. This was not perfect, but it helped a whole lot. She carried this notebook in a backpack on the back of her wheelchair at all times.

I loved teaching at the Endependence Center. I could name my own hours for the most part. I did not have to spend countless hours writing up progress reports since that was my supervisor's job, I guess. This meant I had much more time to devote to my students and their lessons. Teaching materials were very limited and often inappropriate for my students, so I needed to create my own. Progress was often slow but the rewards were so great.

I started teaching there in 1993 and would continue on until a few days before I retired to Tampa, Florida in 2001. In 1994 I was presented with the Volunteer of the Year Award for outstanding service to my students and to the Center. I would receive many more citations in the years that followed.

Norfolk Community Service

Volunteer Achievement Award

I had already received an award from Volunteer Action a couple of years before for my work in the community, so when I got a letter from them again in 1997 informing me that I was to receive another one, I was very surprised.

I thought this award was given to a person only one time. I phoned my friend Nancy who worked in the office there and asked if there had been some mistake. "Oh no" she said. "Your name came up and we saw all the work you have been doing to make this community a better place for so many of its disabled residents and everyone in this office thinks you deserved to be recognized." I attended the ceremony and proudly accepted my award for the second time.

LaVerne and Me

I don't recall where Laverne Watts Avant and I first met, but most likely it was at some fund-raising event for United Cerebral Palsy. In any event we soon became good friends. She, like me, has cerebral palsy and also like me she is a college graduate. But unlike me she is married and has a very healthy child and drives a car with no special adaptations.

Because we were both working, she at the Norfolk Naval Base and I in the community, we didn't see very much of each other. We often met at the Greek Festival in Norfolk or at some special event at Waterside. We often celebrated our birthdays together by treating ourselves to dinner or lunch at one of the many good restaurants in the area. Distance separates us now. But we still keep in touch by phone and E-mail.

The Anchorage – Housing for the Mobility Impaired

Housing for the physically handicapped is a huge problem all over the country. The physically disabled either have to live at home with their parents, go into nursing homes, or go into senior housing. Most of the physically disabled are on fixed incomes and cannot afford to move into their own apartments even if the apartments are wheelchair accessible.

I had been working on this problem for quite some time when I met Bob Horan, who was working to get a federal grant to build an apartment complex designed specifically for wheelchair users. I asked if I could join his team and he was delighted to have me. Accessible Housing Corporation of South Hampton Roads is a volunteer non-profit organization whose members are dedicated to building independent living accessible housing for low income persons with mobility impairments, primarily wheelchair users. This organization partnered with Accessible Space Inc. and together they received a 1.4 million-dollar grant from HUD to build a 25-unit apartment complex. In 1995 a local firm contributed a piece of land in the Wards Corner area of Norfolk. This is one of the oldest shopping areas in the city and it has three senior-citizen apartments all within walking distance of it. The Norfolk City Planning Board approved a very generous sum of ten thousand dollars to our project. This was approved by the City Council.

When it came time for a name for this building, it didn't take me long to put my thinking cap on. Bob had been a Navy Captain and Norfolk has the largest naval base in the world, so I tried to think of an appropriate name. Since this was our first of what I hoped would be many more to come, I thought "Ah! We threw our first anchor over and

A Wheelchair Accessible Kitchen
Bob Horan

it held our ship in place". Thus I came up with the name "Anchorage". The whole board liked the name and it stuck.

The Anchorage was ready for occupancy in 1999, with many applicants having to be turned away and put on a long waiting list. In 2005 a second apartment building was completed in Chesapeake. We hoped that AHC could build at least one apartment house in each of the Hampton Roads cities to provide accessible housing to each city's mobility impaired citizens.

Most senior citizen apartments are considered wheelchair-accessible but what I have found in my own search is that if a wheelchair user can get through the doorway, the unit is considered handicapped-accessible by the owners. Here is where the "accessibility" ends, making it impossible for most wheelchair users to function independently without outside help, or without making expensive modifications to the apartments. Light switches and electrical outlets are often out of reach for example. While I never lived in the Anchorage, I will use pictures from the Anchorage to show a *real* wheelchair-accessible kitchen.

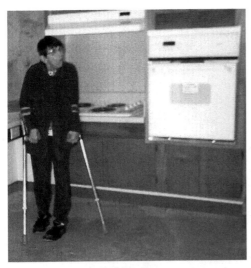

Bob Horan

The Stove and the Oven. The Stove Controls are on the Side, not at the Back. Also, when the Oven Door is Opened, the Bottom Rack is Level with the Top of the Stove, for Easy and Safe Transfer of Food.

Furthermore, a Wheelchair will Fit Under the Oven Door when it is Open.

The Sink. Note the single-lever faucet, the electrical outlets and switches on the front, also the open space under the sink and the pipes to the rear for wheelchair access.

Bob Horan

Planning the Big Move

I had been visiting with Diane at Christmas time ever since she and David moved to Spring Hill, Florida. I noticed a big difference in the way my body felt during these visits. I had less of a problem with the joints and the arthritis flare-ups in my shoulders and right knee. I was able to reduce the amount of medication I was taking to none at all by the time I was ready to return home to Norfolk and the cold winter climate. For this reason alone, I decided that I wanted to move to Florida.

I knew I could not live in Spring Hill because I needed to be where there was a good transportation system and where I would have easy access to good medical help should I ever need it. I took a look at the map of Florida and discovered that St. Petersburg and Tampa were within reasonable driving distance of Diane's, roughly about one hour. This meant that even though I would not be in her back yard, we could visit each other often and I really liked this idea. We hadn't had this kind of a friendly relationship since before I started working back in the early 1960s.

There was one very big concern for me and that was finding accessible and affordable housing. For the past several years, I had been living in federally assisted housing programs for most of the time and I knew I could not afford to just pick up and move anywhere. This move would have to be very well planned. The apartment I was living in in Norfolk was under a federal program known as Section 8. I had been granted a certificate to live there. This meant that, if and when I moved from this apartment, I would lose my Section 8 benefits. What I needed now was a Section 8 voucher, which was portable, so it would move with me to anywhere in the United States that accepted Section 8 vouchers.

These vouchers are very hard to obtain. One has to know just when to apply. The date was usually published in the local newspapers with a telephone number to call at a certain time of the day. At least this was the way it was where I was living at the time I applied. I was very lucky because I did not get a newspaper, but one of my friends did, and she knew I needed the information so she sent the clipping to me right away. The notice said to call any Saturday during the month of March. So I called on the first Saturday. I was on the phone all day trying to get through but I couldn't get to talk to anyone. I tried again the next week and toward the end of that day, I finally got through to the office and was able to get put on a waiting list. Now I would have to call every so often to find out where I was on this waiting list. I could do nothing now but wait...and wait some more. It was over two years before my name moved up enough so that I could even think about moving anywhere. In the meantime, the apartment I was renting on Ogden Avenue had discontinued offering Section 8 certificates to its tenants and I was going to have to move from there by September 2001. This left me sitting on pins and needles. I knew by now that I was definitely going to move to Florida. My only hope now was that my Section 8 voucher would come through before I was forced to move out of where I was at that moment. There was no place I wanted to live in Norfolk and I definitely did not want the expense of moving twice. Moving one time was almost more than I could handle at this time.

When my name moved down to about number fifteen on the voucher housing waiting list, only then could I think seriously about my move to Florida. I wrote to Housing and Urban Development (HUD) in Washington, D.C. for its housing listing of apartments for St. Petersburg and Tampa area that accepted Section 8 vouchers.

When the packet finally arrived and I looked it over, I knew I had my work cut out for me and I was the only one who could do the job of sorting things out. The packet contained a listing of somewhere between three and four hundred pages with one listing to a page. Each listing was very descriptive, so much so that I could visualize the inside of each apartment.

I began by making a pile for anything that accepted Section 8 vouchers. Anything that didn't was put into a discard pile. Next I looked at the amount of square footage in the apartment. The apartment I was living in had 600 square feet. So I knew I needed at least that to accommodate my furniture and my wheelchair. Anything under 550 square feet got put into the discard pile as well. I have a washer and dryer so I needed to be able to hook them up. I knew also that I needed to be where I had access to public transportation. After three days, I was able to narrow my search down to six apartments, two in St Petersburg and the rest in Tampa. I sent for applications for all six. Within the next two weeks, I received only three applications back. I knew I was disqualified for the only one in St. Petersburg when I read what the income level was, even with the voucher, and I tossed that application in the wastebasket. This narrowed my choices to the two in Tampa. So I wasted no time in filling out these two applications and mailing them off.

In the meantime, I was notified by the Norfolk Housing Authority that my turn had come, and I was to bring all the necessary papers with me to an interview with them, and to fill out all the required papers, which I obligingly did. I think I had to make two more trips before everything was finalized. I then had only sixty days to get everything together and move or I would lose the voucher. I wasn't moving within the city of Norfolk, but I was moving to Tampa, transferring this voucher.

The people in the Norfolk office were not very helpful in this matter. As soon as I got the final papers, I took them to the Endependence Center to the lady who was in charge of the housing office there. I had been teaching at that center for several years and I was familiar with all the departments and knew all of the people who ran them. But this was one of very few times I ever had to use its services.

By now everybody there knew that I was planning to move to Florida. It was a question of when and how. Van (in charge of the Endependence Center's housing office) knew her job well. I knew she was the one I needed to help me with the final details and what I needed to do next. After making a few telephone calls to the local Housing Authority to verify my status, she called Tampa to find out what I had to do next.

"No", the paperwork could not be sent from the Norfolk office to the Tampa office. And "No", we could not set up a teleconference. I had to attend a meeting in the Tampa office that next week at 10 am or lose the voucher.

In the meantime I had already decided on where I wanted to live in Tampa and had been in contact with the rental office there trying to make plans with the office manager to make the move as soon as possible. I had not planned on having to come to Tampa until I moved down to stay. I thought that a voucher was portable and that this meant that the paperwork could be transferred from Norfolk to Tampa. But this is not the way that system works.

I had to make a special trip to Tampa to attend a meeting and fill out the exact same papers I had filled out in Norfolk. This did not make any sense to me, especially in this day and time, when the paperwork could have been faxed from one city to the other.

As it was, I had the added expense of a round trip to Tampa and an overnight hotel and taxi bill on top of the move.

At first I was going to take a late night flight and spend the night at the airport to avoid the hotel expense. But my friends said that would be too dangerous, and talked me out of it. One of my friends made the reservation for me at one of the hotels. It had limo service to and from the airport, but there was one catch. It did not transport people in wheelchairs. My friend Lorraine said this was a violation of the ADA law, and let the manager of the hotel know that if I was denied this service she would see to it that proper action would be taken. She faxed this using her attorney's letterhead stationary. I had no problems either at the hotel or at the airport. If Diane had been at home at the tine, I probably would have spent the week with her, but she was in Massachusetts visiting with her family. I had no other choice but to make the trip, and then get home as soon as I could. I knew I had a lot to do in a very short time.

It was very late by the time I got to the hotel and I knew I had to get up early the next morning to get to my orientation meeting by 9:30 am. I was traveling with a backpack with my night clothes and personal items. When I got to my room, I wasted no time in getting to bed. The room was very cold but I was too tired to be bothered finding the thermostat to turn the air conditioner off. I just slipped under the covers and wrapped myself in the quilt and soon fell asleep. I had drunk a glass off water before going to bed. Therefore I would have to wake up early in the morning to use the bathroom, a built-in alarm clock for me. It worked quite well.

The next morning I ate a big breakfast at the hotel and made an egg sandwich from the toast and scrambled eggs I had ordered. I then asked for a doggie bag to put it in. This was my lunch and it would tide me over until I got back to Norfolk that evening around 7 pm.

I took a taxi to the meeting. It was started on time and it was an exact duplicate of the one in Norfolk two weeks earlier– even to the paperwork! I now had sixty days from that date to secure a place to live.

I knew I had to work fast and, at the same time, coordinate a move-out date with the move-in date. Getting packing boxes was always a big problem whenever I moved to a new location before. People would go around to the grocery stores on delivery days and pick up a few here and there so I was prepared for a long drawn out packing process. But this time I got very lucky. One of my neighbor's daughters lived in military housing near the Norfolk Naval Base. There were people moving in and out all the time and they used professional packing boxes that were provided by the Navy. As soon as Kim saw a moving van pull in she would watch for boxes to be thrown out, and she would rescue them before they got put into the dumpster. By the end of the second week, I had more than enough boxes and they were fairly uniform in size, so they stacked easily when they were packed. They were also well marked as to which room they belonged in. This made my job a lot easier than my past moves.

The first thing I did was to empty my storage closet in order to make room for all of the packed boxes so I would have a clear passage way from the bedroom to my front door at all times, just in case I should ever have to get out in a hurry.

I am a book worm and had accumulated quite a large collection over the years. They were stacked from floor to ceiling and I knew I needed to get rid of most of them. So I sorted them out and packed only the ones I treasured most. I then called a second-hand book store to come and take the ones it wanted. The man gave me $250 for them and I was happy to get it. What the bookstore didn't take, I donated to the Anchorage for its library. I never throw books away because someone somewhere can read them. It was clean out time too. I knew I would not be wearing very many heavy clothes in Florida. I had too many, even for Norfolk, and it was time to weed out what I knew I would never wear again, heavy coats, jackets and sweaters. I packed a large trash bag full and took it to the Endependence Center to give to one of my students who was about my size. I knew she didn't have much and I felt good about my choice. I don't like to throw away anything good that somebody might be able to wear or use.

When I started packing the kitchen supplies, I saw that I had more pots and pans and dishes than I would ever use. Some were stored away, just taking up room. So anything I hadn't used in two years, I packed up and took to my friend, Mary, who was living at the Anchorage at the time. She placed them in the recreation room with a sign that read "HELP YOURSELF". She told me a few days later, that everything was gone the next day. And, you know to this day, I haven't missed anything!

Planning the Big Move

I had plenty of help when it came to packing. I really didn't care how most of the things were packed, as long as they were put into boxes that were properly marked as to which room they were going to.

But there was one thing I would not let anybody touch. And that was my china cabinet. I had acquired my parents' Royal Albert bone china dessert set and I did not want anything to get broken in the process of moving. It is six settings of cup and saucer, cake plate and dessert dish. It was given to my parents on their 25th wedding anniversary in 1955 by my mother's coworkers from the school cafeteria. I had planned a surprise afternoon tea and invited them all to attend. Diane helped me prepare the refreshments for the occasion. I don't know how I ever pulled this off, but it was a very special day, one that Mother talked about for many years.

I had packed this china many times before, and only I would take the responsibility if anything got broken. With masking tape, I carefully taped together the six saucers, the six cake plates, and the six dessert dishes before wrapping them in bubble packing material then in thick layers of bath towels before placing them in a small packing box. The cups were also carefully packed in this box. Then I put the small packing box into a bigger box and before placing that box containing the china in it, I then used all my towels to fill up the bigger box. I used this method to pack my other good china as well. Needless to say, nothing was broken during the move.

The plan was I would pay someone to drive a U-Haul truck to Tampa, and my cat, Lucky and I would fly down and meet the movers at my new apartment. This meant that everything had to be out of my apartment late on Friday so the movers would be ready to hit the road on Saturday. My friends Lorraine and Karen had invited me to spend the weekend with them in Virginia Beach. I put Lucky in the kennel for the weekend. Lorraine and I would pick him up early Monday morning on the way to the airport. The movers packed everything in the truck, even my power chair. I had to use the walker which has a seat on it. This wasn't the most convenient way for me or my friends, but it served the purpose for the weekend. It had to be used as a wheelchair. But it sure didn't push like one.

Lorraine and Karen took me for a stroll along the Boardwalk on Virginia Beach. It was the first time I had ever been on one of those big four wheel peddlers. It was a lot of fun.

I remember another time when we three had gone to the beach for the day. We packed a lunch and a few books for an afternoon of relaxation. I always took along my handicapped parking permit whenever I went out with them, so they could park in a handicapped parking space if there was one available, and they wouldn't have to push me so far. On this particular day, Lorraine parked in such a space, put the permit on the mirror, took all of the stuff out of the trunk and we were off for a day at the beach.

When we got back to the car toward evening, the first thing Lorraine spotted on the front window was not one, but several parking tickets. My permit was nowhere in sight. We all knew she had put it in the proper place before we left for the beach. We were very upset because we all knew the permit was there and now it had mysteriously disappeared. And the last thing Lorraine—as an attorney—needed was a parking ticket. Even if I paid the fine, it would go on her record.

When she opened the door, she saw the permit lying on the floor just under the mirror. We guessed it must have fallen off when one of them slammed the trunk lid shut. It shook the car enough to jiggle the permit free. The permit was old and badly damaged at the top.

The first thing Monday morning Lorraine took me and the damaged parking permit to the police station and explained what happened. The tickets were written off. Lorraine fixed my permit so this cannot happen to us or anyone else I should ride with in the future.

From Walking to Crutches to Wheelchair

In early 1989 I began having difficulty with balance, and walking became increasingly more clumsy. When I bent my head forward, I notice a tingling sensation in my right leg. I became very concerned about this and when I consulted my neurologist, he immediately performed some nerve tests. The results of the tests showed that I had a slipped disc in my neck. The only way to prevent further damage was to have surgery to repair it.

Following the surgery I spent three months in a halo neck brace. It was most uncomfortable but bearable. My balance was not as good as it once was. But I was managing as well as possible. I was working out at the local gym five days a week trying to maintain what muscles I could and strengthening others. I would never regain full balance and walking became increasingly slower and my gait more awkward. Things just were not what they once were and I knew it.

In 1998, I suspected that the disc in my neck had slipped again. I was right. I had a repeat of the surgery that I had in 1989.

I told the physical therapist who was working with me following this surgery that I had a pair of loftstrand crutches and was going to bring them in for her to show me how to use them properly. I had used them once before when I had surgery on my leg. But this time I knew it would be permanent. I would have to be taught the best way for me to get up and down stairs so I could ride buses. I felt good about this. I was on my way to getting about safely and that was what mattered to me most, safety first, the heck with looks.

I did okay with the crutches for a couple of years. Then my shoulders started hurting and my right knee began to give out from under me when I least expected it causing me to fall. I had a very difficult time getting to my feet again and walking became increasingly slow and awkward.

When I discussed these problems with my orthopedic doctor, he ordered x-rays of the knees. When I saw them he pointed out to me that the cartilage was completely worn out in the right knee. Due to cerebral palsy, he advised me against having a knee replacement. He said it could cause more harm than good. The knee didn't hurt. Because of the nerve damage caused from the neck, I can't feel pain or heat or cold in that leg. I decided to leave well enough alone. I had had surgery on my left shoulder the year before by another doctor and it did not help any with the problems. And when he wanted to do more surgery to fuse the shoulder, I refused to let him. I never regretted my decisions. By 1999 my walking had slowed to a snail's pace and my shoulders were hurting so badly that I made several visits to the doctor's to get them injected with cortisone. I was also put on anti-inflammatory medicine but nothing did any good. The pain in the shoulders was making me very irritable no matter what I did. I wasn't sleeping well either. Walking with crutches was wearing my shoulders out and I knew it.

I knew I could not deal with the pain and the clumsiness much longer. I went to Washington, D.C. with the Endependence Center to take part in the Olmstead Rally to keep disabled people out of nursing homes and to provide them with the services they need so that they can remain in the community. As long as I had a wheelchair to push, I was quite used to this arrangement. I had done it for many years and this was just another day. I would make out okay.

We were parked in the parking garage at Union Station. We joined several other groups on the lawn of the Capitol Building for a picnic lunch. After lunch we all marched to the United States Supreme Court for the big rally. It was very slow going, but I hadn't noticed just how slow. All I knew was that I was getting very tired way too soon. I was used to pushing wheelchairs all day on some other outings. This should not be happening, but it was. By the time I got to the Supreme Court, my right knee just would not hold my weight and I was literally hopping, trying to balance myself and push the wheelchair. It was really hard, and I knew I had the long walk back to Union Station.

When we started back, one of my co-workers and some of the other participants saw that I was in real trouble and wanted to know what was happening. I told them that I thought my right knee was giving out. A young fellow using a manual wheelchair asked if I needed help. He said he would go along ahead of the rest of the group and send someone back with his wheelchair when he got to the station. Tears welled up in my eyes, but I knew I had no other choice but to accept his offer and be thankful for it. I knew we had a four hour drive back to Norfolk. I was exhausted and not in a very talkative mood.

When I got home that evening it was quite late. I took a hot bath hoping it would help me unwind and relieve some of the tension caused by the events of the day, but I was too upset with what was happening to me.

I knew I was in big trouble when I saw how swollen and hot the right knee was. It didn't hurt due to the nerve damage and I had no warning that something was wrong until I could no longer use it. I guess I was too busy with work and just wasn't paying any mind to me.

By now I knew I was in big trouble. Walking was becoming much too difficult even with the crutches. My shoulders would not take the increased pressure on them that I needed to maintain balance. I went to visit my friend and neighbor, Mary, the next day. She is a paraplegic and I told her what happened in Washington the day before, and that I just didn't feel safe using crutches anymore. She took one glance at the swollen knee and we both knew I would have to get a set of wheels if I was going to remain active and continue working in the community. I just could not procrastinate any longer. For more than a year now I have had to think about how far I had to walk whenever I planned to go anywhere and this was not at all like me.

The power chair was a whole new adventure for me. When it finally arrived at my door, the lady who brought it to me gave me the manual. She told me that all I needed to know to operate and care for my wheelchair was in the book, and then she left.

I was on my own. I had never used a motorized wheelchair before. Those first three weeks were a nightmare trying to get used to it. I bumped into everything. My walls were pretty banged up even driving it at the lowest speed. It was about four days before I got up the nerve to take a stroll to see Mary. She lived in the next set of apartments in the same complex as I did. I was still driving this thing at low speed so it seemed to take me forever to get there. I hadn't anticipated any problems, a straight drive up the sidewalk. But I had forgotten about the speed bump in the road. I almost turned around and went home. Then I realized I would have to deal with these things sooner or later and I decided to tackle it head on. I would never do these bumps in any speed but low. They were just too dangerous, even at low speed.

Getting on and off the van made me very nervous due to the very limited space on the lift. I knew that if I turned my chair just a little too far one way or the other I could have gone over the edge of the lift. To this day, I never back off a van lift no matter how little turning space I have inside a van. Most of the main line buses I use now have ramp access. I just keep my fingers crossed every time I get off a bus that I don't go head over heels. The incline is very steep in most locations. Getting on is no problem because my wheelchair tilts back so there is no danger of sliding off my seat.

Norfolk – The Wards Corner Incident

One sunny warm Saturday I set out to do a little shopping at Wards Corner only to wind up at DePaul's emergency room after my wheelchair tipped over trying to access a broken curb. My front left wheel got caught in a crack and over I went in the very busy traffic. My eye glasses cut into my forehead before they fell off and broke beyond repair. A young policeman came to my rescue and wiped the blood from my face as best as he could and, seeing that I wasn't seriously injured, got me back in my chair. He said the cut would require some stitches. A few minutes later, I was being stitched up and sent on my way.

I did not go directly home from the hospital but, instead, I had other ideas. My first thought was that the city was going to hear about this incident. I went directly to the Anchorage to see my friend Mary and ask her to help me organize a group of disabled citizens living at the Anchorage to speak before the City Council on Tuesday to let the city know just how badly run down this area had become. Mary Colucci, Julie Marshall and I worked on the project the whole afternoon. Julie worked on the presentation to City Council while I rounded up some of the disabled people to accompany us to City Hall on Tuesday. There are three other apartment complexes in the same area, all of which are for senior citizens, many of whom are disabled and encounter many of the problems as those living at the Anchorage. Most of us would need to set up our transportation well in advance for this trip. So it had to be well planned in order to get everybody there on time.

When I got home that evening, I called my friend Fran to tell her what had happened and asked her if she would like to join us on Tuesday at City Hall. She said she was busy and wouldn't be able to, but did I want the media? "Of course I do" was my reply.

"OK, I'll see what I can do and get back with you early Tuesday."

On Tuesday I was in the middle of breakfast when the phone rang. "Hello, This is Fran, I have channel 10 on hold. They want to know if you can meet them at 10:30 at Wards Corner to do a walking tour of all the bad areas before they follow you to City Hall."

"Yes, I will meet them in front of the Pancake House". She hung up.

Ten minutes later the phone rings again. "Hi, I got the Ledger newspaper and Channel 13. The newspaper will meet with you at the Anchorage at 12:00 Noon. The TV people will meet with you before the meeting at City Hall."

We chatted for a bit and after I hung up, I called Mary to let her know of the developments to let her know that I would be there as soon as I was finished with the TV people.

It would take me about a half hour to get from my apartment on Ogden Avenue to Wards Corner. I wanted to get there a little ahead of the TV people so I could survey the area and pick out the very worst places to show them and the public, the spots that posed the most hazards to wheelchair users. I selected the area I had just traveled through to get there. It is around the corner from the Pancake House, behind the drugstore at Little Creek Road and Granby Street. The sidewalk was so badly broken, with debris everywhere blocking what little was left of the sidewalk that I had to ride in the street with traffic whizzing by me like it was an expressway. When I got to the curb-cut on Granby Street I paused a moment and said "Thank you Lord for getting me here safely". The other places in urgent need of repair were at the railroad crossings. The one near the post office on Granby Street and the other on East Little Creek Road were so dangerous that a wheelchair user had to be rescued by the police after his chair got stuck at one of the railroad crossings.

When the TV crew arrived, I was well prepared for it, whether or not it was prepared for me. We wasted no time in getting to the task at hand. I had an advantage over the crew. The reporter and cameraman had to travel on foot and, of course, I had wheels. I would find myself having to slow the pace to let them catch up with me. It wasn't long before we were at a pace we could agree with and this part of the job was successfully completed. We would meet again in a couple of hours at City Hall.

I kept my fingers crossed that our transportation would not be messed up as it often was. We all got to our destination in good season. And everything went smoothly. Julie did an excellent job with her presentation. She told the councilmen how she and other wheelchair users had to break the law by having to ride in the street for lack of curb cuts, and broken or cracked sidewalks in the whole shopping area. She said she and others have a right to be able to shop safely in their own neighborhood. If they didn't ride in the street, it would be impossible to access the many stores in this area.

We had complained before, only to be told that there were no funds available for these kinds of repairs. We invited some city officials to do a walking tour of the area and, much to my surprise, they accepted the invitation. They met us on Thursday at the Anchorage. We offered loaner wheelchairs so they could experience firsthand the many problems we faced every time we went shopping. They did come, but they said "No, Thanks" to using the wheelchairs. "We will walk with you."

I think the city officials were appalled and a little ashamed at what they saw. We began to see some improvements within a week.

At this time, I was getting ready to move to Tampa, Florida and would not be in Norfolk to see the work completed. I was serving on the Mayors Commission for Persons with Disabilities. The last meeting I attended was turned over to me so I could give a detailed report on everything that needed to be done in the Wards Corner area. This report would be turned in to Mayor Paul Fraim. It would be up to him to see that the repairs were completed in a timely manner.

A few days before I was to leave the city I requested a private meeting with the mayor to discuss the importance of work I had begun. I told him I hoped these repairs would get done before somebody was seriously injured or killed. We discussed my proposal and the safety issues for all of the residents who live in the four apartment complexes in that area. He promised me that my wishes would be fulfilled. And they were.

I was very touched when I received this letter from Mayor Fraim shortly after I moved.

Text of Mayor Fraim's Letter to Me

"Dear Arlene:

On behalf of the City Council, I want to thank you for your service as a member of the Commission for Persons with Disabilities. I am sorry you will be moving out of the city, and regret the city will lose the benefit of your considerable talents. I know Chairwoman Helen Brown, other members of the Commission and staff will also miss you and the contributions you made during the time of your service.

Because of the wide range of disabilities that affect young and old alike, the Commission for Persons with Disabilities plays an important role in addressing issues such as accessibility, programming and employment opportunities as well as assisting disabled citizens to achieve independent lives. Your interest and advocacy around these areas was well known and effective, and helped Norfolk become a place where life is celebrated daily. We are fortunate to have citizens like you who are committed to community service and to working for a better Norfolk. I appreciate your willingness to devote so much time and energy to the city, and wish you all the best the future has to offer."

City of Norfolk
Virginia

Paul D. Fraim
Mayor

1109 City Hall Building
Norfolk, Virginia 23510

November 5, 2001

Ms. Arlene M. Sollis
7824 Ogden Avenue, Apt D
Norfolk, VA 23505

Dear Arlene:

On behalf of the City Council, I want to thank you for your service as a member of the Commission for Persons with Disabilities. I am sorry you will be moving out of the city, and regret the city will lose the benefit of your considerable talents. I know Chairwoman Helen Brown, other members of the Commission and staff will also miss you and the contributions you made during the time of your service.

Because of the wide range of disabilities that affect young and old alike, the Commission for Persons with Disabilities plays an important role in addressing issues such as accessibility, programming and employment opportunities as well as assisting disabled citizens to achieve independent lives. Your interest and advocacy around these areas was well known and effective, and helped Norfolk become a place where life is celebrated daily.

We are fortunate to have citizens like you who are committed to community service and to working for a better Norfolk. I appreciate your willingness to devote so much time and energy to the city, and wish you all the best the future has to offer.

Sincerely,

Paul D. Fraim
Mayor

Mayor Fraim's Letter

Tampa, Florida

It was late afternoon by the time my cat Lucky and I finally arrived at Tampa International Airport from Norfolk. We had to change planes in Atlanta, Georgia. It was the first time I had ever taken Lucky with me and I was very worried about him since he couldn't ride in the cabin with me. He had to ride with the baggage. He had spent the weekend in the kennel and the vet had given him a sedative just before we left for the airport in Norfolk to help keep him calm during the trip. By the time we reached Tampa I knew the sedative would be worn off and he would be very upset. I just wanted to get to him as quickly as possible so he could see that I hadn't deserted him.

Since I hadn't even seen my new apartment, I had no idea where it was. The taxi ride seemed to take forever and Lucky cried all the way. I kept talking to him but it didn't help. I knew he was very upset and scared. I had traveled with a cat before, but never with Lucky, and I hope I never have to again. I know the poor cab driver was very happy to get us to our destination. I had no idea where Williams Landing Circle was and I had to trust that the driver knew where he was taking us. When he got to the corner of Williams Road and Martin Luther King Boulevard, the driver asked me which way to turn and of course I had no idea. He took a chance and turned left. He drove about a quarter of a mile before he realized the numbers were running in the wrong direction from the address I had written out for him the day before. So he had to turn around and cross over MLK and head south for only two blocks.

By now it was close to 5 o'clock. I had expected the movers to have been and gone, but much to my surprise, they greeted me at the office. They were very upset because the landlord would not open the door to my apartment until I got there and filled out all of the paperwork and gave them a check with my first month rent and pet fee. Only then did the landlord hand over my keys.

I was exhausted and knew I could not make it to my apartment without my power chair. I was using my walker with the seat on it.

I knew the wheelchair was the very last thing that had been put into the moving truck, this along with Lucky's litter box, food and dishes. I had a little better balance then than I do now, but when I got tired, no part of me worked. The movers drove the truck around to the clubhouse and brought the chair to me. The landlord handed me the keys and left. When I finally got into my new apartment, I had the movers set Lucky up in the bathroom and close the door so he wouldn't be in their way. At this point, I didn't really care where they put anything but the large pieces of furniture. I would have plenty of time to juggle things around the way I wanted them later. All I really needed for now was to have the bed set up so I would have a place to sleep that night. There was one other thing I requested of the movers, and that was that they leave clear floor space between the front door and the bedroom in case I needed to get out in a hurry.

It was seven o'clock before the movers got everything in and I was alone. I was very tired and had a headache. I needed to unwind and find something to eat. I knew I had packed a box marked "moving day food" which contained things like a box of crackers, a package of cheese, and some canned food. The note on the top of the box read "Please place this box on the kitchen counter" and I had no trouble locating it. I knew I had packed enough food for a few days. This would tide me over until I could get some of my things unpacked and get some of the boxes out of the way.

My first big concern was for Lucky. He had been in the carrier since early morning without food or water. The airline gave him water before we left Norfolk, but I knew he was too upset to drink it. I pulled his carrier out of the bathroom and into the bedroom and opened the door to let him out. I guess he was still too scared to move. I tried to entice him to eat with his favorite food and some water, but still this did not help. I got my food and sat on the floor next to him and talked to him while I ate crackers and cheese and drank a bottle of warm juice.

By now it was getting dark and I just wanted to put this day behind me and get to bed. I had left the bottom sheet on the mattress and put the top one under it before I left Norfolk because I knew I would not be able to find the box of linens for several days. It was June and I knew I wouldn't need any blankets for a while.

I Came – I Stayed

Lucky

When I awoke the next morning, Lucky's food and water dishes were empty and he had used the litter box sometime in the night, but he still wouldn't leave the carrier. I knew the only thing I could do now was to leave him alone and let him set his own pace. It was over two weeks before he ventured into the living room and I could put the carrier away. He stayed under the bed during the day for several weeks, coming out only to eat.

I soon got acquainted with some of the residents. Everyone was so friendly and very helpful. One of them connected my washer and dryer. Another one put additional shelves in my bedroom closet which serves as a pantry, a linen closet, and my watered-down library. One of the ladies from my building sent her teen-aged granddaughter down to help unpack some of the boxes. Together, we got my good china stored in my hutches. I have two, one in the dining room and the other I put in the living room.

By the time I got everything in place and most of the boxes out of my way, Diane and David were back from their summer retreat in Plymouth, Massachusetts. They had a camper on Diane's daughter Heidi's property where they spent several weeks during the summer. I was anxious for Diane to pay me a visit so I could show off my new apartment. This would be a real treat for me because I hadn't seen her since our yearly get-together at Christmas time. I felt so excited that we were only about an hour's drive apart. We hadn't lived this close to each other in over thirty years. She and Johnny, her first husband, had visited with me a couple of times when I lived in Norfolk. I remember one of those visits like it was yesterday. They were on their way home from someplace and they surprised me with an overnight stay. I was living on 52nd Street at the time. Barbara and Lee lived upstairs over me. We had planned to go and see the movie "Joni" at one of the local churches. I phoned Barbara and told her that I would have to take a rain check as I had unexpected company. "Oh!" said Barbara, without asking who my guests were, "Just invite them to join us." I thought that was a splendid idea. I told her to tell Lee that I would order a Pizza before we headed out. That would be a quick and easy supper and no dishes to mess with.

When we got back from the movie, Johnny said he was going out to explore the town. He was gone for quite a while. Diane started to worry that he had gotten lost. I told her I knew right where he was. She looked at me surprised. I said it wasn't very far, just up the street. When he came in a couple of hours later, Diane ask him where he had gone. I answered for him "The Coach House". He just laughed. He had gone for a couple of beers and forgot the time.

The last time I saw Johnny was just a few months before he passed away from a long battle with cancer. They had stopped by for a short visit. Diane and he were on their way home from somewhere and on their way to Washington, D.C. He said he just had to go a little out of the way to see me. I think he knew it would be his last visit and I did too.

Diane and David had picked me up at the airport in Tampa many times. But I was now living way across town from there. I didn't know much about Tampa. All I knew was that I was just one stoplight from I-75. I told them that if they found their way to I-75 the rest would be easy. I gave them directions from the interstate and they had no trouble finding me. Diane told me later that no matter what roads she took, it always took an hour to get here, a half hour to get to the interstate and another half hour on it. Diane's first remark to me when she saw the apartment was "I guess you won't be moving from here any time soon." I told her "I never want to move again" and I meant it.

The first time Diane and David came to see me, they took me shopping for groceries. I spent over three hundred dollars that day. Diane asked me if I was going to feed the whole complex. I told her that I had to buy enough food to last a while as I didn't know when I would be able to get any more, even though I lived only three blocks from the supermarket and I could use the main line bus to get there. It isn't easy for a wheelchair user to carry enough food for one week's supply. Also, any perishables would spoil before I could get home and put them away.

Within two months Charmaine Andrews (activities director for Williams Landing Apartments at the time) had this problem solved. She contacted an organization known as *Seniors in Service*. This organization is made up mostly of retired senior citizens. They are volunteers whose job is to help other seniors in need. They are paid a very small sum of money for their time. They are not homemakers, but they are companions to those who are more or less shut-ins. They can tidy up the house and run errands and this was all I needed at that time.

Hattie McGee was assigned to me for three hours one day a week. Together we did my grocery shopping. Sometimes I would take the bus and meet her at the store. Other times I would send her with a shopping list. She worked with me for about a year. When she got sick and had to undergo surgery, another lady, Mary Ann Griffith, was sent in her place. Mary Ann and I developed a very special friendship over the years. She worked with me in another situation until she moved away in 2009. My readers will learn more about that in a later chapter.

Diane phoned me a couple of weeks later and said she and her sister Darlene were coming down for a visit. When they got here, Diane noticed that my walls were bare and asked me if I had any pictures to be hung. I told her I had a couple of boxes of them stashed away in the closet. She said "Well, Arlene, where are the hammer and picture hangers? Darlene and I need to get to work here." That afternoon before they left, they had my apartment looking like an art gallery. Now that my apartment was in order, the next big thing I needed to concentrate on was finding out where to obtain the services I needed before I really needed them. I knew that once I established residence in Florida, all the medical programs I had in Virginia would be discontinued. Charmaine Andrews was very knowledgeable about services and programs that were available to me and how to go about getting the ones I needed.

One of the very first things I knew I needed to do was to transfer my state medical insurance from Virginia to Florida before I really needed to use it. A social worker came to see me and together we filled out all the necessary papers. The transfer would take about a month from the day I signed all of the papers.

The social worker saw that I have a cat. She informed me of a program that was offered by the Tampa Humane Society to qualified individuals. She signed me up for this program. Once a month, a very nice volunteer brings Lucky a large bag of dried cat food, more than enough to feed him for the whole month. I am most grateful for this program as cat food, like every thing else, is very expensive. I also look forward to a friendly chat with the volunteer each month.

I had to find a primary care physician. One day not long after I moved here, a nurse practitioner came to speak to the residents of Williams Landing. She told us that she worked under a primary physician. She said she would be making a house call to anyone who wanted it. I thought this was a great idea and sighed on for the service.

This meant that didn't have to spend hours using public transportation to get to the doctor's office. It has been working out just fine for me. She comes to see me once a month. She checks my vital signs and calls in any prescriptions I might need, which are none at the moment. She orders blood work every so often. The lab technician comes to me. Once I had a very bad cold. To make sure it wasn't developing into pneumonia she sent an x-ray technician to the house to x-ray my lungs. It is just great not having to sit in a waiting room full of people for hours when I don't feel well.

One time I discovered a big lump on my upper leg. It wasn't bruised and it didn't hurt. It was just there. I became very concerned when, after a couple of weeks, it didn't go away. I showed it to the nurse practitioner and she ordered an MRI to find out what was going on.

When I got to the medical building with all the paper work properly filled out, I was ushered to a waiting room. There was nobody else there. So I sat patiently for about twenty minutes reading a book. When the nurse called my name, I replied "Here I am". She looked at me with a puzzled expression on her face. I said, "I am Arlene Sollis." Then she wanted to know where my next of kin was. I told her that my uncle is up in Massachusetts. She wanted to know how I got to the medical center. I told her I took the Hartline van. She wanted to know who came with me. I told her "nobody", then she asked me if I was all alone. I was getting very irritated by now and replied, "It looks that way, doesn't it?" She said "Well, then, there is nobody to sign for you to have an MRI." I told her that I could sign my own papers. She insisted that I needed the next of kin to sign for me. And she left the room. A few minutes later, she came back and told me that I could not have the MRI. I told her that I wasn't leaving the building without having it. She left the room again. A few minutes later, a technician came in and started giving me the same run-around. I told him if I am denied this MRI, I would own this darn center ten times over and the staff had better be prepared to meet me in court. I told him that I didn't order the MRI, my doctor did. The technician left. I think he called my doctor. Another few minutes went by before the nurse come in and handed me the papers, and I signed them.

I get very annoyed with people when they think because a person is physically disabled, he or she is also mentally incompetent as well. Things like this happen to me more times than I care to write about.

I think I could write a whole book on such incidents, but I wouldn't want to bore my readers. I can excuse the general public, but people in the medical profession should know better. Incidentally, the lump disappeared in about two months just as mysteriously as it came.

My social worker comes to see me once a year to fill out all the paperwork so that I would not lose my state medical benefits and to make sure I was getting all the services I needed. She decided that since Mary Ann would no longer be working with me, it was time to give me more service with another agency. The service with the new agency was pretty bad. The ladies who were assigned to me were hardly ever on time, and the "no shows" became increasingly more frequent. I never knew from one week to the next who would show up, or when. When my social worker came to review my case, she saw for herself the inconsistencies of their hours and days when I showed her their time sheets. She asked me if I wanted to change companies. I was very reluctant to do that as I didn't want to go from the frying pan to the fire and get worse help than I already had. But after much discussion we both agreed that the present situation just wasn't working out. She told me of another company in the area that had a very good reputation. She told me to give it a three months trial to see if it was any better. So I agreed to her suggestion.

Bayada took me on as its client and has been providing me with excellent homemaker service for a number of years. No company can guarantee that its workers will do their job well, but if there is a problem with any of them, it is resolved in a timely manner. I am most fortunate to have two very good workers. Since I am home most of the time, I am able to adjust to their busy schedules. A time clock really doesn't matter to me as long as the work gets done right and the ladies are friendly and trustworthy.

I remember once while I was living in Norfolk and receiving similar services, I went to cash a check at my bank. The teller told me I had insufficient funds in my account to cover the small amount of the check. I couldn't believe what I had heard and I think I let the whole world hear me. The teller calmed me down and went to get the cancelled checks. I looked at them in disbelief. I saw three checks that I didn't write. The three checks totaled over one thousand dollars. I looked at the signatures on those three checks. They definitely were not mine, even though my name was spelled correctly. Then I recognized one of the names to whom one of them was made out. The writing of her name and *my* signature matched. Rosalyn had been working with me for only a short time, maybe two or three months. The head of the bank took me to a cubicle. I told him I wanted to press charges against this person. He told me that if I did, the bank would no longer be responsible for replacing my money and advised me not to do it. It upset me that this person would be getting away with this, but I had to leave the problem in the bank's hands. Before I left the bank, I had that account closed out and a new one opened. When I got home, I wasted no time in contacting my social worker to tell her of the incident. I discovered that six checks were missing from the back of one of my checkbooks. I never saw Rosalyn again.

When I got to work the next day, I told everyone at the Endependence Center of the incident so the peer counselors, all of whom are disabled themselves, could warn their clients of what could happen to them. I advised them to put all money and valuables under lock and key. I sure did after that. The disabled and the elderly are very easy targets for such crimes. We don't expect our care givers to be *thieves,* and for the most part they *are* trustworthy.

My New Life in Tampa

Diane and Emogene at Lowry Park Zoo

Diane came to visit me often. Sometimes when she came, she would bring her very good friend, Emogene Hobbs, with her and we would do something special. One time we went to Lowery Park Zoo and another time we went to the Museum of Science and Industries (MOSI). Since we are all Yankees and hadn't been living in Florida very long, the three of us had such a good time exploring the area together. Sometimes we went out to lunch. I was always careful to select a restaurant they, and most of the time I, hadn't eaten at before. This always made the day seem very special.

One time we were headed for the Cracker Barrel on Route 60 but never quite made it there. I spotted the Oaks Bar. It looked very inviting to me. Seeing its name, Diane was very reluctant to try it. I guess she thought it was a place where mostly bums hung out. I asked her to check it out as I didn't see an access ramp. I told her if there wasn't any, there would be in the not too distant future. When she came back to the car, she told us we would have lunch there. I told her "See Diane, you can't judge a restaurant by its name any more than you can judge a book by its cover". The food and the service were excellent. The only disappointment for me was that I couldn't turn the restaurant in for violation of the ADA because the wheelchair access ramp was in the rear of the building.

Diane was always very sensitive to the needs of others. Whenever she would bring Emogene with her and we planned to go out to lunch, she would always keep track of the time as Emogene is diabetic and had to eat at regular intervals. When my birthday rolled around and she and Emogene came to take me to lunch, Diane always bought a small cake. She made sure it was sugar-free so Emogene could enjoy it with us.

It was so nice having Diane living just an hour's drive away. Whenever there was a special event like the State Fair or the Strawberry Festival and I wanted to go, I would invite her to come with me for company.

Ever since Diane moved to Spring Hill sometime in the '90s, I had been considered one of the family at Christmas time even when I lived in Norfolk. Now that I am living in Tampa, not only would I be spending the Christmas holiday with her but Thanksgiving as well, without having the worry about catching the plane to go home. And it was sure cheaper. Even so, I still had to limit my stay as I have a cat and have to get one of my neighbors to feed him while I am away.

David, Me, and Diane

On a beautiful Florida day in 1999, while I was visiting Diane for my annual Christmas visit before I moved to Tampa, her sister Darlene and I decided we would all go to Busch Gardens for the day. I had been to Busch Gardens in Williamsburg, Virginia and always enjoyed it so I thought the three of us would have a wonderful time at the one in Tampa. Diane's home was an hour's drive from Busch Gardens and I knew it was something we could do in one day. It was a typical Florida sun-shiny day. There was so much to

Darlene and Diane at Busch Gardens in Tampa

see and do there. One of the animal attractions we enjoyed was the bird sanctuary. We bought bird feed and the birds came right to us. One of them landed on my arm and did not want to leave. He stayed with me even when Diane pushed me in my wheelchair.

We decided to go see one of the stage shows. The line was quite long and we thought we would have an hour's wait to get in. While we were deciding whether or not we wanted to wait that long in line, one of the theater employees spotted my wheelchair, came over and pulled us out of line and told us to follow him to the door. I will have to say that we saw a few very disgruntled people who looked a little envious that we did not have to wait in the line. We enjoyed the show very much.

We had a wonderful lunch at an open café. There were peacocks walking freely and they put on a wonderful show for us. They opened their tail feathers and they were like the most gorgeous, colorful fans. We took the Serengeti Railway Ride through the African Safari-inspired-park and saw the desert animals in their natural habitat. There were lions, tigers, giraffes, elephants, antelope, ostrich and zebras, among others. Isn't it amazing how animals of all different species can get along so well...while we humans can't?

We enjoyed going through the gift shops, just looking! We also enjoyed snacks alone the way, like their delicious popcorn.

There were so many exciting rides. I wanted to try the Tanganyika Tidal Wave Ride where we could take a scenic ride through a mighty jungle, but you must beware as there are surprises. It ends with a sudden fifty-five foot drop into the waters below. I really wanted to go on this ride but I was denied because I am disabled. I felt that if this ride wasn't safe for me, it wasn't safe for anyone else. I had been to other theme parks and was never denied the right to participate in anything, including the rides.

After a wonderful day of excitement and fun, we headed for Spring Hill. Diane and Darlene were exhausted, but I could have done the day all over again.

Diane's house on Dow Lane was wheelchair accessible and quite spacious so I had no problem getting about. I entered through the back porch and I could manage the big sliding glass doors going from the back porch to the living room just fine. They were left open most of the time during the day and we often sat out there for our meals. Occasionally Diane and I enjoyed a game of Scrabble there. I spent many hours relaxing with a good book there also. Whenever I came for a visit, even before I moved to Tampa, Emogene would come to see me and would bring me magazines or some little gift that she handcrafted. These visits were so very special to me.

David watched the TV in the living room while Diane and I often settled in the den. The den was added to the original part of the house and had one step down from the living room. Before I came for a visit David took the door off and put in a portable ramp which he built for this purpose so I could use the den safely. The computer was here and I liked using it, especially if Diane and David went off somewhere for a few hours. They often had a house full of company on holidays and the den got used for sleeping quarters as well. Heidi and her family came down from Plymouth, Massachusetts. Mark and his family came up from Naples and David's daughter JoAnne and his son Bobby would come for the day. The bedroom where I slept was often referred to as Arlene's room even when I wasn't there. Over my bed hung two tiny sweaters I had knitted for her first born son, Rusty, oh so many years ago.

Diane always let Emogene know when I was coming. Together they would plan something special. We often went off for the day. On one outing, we went to Homosassa Springs Wildlife State Park. This is one of the most beautiful wildlife parks I have ever visited. We took a very relaxing pontoon boat ride on Pepper Creek to get to the wildlife park. Once in the park, we strolled along an elevated boardwalk where we observed a large number of animals in their natural habitats. These included alligators, bears, bobcats, cougar, deer, and many different kinds of birds.

I think we all enjoyed The Fish Bowl very much. It is a floating underwater observatory. It houses a wide variety of fish of all sizes and colors, and also a manatee. Once outside, we watched a care taker standing knee deep at the edge of a rocky pond feeding a friendly manatee.

At a distance we saw many alligators sunning themselves at the water's edge. They looked so friendly, but from stories I have read about them, they are very vicious creatures. I have seen a couple of them in the retention pond from my apartment window and this is as close as I care to get to them.

We wandered into the Children's Education Center. It was here that we saw a two-headed turtle among the many other small creatures.

There is a building for reptiles here also. It is home to many species of snakes, many of which are native to Florida. However, I haven't seen any since I've lived here, except in captivity, and I hope I never do. I have seen turtles and frogs of many sizes in and around the retention pond and occasionally one has strayed to my doorstep.

I would like very much to return to this beautiful state park some day.

When Diane would come down for the day, she often took me to run errands. Something that took fifteen or twenty minutes in a car often took me two or three hours using public transportation. If I needed to go to the bank, for example, which is just down the road a piece, and I needed to drop something off at the local drugstore, I would wait until she came down so I wouldn't have to sit out in the scorching sun for almost an hour waiting for a bus, or worse yet, get caught in one of those sudden thunderstorms that seem to come out of nowhere at any time of the day. These storms occur most frequently during the late afternoons of the summer months. These sudden downpours could ruin my five thousand dollar motorized wheelchair, so I pay very close attention to the weather forecast before I head out. If I am at the clubhouse and it starts to cloud up, I waste no time in getting back to my apartment before the rain, and often the lightning, come. I had been shopping at Walmart one day and was waiting for the bus to get home when suddenly it got very dark and even before I could get back to the store the rain came down in buckets. I had to wait another two hours for the rain to let up so I could get home safely.

For the past couple of years a very nice neighbor, Pat, has been taking me to church on Saturday afternoon. Mary Help of Christian Church is very small, much like the one I attended as a child, and the congregation is very friendly. The parking is also very good here. Even if we didn't bring my handicap parking permit, there would be no parking problems here. When we get to church I just transfer from the car to my lightweight portable wheelchair and she pushes me into the church. This had been working very well, at least until the rainy season came. Since it takes me about five minutes to transfer to and from my wheelchair, the both of us would look like drowned rats if we got caught in one of those famous Florida downpours. I really don't mind getting a little wet, but in trying to hurry so we won't, I could have an accident and we both could end up in the emergency room. As much as I need to go to church, I have to put safety before God. I believe He understands that.

Pat has recently moved to another town but still comes to my home once a week to bring the church to me. We pray together reciting most of the prayers used in the Sunday Mass. She reads the Gospel of the week and brings me Holy Communion. If someone drops by to see me while she is here, he or she usually participates in the service with us. Even my cat Lucky lies quietly at my feet during these prayer sessions. I think he wants God's blessing also.

During the first year I was here, Lorraine and Karen came down to spend a week with me. They rented a car when they got here so we would be able to do a little sightseeing. We decided that since none of us had ever been to St. Augustine and we all liked historical places, we would go there. Since it is a good three hour drive from Tampa, we knew we would need to spend a night in a motel.

One of the first things we did after we found a motel was to take a guided tour of the city to learn all about its history and to locate places where we thought we wanted to spend time. I already knew that it was the oldest settlement in the United States. It was founded in 1565 under the Spanish Admiral Pedro Menendez de Aviles on the feast day of Saint Augustine, from which the city was named.

We knew we just wouldn't have time to see and do everything in the short time we were there. After the tour we made a mental note of where we would spend the rest of our two days. We soon realized that there was more to see than we had time for. I don't recall who made the suggestion, but we all agreed to spend another night in the motel so we wouldn't be pressed for time. Some of the places we visited at our leisure were Flagler College, Lightner Museum and City Hall, St Augustine Lighthouse and Museum, San Sebastian Winery, the Oldest Wooden Schoolhouse, and Old St Johns County Jail.

The girls decided that I had to go on a ghost walk that first night we were here, something I had done only once before and had forgotten just how scary they can be. It was February and the evening was quite chilly for Florida, so I bundled up in my heavy coat. Our storyteller was almost too good. One of her stories was "The Shaking Bed".

When we got back to the motel, I was very cold from being outdoors for over two hours and the bed was so inviting that I wasted no time getting under the covers to get warmed up. I must have fallen asleep almost as soon as my head hit the pillow. Suddenly I was awakened, and my bed was shaking. At first, I thought I was dreaming. Then the girls started laughing. Lorraine was the ghost.

I think it was during this visit that we ventured to Ybor City for dinner at the Columbia Restaurant. We had checked it out earlier in the day and had decided that it looked very inviting. I was using the portable wheelchair that Mary's grandson, Michael Layman, had outgrown and passed on to me. Late that afternoon, while we were strolling through the streets of this historic area, one of the front wheels came loose and fell off. The girls were unable to retrieve the screw and nut that held the wheel to the chair. They left me sitting on a bench while they went to find a hardware store to buy a replacement screw. They came back a half hour later empty handed. Wheelchairs require special screws and I would have to take my chair to a place that does wheelchair repairs.

In the meantime here we were in Ybor City with a three-wheeled chair that is supposed to have four wheels. It was impossible to push it. Karen took a hold of the side of the chair with the missing wheel and held it up while Lorraine pushed from the back. Together they managed to get us to the restaurant where we all enjoyed a delicious meal and a very enjoyable floor show. I wasted no time in purchasing a *new* light weight portable wheelchair.

The three of us also enjoyed a day at Tarpon Springs. I had been there a couple of times before. I was really looking forward to returning for some mouth-watering Greek food. I don't think Karen had ever been there. We spent the whole afternoon browsing through the many gift shops before taking the sponge boat tour. I had taken it when I was there a few months earlier and the ticket cashier recognized me. He not only gave me a free pass for that day, but he also gave me a VIP pass and told me it was good for any time I should return. Needless to say, I felt honored. Getting me aboard the boat was no easy task, but somehow we managed.

Karen, Lorraine, and Arlene at Tarpon Springs

By the time the sponge diving tour ended, we were quite hungry and my mouth was watering for some Greek food. I told Lorraine and Karen we wouldn't have to go very far. I had eaten in the restaurant right at the sponge tour boat dock on my previous visit and the food was excellent. By now the girls knew when I said a restaurant was good, they could take my word for it. We all had a delicious meal including a bottle of wine. I don't eat out very often, so when I do, I don't mind splurging a little on good food.

I hadn't been living at Williams Landing Apartments very long when I saw a need for a newsletter. I approached the activities director about the idea and told her what I had in mind. I wanted this project to be the work of the residents and I would be its editor. She thought that was a great idea. I thought about an appropriate title for it for quite some time. I wanted it to be unique. I thought of *The Landing News*. But this sounded too ordinary and I really didn't like it all that much even though the residents accepted it. So I went to my computer's thesaurus and found many words for *news*. The word gazette stood out above all the others and had the perfect meaning, **a penny's worth of news.** I was very satisfied with this definition and called the paper *The Landing Gazette*. The residents really liked this name as much as I did. I knew I had a deadline to meet in order to get the paper printed by the first of each month. The residents were very cooperative in getting their stories, jokes, and any announcements to me in time for me to work on them. Each month I would get the resident birthday list from the office. The manager usually had some short announcements for me also. In no time, I had enough material from the residents to increase the number of pages from two to four. I was delighted with all the participation from them. It was what I had hoped for. This meant that I didn't have to spend time dreaming up things to write about.

There was only one complaint. The activities director said the paper was **too long**, it was taking **too much** of her time at the copy machine and I was wasting **too much** office paper. She told me I had to cut back to two pages, one sheet of paper. I was very upset with this. And I knew the residents would not like it any more than I did. I told her that I was volunteering my time to make the residents happy, not her. I quit. The residents were very upset and offered to buy me paper if I would continue. But I felt that the activities director would find some other reason for not wanting me to continue with the project. The lady who tried to fill my shoes ran into similar problems and also quit.

One morning not long after I moved to Tampa, I ran out of milk and decided to venture to the convenience store at the Shell Station located just up the street from my apartment. I had made this trip many times before and thought nothing about it. I was about three quarters of the way there, when I glanced up and saw that a police car had come to a stop a few yards ahead of me. At first I paid it no mind and continued on about my business, until I looked up and saw this young blue eyed blond policeman standing right in front of me and I could go no further without asking him to move out of my way.

He didn't give me a chance. He said to me in a gruff tone of voice and pointing his finger at me, "What are you doing riding in the street, don't you know it is dangerous? Where do you live any way?" When he had finished lecturing me, I turned my wheelchair to face the side of the road and looked up and down the street moving my hand as I did and said, "Officer, I don't see any sidewalk here, do you?"

He looked and just shook his head. "Well, no."

"Well, then, Officer. I guess I have to ride in the street, don't I?"

With that, he got back into his cruiser and drove off and I continued up the street.

A week or so later, I was called to the rental office. The county sheriff and the local newspaper reporter were there and wanted to do a story about the lack of sidewalks here. I talked about the dangers that all of us wheelchair users face every time we venture out to the bus stop which was on MLK Boulevard at that time. After a briefing in the clubhouse library, I led them out to show them just where the problem was. I went ahead, not paying too much attention to them, until I got to where the sidewalk ended at the end of the apartment complex and I had to stop. I glanced up, only to see that they were several yards behind me. I waited patiently for my guests to catch up to me. And when they did, the sheriff called me a "hot rodder" and this name has stuck with me ever since. A few weeks after this story was published—with my picture to boot—the sidewalk was completed, and we no longer 'have to' ride in the street to get to the convenience store at the corner of Williams Road and MLK Blvd.

No Sidewalks on Williams Road !

Our Swimming Pool

I was overjoyed when I learned that my apartment complex had a swimming pool and I couldn't wait to get moved and settled in so that I could use it.

My first day at the pool was quite an experience. The public pool I had been using in Norfolk had an access ramp at the shallow end so disabled people could get in and out with no difficulty.

Arlene Getting Out of the Pool

The new pool was designed quite differently from the one I had been used to using and I knew I was going to have to find my own way to access it. It has a single railing in the middle of the steps. Because of my disability, I knew I would have to go down one side to get into the pool and up on the other side to get out. The first time I tried, I hadn't thought anything about where I would park my wheelchair. I parked so I could grab the railing and pull myself to a standing position. With both hands on the railing, I managed to get down the steps. I sort of half fell in. That worked OK.

Getting Out, Stage Two

Me in the Pool

It was much more difficult getting out than getting in because the steps are just too steep. I could manage the bottom step okay because the buoyancy of the water helps with balance. It is almost like weightlessness and there is very little pressure on the joints. I soon discovered that my wheelchair was on the wrong side of the railing. In order to get out I had to sit on a step and slide my body under the railing to get to my chair. I then had to get to a kneeling position and pull myself to my chair. In the future, I knew I had to put my chair on the other side of the railing. It would be a little harder to get into the pool, but a lot safer to get out and I always put safety first.

There was one other problem: the pool railing got very hot with the Florida sun beating down on it for hours. I had to bring a washcloth with me and dip it in the water and place it over the railing to cool it down before I could use it. Even with these difficulties I was using the pool almost every day when the weather cooperated. I wasn't the only disabled resident having problems at the community's swimming pool. For many of us, the gate latch was too high and out of reach, particularly from the outside. One had to reach over the top of a six foot high gate and pull up on the latch to release it so the gate could be pushed open. Many of us found this impossible to do even from inside the pool area. Most of the time during the week I had to enter the pool area by parading through the clubhouse and the lanai if there was no one at the pool to let me in. On weekends, I could not use the pool at all unless someone was there to let me in. On a few occasions I was locked in and had to wait for someone to come along to let me out. One day I waited for more than two hours. Most of the time people would fix the latch so that it didn't catch and I could pull the gate open to let myself out.

One day the manager called me to the office. She wanted to know if I could manage the latch to the gate out by the street. I told her that I had no need to use this gate and hadn't even tried it. Together we took a stroll to this gate so I could try it out. It worked just fine, no problem. She told me she would order one like it for the front gate of the pool and maintenance would have it installed in a week.

Three weeks went by and still the new gate latch had not been installed even though I was told that it had come in. One afternoon when I went to leave the pool area the gate latch was caught and I could not get the gate open to get out. And nobody was around, or so I thought. I was very angry and I cursed, using nasty words I don't normally use. I heard a loud laughter coming from the lanai. The whole staff heard me and was in hysterics. Mike, the head maintenance man, came and let me out. The new latch was put on the next day.

I soon learned that there were a few residents who could not access the pool at all. One of them told me she cried when there was an exercise program at the pool because even though she wanted to participate in it, there was just no way she would be able to pull herself out even if she got in. There were a few others who had problems with using it also.

I decided that since I wasn't the only one having a very hard time with pool access, I would explore ways to remedy the problems. Having studied the Americans with Disabilities Act (ADA) so well that I can find anything it covers, I knew that it does not cover swimming pools. For some reason, swimming pools were overlooked when the laws were written. I hope to bring this very important activity for many disabled people to the attention of some ADA lawmakers to work on getting this activity added to the law. At that time, the way the law covers the issue is that if there is a program at a public pool, and a disabled person wants to participate in that program the one running the program has to find a way to get the disabled person in and out of the pool or find some other way for him to have access to the program.

I was told that one of the local YWCA's in Brandon has a portable lift for its pool. I had one of the residents drive me to that pool so I could have a look at it and see whether or not it was something we could use at our pool. I had phoned and set up an appointment the day before so the pool director was expecting me. He showed me to the pool area and rolled the lift to the edge of the pool and demonstrated just how it worked. He told me it was battery operated like my motorized wheelchair and the battery had to be kept charged. I thought this was too much of a responsibility for anyone at the apartment complex and the care and upkeep was more than I wanted, even though I liked the way it worked. I asked him if there were other types of pool lifts. He told me there were and took the time to tell me how they worked. Before I left he showed me a catalog with all kinds of pool equipment in it and showed me the other types of lifts and told me how each one worked. He gave me an extra book with a separate price list. I knew I had my work cut out for me.

When I got back home that afternoon, I went straight to my apartment to digest everything I had just been told by the patient pool director. Somehow I knew our pool was going to have a lift. And I also knew I had a lot of work to do to make this wild dream become a reality.

In reading through the Fair Housing Act, I found what I was looking for so that I would have some legal grounds to stand on. It read in part that "disabled tenants can make modifications to their apartments and/or the common use areas at their own expense." With this statement, I knew the pool area would be covered.

Next I needed the support from the residents that the lift was needed so that all the disabled residents could have access to the pool. The disabled residents could then take an active part in the water exercise programs. I wrote up a petition stating the need for a lift. I gave myself two weeks to get it signed. I did not have to worry about meeting my deadline. As soon as word got out, the residents came flocking to me to sign it. I was very surprised at the enthusiasm everybody showed me. Nobody refused to sign it.

In the mean time I got permission from the owner to purchase a rail cover to prevent me and many others from getting burnt hands. This helped a great deal as it gave me a firmer grip and prevented my hands from slipping.

Kathy Yeomans Using the New Pool Lift

By the end of the summer of 2005 the owner and I had finally come to an agreement about the best lift for the residents and the one which required the least to maintain once it was installed. We all agreed that the portable one like the lift I saw at the "Y" required too much of an added expense because of the batteries which would have to be recharged frequently and eventually would have to be replaced, and the lift would have to be taken in at night. We needed one that would be permanently attached to the side of the pool. Besides the safety issues, there were the financial and insurance issues to be dealt with by the owner. He said he would pay half of the cost. I was very surprised at his offer and delighted that he had accepted some responsibility to make my dream happen. I told him I had been saving up for the past three years and would pay what I had saved which was considerably more than half the cost.

Resident of the Year Award

That year I was voted *"Resident of the Year"* and they presented me with a special plaque which I have hanging in my living room.

My Hip Ordeal

One evening in November 2005, while I was getting ready for bed and putting on my pajamas I lost my balance and fell. I landed between the bed and my computer table. My left leg got caught under the bed and I couldn't move. I didn't know what to do so I screamed at the top of my lungs for HELP hoping that one of my neighbors would hear me. After about five minutes Eva, my neighbor behind me, came in and saw that I had fallen. She went and got a friend to help her get me into bed. My left leg was hurting me quite badly. I knew right away that something was seriously wrong. So we called 911.

I was taken to the Emergency Room at Brandon Regional Hospital where I underwent x-rays of the hip. When the x-rays came back they *apparently* showed that nothing was wrong with my hip. They were going to send me home. When I told them that I lived alone and that I couldn't move as my leg was hurting me quite badly, the emergency room doctors really didn't seem the least bit concerned. I told them that I was having a problem with my neck also and that I needed an MRI on my neck as I thought I had slipped a disc. They told me the MRI machine was broken. This was a Saturday night. I told them I wasn't leaving the hospital without an MRI on my neck. So they kept me in the Emergency Room that night and all day Sunday. They kept giving me pain pills for the leg but nothing really helped. They didn't give me any food either. The Emergency Room doesn't offer food. Because I was not registered as a patient, they didn't feed me anything all the time I was there. I was there a day and a half. The only water I was given was the water the nurse gave me to wash down the pain pills every four hours.

On Monday they came and got me and took me for my MRI. When it was read they discovered that I **did** have a slipped disc. The fourth and fifth vertebrae were slipped. That was when they called in a neurosurgeon to look at the x-rays and examine me. They moved me to a room where there was a real bed and FOOD. The neurosurgeon read the MRI and said that I needed surgery on the neck to correct the slipped disc. She scheduled me for surgery, but it wouldn't be for another two weeks.

In the meantime she sent me home. The leg was still hurting me really badly. I knew I was not ready to go home because I would have no help at home but they discharged me anyway.

When I got home the leg was no better. I had a really difficult time transferring from my wheelchair to the toilet and the bed but somehow I managed to get the job done.

In the meantime I had previously planned to go to Washington to visit with my friends, Lorraine and Karen. We were going to celebrate my seventieth birthday. They had planned to take me to the Great Smoky Mountains and Dollywood. I didn't feel that I was up to the trip and called them to tell them that I would have to cancel the trip because my leg was hurting me too badly and I was going to have surgery on my neck in two weeks. Plus I knew I could not climb the stairs to their second-story apartment. They were very disappointed and told me to plan to come anyway and they would get me up over the stairs. They knew we would be spending several nights in a motel so I would only be climbing the stairs one time. I was still very reluctant to do this, but they said that as I was going to have surgery anyway, that I might as well enjoy my time before the surgery. So I went.

They met me at the airport in Washington and we drove back to their apartment in Spotsylvania, VA, just outside of Fredericksburg. It is an hour and a half ride on the train. They managed to carry me up over the stairs that evening and get me down the next morning. We headed out for our Smoky Mountain trip.

We enjoyed several days in the Great Smoky Mountains and Dollywood Theme Park. I had never been to Dollywood before and had no idea what to expect. I thought it was just the home of Dolly Parton and maybe a music theater where I would be hearing a lot of country music. I didn't know it was a big theme park so I was very surprised when we arrived to see how well it already was decorated for Christmas. Several of the shows were Christmas oriented.

The girls decided to put me in a car that was a replica of one that Dolly Parton drove. It was on a track. So they put me in the driver's seat like I was really driving it. I have never driven a car in my life and I don't think anyone would want to be on the road with me if I did.

We all enjoyed the ride around the park on the Dollywood Express train one evening. The ride through the park at this time of the year was so beautiful with all the Christmas lights aglow.

We also enjoyed browsing through the many gift shops and sampling some delicious southern cuisine. All in all we had a great time here.

On our way home from the Great Smoky Mountains we decided to stop at Monticello, Thomas Jefferson's home. I had never been there and one of the other girls hadn't been there either.

We learned that Thomas Jefferson's home, which he designed himself, was built on the summit of an 850 foot high peak in the Southwest Mountains in Charlottesville, Virginia in 1772. The house was once the center of a plantation of 5,000 acres maintained by 150 slaves. Because

Monticello

Monticello appears on the reverse side of the two-dollar bill, the gift shop at Monticello hands out two-dollar bills as change.

A row of functional buildings and slave dwellings known as Mulberry Row was near the home to the south. A cabin on Mulberry Row was for a time the home of Sally Hemings, a mixed race slave of Jefferson's and said to be a half sister of his wife. On the slope below Mulberry Row, Jefferson maintained an extensive vegetable garden.

It was the day before Thanksgiving when we got back to Spotsylvania. Once again I was carried up the stairs to their apartment. I would not be going out again until Monday morning when I was driven to the airport to return to Tampa. The girls are excellent cooks and together prepared a delicious dinner with all the trimmings and, of course, a bottle of wine. All in all I had a very enjoyable week. As long as I sat quietly and didn't have to put any weight on the left leg, the pain was bearable. I thought I had just badly bruised some muscles in it and it would have to heal in its own time.

When I returned home I was exhausted and very worried about having to undergo neck surgery for the third time and by a doctor I did not know very well. I had to trust that the operation would go well.

Before the surgery, I was told I would have to wear a neck brace for three months after the operation. I was very relieved when I was told that it would ***not*** be the halo brace I had to wear after the previous two neck surgeries I had in Norfolk– about 1989 and 1998.

The halo brace was most uncomfortable, and it required a lot of professional care daily to make sure that I didn't develop any infections from the screws that attached to my head. Once the halo brace came loose and detached itself from my head during the night. I was terrified. I didn't dare move for fear that I would undo the work the surgeon had done and it would have to be done over again. All I could do was to wait for someone to come in and call 911. Even though the telephone was right by my bed I could not reach it without disturbing the neck part of the brace even more. It was four hours before the nurse came to clean around the screws. I was taken right to the emergency room. The doctor had to take the whole brace off. He was also worried that I could have undone the work he had done several weeks earlier. We both took a big sigh of relief when I got back from x-rays and everything was intact. He had the nurse wash my upper body before he put a new brace on. That felt so good. I felt clean. The upper body hadn't been bathed in several weeks. The body part of that brace was lined with lamb's wool to prevent sores. It got very smelly from body odors and there was nothing anyone could do about it. I was very happy when it finally was taken off after having worn it for three months. One of the first things I did was to soak in a tub of hot water for an hour. It felt *so* good.

I thought this next surgery would be a piece of cake compared to the last two times. I would not have to wear the halo brace, just a stiff neck brace. I could deal with that just fine. I would have the surgery and remain in the hospital for a few days, and then would be sent to some rehab place for a couple of weeks, long enough to regain my strength and make sure I would have no complications from the surgery. I was still having a lot of pain in the left leg from the fall I had taken a month earlier. I thought the bed rest would be just what I needed in order for the bruised muscles to heal properly. I was really looking forward to getting the surgery done so I could get back to living a pain-free life once again. I thought I would be well mended in about a month's time and home again. I got one of my neighbors, Jessie, to tend to Lucky's needs while I was in the hospital. By now Jessie was used to taking care of him while I was away. They seemed to get along pretty well. It's a good thing they did because it turned out that I would be in rehab for five months. Jessie took care of him all that time. I guess that's what good neighbors are for.

A few days after the surgery the doctor came in and said I was ready to go to a rehab for a while. The hospital made arrangements for me to go to Tandem Rehab in Brandon. I thought I would be there for about a month or maybe two at the most.

My first two weeks there were very, very difficult as the leg was still hurting me and I was not permitted to have my motorized wheelchair brought in. This meant that I had to stay wherever the staff left me since I could not manage a manual wheelchair because of the arthritis in my shoulders. When I asked if I could have my own wheelchair, I was told that I could not because they didn't want me running around the nursing home running into people and things. I told them that I had driven this motorized chair for a good number of years and have never had an accident with it. I told them "I have a physical disability but my mind is probably better than yours." They finally consented to my wishes and we drove in their van to my apartment to get my motorized wheelchair. This gave me a little more freedom and relieved the nurses of having to push me to therapy. There was a beautiful courtyard there and, when I asked if I could go outside in the courtyard, they told me that no patients were allowed outside at all. I think the staff was afraid I was going to leave.

I was taken down for physical and occupational therapy daily. I was able to transfer from my wheelchair to the toilet on my own but only because there was a grab bar in the bathroom and I was able to pull myself up between the toilet and the wall, using the grab bar for balance. I still could not put any weight on my left leg because the hip hurt too badly. I could not stand on my right leg for more than a few seconds because the right knee would give out from underneath due to the arthritis in it and the worn out cartilage. I had a stabilizing brace at home. I used it only on rare occasions for climbing stairs. I thought that if I had the brace it would help because I could lock the knee so it wouldn't buckle. They were reluctant to even give it a try but I insisted and they finally relented. It worked! Now I was able to stand on the parallel bars but I was not able to walk with it, because I was not able to put any weight on the left leg as it hurt too badly. As they were in the medical profession, I did not understand why no one investigated further as to why I still had so much pain in my left leg. They just kept giving me muscle relaxants and pain pills thinking this would keep me quiet but the pills didn't help to alleviate the pain. I still could not transfer from the wheel chair to the bed, even with the brace. I complained that the mattress on the bed was very uncomfortable and I couldn't sleep well. They changed the mattress, but this did not help at all. So they just gave me more muscle relaxants.

Not only was I in excruciating pain but the food was almost inedible and I went down to 72 pounds. I only weighed about 85 to 90 pounds to start with, so going down to 72 was a loss I could **not** afford. One time they gave me boiled eggs for breakfast and scrambled eggs for supper. They often served beans and hot dogs which I don't eat. The dietician, if there even was one, never came near me to see why I wasn't eating.

I was in a private room for the first two weeks that I was there. Then they decided that I no longer needed a private room so put me in a four-bed room. This really didn't make any difference to me but they were very sarcastic about the fact that I didn't warrant a private room. This made me very angry. They were just plain nasty.

My long-time friend Diane came down from Spring Hill a few times to visit with me and see how things were going. She was very dissatisfied with my care. I was losing weight and they were doing nothing about it. It was like they put blinders on because they just didn't care. Diane said she didn't want me to spend Christmas alone, so on her way to Naples to visit with her son Mark and family, she stopped by to pay me a visit. I was so thrilled to see her. She brought me gifts so I would have a special Christmas. I hated to see her leave.

I had been there about three weeks when the director and other members of the staff decided to have a teleconference with my uncle and aunt, Philip and Sheila, to discuss my progress. Philip has the power of attorney so he was the contact person. The gist of the conversation was that I was making progress and that they thought that I would be there for another week. I agreed to that because I knew I was not ready to go home just yet.

The next morning the head nurse came in my room and told me to get ready because I was going home that afternoon. I was **very** upset because they had told me that I would be there for at least another week. I knew I was not ready to go home since I knew I needed help for my basic needs, getting in and out of bed and on and off the toilet. I went down to the director's office and I asked him what was going on! He said, "What do you mean?" I told him that he told my aunt and uncle that I would be there for at least another week. I figured by that time I would have services in place for when I got home. He told me that he was discharging me because he felt that I was "becoming too dependent on their help." I said "But I am not ready to go home yet. I can't even get in or out of bed, and I will have no help at home." It was like he just didn't care. I told him I wasn't going home. He told me I was and, if I stayed any longer I would be responsible for the bills. He forced me into signing the release papers. He threatened me with having to be responsible for nursing home care which would be $155.00 per day which I knew I could not afford. I left his office terrified. What was I going to do? Where would I turn to for help? There were no provisions for home care after discharge and I would be alone.

The director told me to be ready at 1:00 pm and he would have one of his staff member's drive me home in their van. At this point I called Diane and told her what was going on. She was horrified that they could do such a thing. She said she would come down and spend the night with me. When the lady dropped me off she just left me in the living room, not even offering to help me in any way. I don't even think she said "goodbye". She just left me. Probably due to stress, I was not feeling well. I had diarrhea. Not badly, but enough to be annoying. When I read the report several months later it said that I had "incontinence of the bowels and bladder." Knowing how sick I was, how could they just ***"patient dump"*** me, knowing that I lived alone? I guess that they just didn't care.

Probably due to stress, I was not feeling well. I had diarrhea, not badly, but I knew I had it. It was enough to be annoying. When I read the report several months later it said that I had 'incontinence of the bowels and bladder'. Knowing how sick I was, how could they just ***"patient dump"*** me, knowing that I lived alone? I guess that they just didn't care.

That was a Tuesday. I had to make arrangements to get to the doctor's office for a checkup on the neck surgery the next day. Diane would follow the van in her car. The checkup went well. I was told to come back in a month.

When I got home I went to the office at the apartment complex where I lived and asked if there was anyone who could help me. I told them what was going on and that I needed help getting in and out of bed. One of the residents here is a CNA and she offered to help me. Since I could not put any weight on the left leg, she suggested that I get a hospital bed to make it a little easier on the both of us. I did. But it didn't help all that much. It was even more uncomfortable than the one in the nursing home and I just could not sleep.

She came in several times a day for the first few days I was home to get me up in the morning and back to bed at night and she also came in several times during the day to make sure I had enough to eat.

On the third day that I was home my friend Bessie, a neighbor, came in to talk to me. She told me that I didn't look well. She thought I was very sick and needed to go back to the emergency room at the hospital. I was very upset but yet I knew she was right. I was **very** sick and needed medical help. The diarrhea had gotten worse and I was spending too much time in the bathroom. I was getting dehydrated and felt very dizzy and lightheaded. She called 911 and the ambulance came and took me back to Brandon Regional Hospital where I had my neck surgery. I told the emergency room attendant that I wasn't feeling well and that my leg was still hurting me. They sent me for x-rays on the leg and then took me back to the emergency room cubicle. The doctor had ordered some pain medicine before I was taken for x-rays to make me a little more comfortable when I was transferred to the x-ray table but it really didn't help any. The doctor came in a few minutes later and said "Guess what!" I looked at him and said "Lord only knows what!" He told me I had a broken hip. That put the pieces of the puzzle together. That is why my leg was hurting me so badly for so long. He said, "We'll take care of that!" He had given me Darvocet to relieve the pain when I first arrived. When he realized that my hip was broken, he wasted no time in giving me a shot of morphine to relieve the pain.

The orthopedic surgeon on call was a young fellow. After he read the x-rays, he sent me up to the orthopedic floor and put my left leg in traction for the night. He said that he would do the surgery in the morning. But that never happened. I did not sleep at all that night. I watched all the animal shows on television the whole night trying to keep my mind off the ordeal of having to undergo surgery in the morning. I just wanted to get it done and over with.

The doctor came back the next morning and said that he talked it over with his senior colleagues and they decided that, since the hip had been fractured for quite some time (since November and it was now mid January) and I wasn't walking, that they would not do the surgery. They would wait to see if it would heal itself. I was very upset with their decision and I think the doctors knew it. I could not see how this fracture was going to heal itself. But what did I know! I was only a patient. I hadn't had ten years of medical school. The doctor was supposed to have all the right answers.

I would have to endure the next three and a half months in agony before surgery was finally done with a total hip replacement. This delay caused me to lose a lot of muscle strength in my left leg which I was never able to regain.

I have no proof of it but it is my opinion that because I have cerebral palsy the doctors were afraid to take a chance on operating on my hip. I think they were afraid of making a bad situation worse. The doctors told me that it had started to heal itself so they wanted to wait to see what happens. In the meantime I was to go back to rehab with orders that I was to put ***no weight*** on that leg for two months.

I told the doctor what happened at the nursing home and that I had been put out. When the hospital sent the social worker to do the paper work to transfer me to a nursing home for rehabilitation, the social worker said that they were going to send me to Tandem Nursing Facility. I said "Over my dead body are you going to send me back to Tandem. I was just dumped out of that place." I told her what happened while I was there. She called around to find another place that had room, but because I had bowel and bladder infections which I probably picked up at Tandem, she had a hard time finding a facility that would take patients with these infections for fear of spreading them to other patients. She finally contacted Central Park Nursing Facility and I was accepted there.

When I got to Central Park I was graciously received. The orthopedic surgeon sent the report and in the report it said that there was to be no weight bearing on the left leg for at least two months. I was on antibiotics for the bowel and bladder infections for three weeks. When these infections cleared up, I began to feel a little better. The first day I was at Central Park the dietician came in to see me and told me that they were going to have to fatten me up. At this time I was unaware of just how much weight I had lost as they never bothered to weigh me at Tandem. She looked at my report and said "You only weigh seventy-two pounds!" I was surprised at that myself and a little scared. She said

"You're going to put us to work before you leave here." I told her that if the food is good I eat. If it isn't, I don't eat! She brought down a sheet of paper with all the foods listed on it and I was to check off the ones I would not eat. The dietitian looked at the list and she said that it looks like I eat pretty well. She said that if I saw something on the menu that I didn't like, they would substitute something for it that I do like. That sounded really good to me. I told her that I did not drink milk, but I like things that contain milk. She always made sure that I had yogurt and some kinds of puddings for dessert. Sometimes I got two or three deserts on my tray. I also told her that I got hungry at nighttime before I went to bed. She made sure I got a midnight snack, usually a peanut butter and jelly sandwich and juice.

The first few nights I was there one of the CNA's on the night shift turned me over and she flipped me too fast and it hurt. I complained about this to the head nurse and the head nurse had a talk with the CNA. I had no more problems after that. That CNA became my best friend while I was there.

I had physical and occupational therapy sometimes six days a week. It was mostly upper body exercises so that I would have the strength to transfer myself from wheelchair to toilet or bed. I requested my motorized wheel chair and they went and got it almost immediately, no questions asked. I had been there for just a short time when the physical therapist decided that I should learn to stand in order to transfer from chair to toilet using the grab bar in the bathroom. This was very difficult as I could not put any weight on the left leg at all... doctor's orders. I knew that the longer I could not use the muscles, the less chance I would have of ever regaining strength in them no matter how hard I worked at it. This really bothered me.

I decided to go back to the leg brace again. They agreed to that. It took a while before I was able to pull myself to a standing position so the aides would not have to lift me from my wheelchair. I was able to stand just long enough that they were able to pull my pants up and down when the right knee brace was locked. This helped a lot. I was still not permitted to put any weight on the left leg and I was still wearing the neck brace. I would have to continue to wear it until the end of March. It was a little uncomfortable, but tolerable.

Philip did not like that the doctor did not want to see me again for two months. He called the doctor and he told them that two months was too long to go without checking to see how my hip was ***healing***. When I went back to the doctor and saw the x-rays a month later I looked at the x-rays and I could see where the break was and my first thought was, "How the hell is this going to heal itself?" There was a space of about an inch long where that bone had broken and become separated. The doctor was still reluctant to do anything.

When I got back to the nursing home, the physical therapist said that I could put a little bit of weight on my leg now. Toe touching, I think she called it. This gave me a little better standing balance, but it did not help all that much because the whole leg was hurting me too badly. The leg just wasn't going to get better and I knew it. I was working out in the gym every chance I got. I still could not transfer to and from my wheelchair even with a special transfer board.

By now the leg was hurting me worse then ever. I was having pain in it even in the middle of the night. A few times I had to ask to be put in my wheelchair. At least here I could find a position where there was less pressure and I could tolerate the pain a little better.

Finally, after three months, when I went to the doctor again, I looked at the x-rays and saw that it wasn't any different than the first time. I told him that he would have to do something about this. That is when he said, "Yes, we do!" He then turned me over to the senior surgeon. He scheduled me for surgery the next week. He told me that I couldn't bear the pain any longer. I said ***"AMEN!"*** By now it was mid April and I fell in mid November, the year before.

I had to go for pre-op tests at the hospital the day before the surgery. One of the CNA's drove me for the tests. The surgery was scheduled for four o'clock which seemed quite late to me. I saw the paper work and it did say four o'clock. The next morning the head nurse came in and told me I could eat a little breakfast because the surgery was late in the day and she felt that eight hours was long enough to go without food before surgery. The hospital wanted me to fast from midnight. Somehow the timing got mixed up and I wasn't at the hospital when the doctor thought I should have been. According to him, the surgery was scheduled for twelve o'clock noon and I wasn't there. The head nurse got very upset because she saw the paper too, which said four o'clock. The doctor was going to postpone the surgery until the next week. I was very upset about all that was going on. The more upset I got, the more intense the pain got. Finally, after much discussion, the doctor told the head nurse that he would do the surgery at six o'clock that evening, so make sure to get her to the hospital right away. By now it was three o'clock. I was not only very upset with all that had gone wrong, I was angry at the hospital for the mix up in the time of the surgery.

The ride to the hospital in the ambulance was **murder**. I was very upset anyway and the leg was hurting me worse than ever. When I got to the hospital I was ready to scream as I was in so much pain. When the surgeon came in, I asked him if he had partied last night. He said "No." I said "Good, because I wouldn't let you touch me if you had partied last night!" He laughed. The senior doctor did the surgery and it was a success.

I was in the hospital for just a few days. The physical therapist got me up in a chair the very next morning after the surgery. I had a lot of pain in the top part of the leg. The therapist told me that this was because of the position the leg was in during the operation. All the muscles were stretched, like I had over-exercised them. This pain would vanish in a couple of days. I was up for about an hour that first time. This was very tiring for me. I think she came back and got me up a second time that day. On the third day, I stayed up most of the day. The therapist was quite surprised and pleased with this, and so was I. I think I had the surgery on Wednesday. I was able to leave the hospital on the following Monday.

I would have to spend about six more weeks in rehab. But at least the worst was behind me now and I could look forward to the day when I could return home to my own apartment and sleep in my own comfortable bed again.

By now it was mid April. The weather was summer-like, and I took advantage of the beautiful courtyard at Central Park. I would take a book or magazine and go sit outside under the shade trees and read. When it was time for my therapy, the therapists got so they just looked out their window which faced the courtyard, before sending someone to my room to fetch me. They knew right where I would be. I think I was the only patient there who had nerve enough to wear shorts so I could get a little tan on my legs. The female CNAs would all kid me about this and say that I just wanted to look sexy for Jorge, the only male CNA there at time.

Jorge was assigned to my room. He worked very well with me. Sometimes, if I needed something done and it wasn't urgent, I would wait for him to come on duty at three o'clock rather then have someone less competent do the job, particularly when it came to lifting me. Some of the others just would *not listen* to me when I would try to tell them the best way to do something so that it put less of a strain on both of us. They just had their own way and what did I know? I was just a patient. Well, I knew my own body and how it worked better than anybody else. That's what I knew. Jorge saw this, and he worked with me. And this made all the difference. I hope he gets to read my book.

Diane came down to visit me quite frequently. If I needed anything from my apartment, she would stop by to pick it up before she came. Once a month she would bring all the mail that was collected daily and left on my dining room table. Much of it was junk mail, of course. We would spend a half hour sorting it out. I made three piles, one for throw-aways, one for bills to be paid and one that stayed with me, most of which was magazines to be read at my leisure. She wrote out any checks so my bills would get paid on time to avoid any late charges for them. My bills are high enough as it is without adding a late charge.

A couple of times Diane's sister, Darlene came with her. Once Darlene saw that I was looking like a shaggy dog and decided I needed a hair cut. The next week she brought her hair clippers and barber scissors and did a first class job. It made me feel somewhat human again. It felt so good to get the hair off the back of my neck as it sometimes would catch on my neck brace and was most uncomfortable.

If Diane came down at lunchtime, she often stopped somewhere along the way and bought us **real food**. We would picnic in the courtyard under the shade trees. A couple of times I shared my lunch with her. What I didn't like, she did. It looked like I cleaned my plate for a change. After the terrible food at Tandem, the food at Central Park was like eating in a gourmet restaurant.

Following the total hip replacement surgery in mid-April, things began to turn around in a more positive direction for me. Until now it was doubtful as to whether I would ever be able to return home to my own apartment since I was not able to transfer to and from my wheelchair without help.

Once I was pain free my progress was beginning to speed up daily. When I was able to get in and out of bed and on and off the toilet without help, I was on my way home and the physical therapist and I both knew it. Once again, I was in the gym working out every chance

I got, whether the therapists worked with me or not. I just wanted to get home to my own apartment. I was very careful not to have any accidents all the time I was at Central Park. I didn't want any of the staff there to find any reasons for not letting me go home.

Before I could go home, the occupational therapist and I went to see my apartment to make sure I would be able to function in it. She saw that my bathroom did not have a grab bar at the toilet, which I needed. It also had a tub. She and I knew there was no way for me to get in and out of it even with help. She also knew that I needed a side railing for my bed.

When we got back to Central Park later that day, we went through all the **special equipment** catalogs until we found just what I needed for the least amount of money and that was the simplest to install. Everything was ordered and properly in place by the time I was ready to go home.

The door on my microwave oven did not work right and it was very hard for anyone to open. Only I had the "magic touch" to operate it with very little difficulty. I kept putting off buying a new one as the old one still did what it was supposed to do cooking-wise. It really needed to be replaced and now was as good a time as any to do it. One time when Diane stopped by my apartment to get the mail, I asked her to try my microwave. She phoned me to tell me she couldn't get the door opened. I started laughing. I told her "I have the magic touch." She told me that I needed a new one right away. I asked her to check out my toaster while she was at it. I knew what she was going to tell me. "It doesn't work right either." I asked her to bring my checkbook with her. Before she left that afternoon, I gave her a blank check and asked her to do a little shopping. She loved bargains, so I knew whatever she bought would be on sale and of the best quality.

It was around this time that Philip and Sheila came down to see me. It was spring break so they planned a family vacation and Lorena, their daughter, came with them. They went to my apartment and Phil put the special equipment together so my apartment would be ready for me when I was ready for it. Sheila and I spent time filling out my annual Section 8 recertification papers so they would get off in the mail right away. It always makes me very nervous that the Housing Authority will find some reason to reject me. I am on pins and needles each year until I hear that my application has been approved and just what my rent will be for the coming year. If I ever lose this voucher, I will surely end up in **Tent City.**

After we got everything done in the apartment and my lease papers signed at the office, the manager couldn't wait to take us to the pool to show me the pool lift that was recently installed. She knew how hard I had worked to get it. I was overjoyed that it finally got here and couldn't wait to see it working. I knew it would be a while before I would have strength enough to use it. But it was ready for me when I was ready for it.

From five months of not being able to use my left leg at all, the hamstrings had tightened up so much that I couldn't straighten the leg at the knee, just one more problem I would have to deal with before I would be able to leave Central Park. I decided that I needed to get standing on **both** feet and asked the physical therapist to put me in the standing table for a short time every day. I had lost my sense of balance and to this day I still cannot stand unaided no matter how hard I try. The standing table did help some, but not all that much.

Between us, we then decided to try an adjustable knee brace at night time. The tension could be adjusted to as much as I could tolerate and was quite uncomfortable for the first few weeks. Later, I could completely straighten my knee without the aid of the brace but this did not happen overnight. I had to wear this brace to bed for almost two years before I felt I no longer needed it. For the first few weeks of use my muscles were quite sore from being stretched. But as time went on, the soreness wore off, and I was sleeping pretty well.

Before I was discharged from Central Park, the social worker and the therapists made certain that I would have all of the services I needed at home as soon as I got there. My homemaker service was notified and somebody would be sent the very next day. Physical and occupational therapy would be continued in my home two or three times a week for a short time.

The rental office somehow knew that I would need a helping hand when I came home and they asked Mary Ann to come over to see just what help I would need. The only help I really needed at this point was someone to help me at bedtime because I could not get the knee brace on. Also, I wear protective underwear to bed so I won't have to get up half asleep in the night to use the bathroom. I have a very difficult time getting them on because I need both hands to hold me up in a standing position and there is just no way I can let go long enough to pull on a pair of pants.

With all the services in place and my apartment set up with all the necessary adaptive equipment in place that I needed to live as independently as possible, a date was set for me to return home. Those last two weeks at Central Park were the very happiest I had had in over six months. The whole staff saw a big change in my personality. I think I got some of the aides in a little trouble one evening. We would gather in the conference room after supper and after most of the patients were put to bed. We did get a little rowdy at times telling stories and jokes. I felt the need to liven the place up a little. I guess the head nurse didn't like this any too well because the conference room was kept locked up for a week. When I inquired about the lockup, the nurse told me, "The aides are here to work, not to party". We all behaved a little better after the lockup. At least we kept our voices quieter.

There was one big problem here. This was the laundry service. For those of us who didn't have anyone to take our dirty clothes home to be laundered, if we sent it out, we hardly ever got it **all** back. It didn't seem to matter how well marked my clothes were, they wound up in the main clothes storage closet or on one of the other patient's back. I complained to the nursing supervisor a number of times to no avail. The day before my discharge she took me to the storage closet and together we sorted through all the clothes until I had recovered some of what were mine. I must have lost around three hundred dollars worth of clothes to Central Park, mostly long pants. When I got home, I would discover that I would no longer be able to wear them because I could not get them on without help, so I guess it didn't really matter that they were lost.

I really did not like being in my room and spent most of my time in the courtyard. When the other patients had visitors, I was introduced to them and enjoyed chatting with them and really looked forward to their visits. On the morning of my discharge I was very surprised when I came back to my room to find that the wife of one of the patients had sent me a most unusual floral arrangement. It was not flowers but, in fact, it was made up of fresh fruit. I have seen many fruit baskets. But never had I seen anything quite like this, flowers made from fruit. It looked too pretty to eat. As soon as I got home, I had to put it in the refrigerator so the fruit wouldn't spoil. I feasted from it for over a week.

Before I could come home, I would have to invest in a new mattress for my bed. The old one was about twenty years old and it had seen its better days and once again Diane did the shopping for me. I told her I needed the firmest one that was ever made. And it had to be heavy enough that it would not slip and slide off the frame as it would have to secure the railing so I could get in and out of bed safely. The mattress would be the only thing holding the grab-railing in place. Part of it slides between the mattress and the box spring. When the bed arrived and it was all assembled I discovered that it was too high and I knew I would have a difficult time getting into bed. Diane suggested that l do away with the metal frame, the part that has the wheels on it. I knew that once the bed was in place, it would not have to be moved. This idea made the bed the perfect height for me to be able to transfer to and from my wheelchair safely.

The week before I was to go home, Jorge and I worked out the details for using a toilet in the main bathroom. The one I had been using at central Park was not in the same position as the one in my apartment. He got a portable one and together we positioned it properly and securely. He wrote a sign that read, "***Arlene's toilet. Do not remove.***" and taped it to the wall over the toilet. I used only this one for the last week I was there.

Diane came to see me a few days before I was to go home. I asked her to take most of my belongings home that day. I knew that I would have to use public transportation to get home and I would not be able to manage all of my things alone on the van and get them inside my apartment. I knew that the van drivers are not permitted to enter anyone's home. Besides that, I was also aware that I could have no more than two carry-on shopping bags.

On the day I was to leave, the aides were supposed to help me gather up my belongings but I guess they were just too busy. I had to ask the cleaning girl for a trash bag from her cart so I could gather up what few things I did have and be ready to meet my driver outside at the main entrance to the building by noon time. It would be so nice to get home and sleep in a comfortable bed again, and eat what I wanted when I wanted.

Once again Diane came down to spend a few days with me to make sure that I had all the services in place that I needed. She also knew that I would have very little food in the house. She and I made out a grocery list with enough to last a week and tide me over until my homemaker could do the monthly shopping.

The social worker at Central Park and my county social worker coordinated everything so well. That next day was so busy with people coming in. This was a Friday. I really wasn't expecting anyone to show up until at least Monday. I would have physical and occupational therapy two or three times a week for the next two months. This was the first of June and, by the end of the summer, I was able to pull myself to a standing position at the kitchen sink long enough to wash a couple of dishes with my wheelchair seat behind me and holding onto the front of the sink with one hand. I still have a hard time reaching the faucets to turn on the water. I sometimes use the bathroom sink to do dishes as it is lower and smaller than the one in the kitchen.

By the end of the summer I felt that it was time to try out the pool lift. I asked the physical therapist who was working with me at the time to come to the pool to work with me on transferring from my wheelchair to the lift chair. I found it very difficult the first time I tried it. I felt that with practice it would get easier, and it did. She worked with me twice a week for the next three weeks. The next time she came, I told her I wanted to try the lift out. I knew she would have to get in the pool with me. She said that she couldn't do that because she wasn't dressed for that. I said "You will be in a few minutes", and handed her one of my bathing suits. It was a little big for me so I knew it would fit her but she was a little chunkier than I so I thought it would be a perfect fit and it was. I had a very difficult time getting off the seat because the water was too deep and my feet could not touch the bottom of the pool. The therapist managed to get me to the shallow end where I could stand up. She worked with me on standing balance for a few minutes before she let me try out my swim-trainer. She was very careful not to let go of me while I took my first steps in the water. It felt *sooo* good just to be able to take those first steps. I hadn't been in the pool for a whole year.

The second session was a little easier as we both knew what to expect. By the end of the afternoon, I was able to walk alone using the swim-trainer for support. Together the therapist and I accomplished my goal. I knew that I would need help using the lift but for now I was very satisfied with just being able to use the lift and once in the pool I was able to walk. By the next summer, the lift had been moved to the shallow end of the pool and I could now get on and off its seat without help.

When I first came home, I had very little time to myself. There were people coming in to work with me every day during the week. I really looked forward to the week end so I could just be alone and do what I wanted. My uncle had sent me a large carton of books, about twenty in all and I just wanted to get to read them without any interruptions. After having had people around me seven days a week for the past six months, I longed for the day when I could lock my door and shut everybody out. I guess I had become very anti-social at this point but I just didn't care to be around a lot of people all the time, even those I liked. Being away from home all that time was so terrible for me. I had no privacy and it made me very grumpy.

I had only been home one day when I realized I was going to have to change my wardrobe since I just could not stand long enough to pull pants on and off. This meant that I would have to start wearing dresses which I hated to do. I hadn't worn a dress since high school days except to funerals and weddings so I never had to shop for them.

One day when I was out with one of my aides, I told her I needed to look at dresses. I was very discouraged when I couldn't find anything I liked or that I could get into without help. She told me not to worry, that she had the perfect solution. She wheeled me to the fabric department of that store and told me to pick out five different pieces that I liked and she would make them into dresses for me. "Now" I said, "we need to find a pattern." "Oh no," she said "I don't need one."

I had forgotten all about the dresses until my birthday. A group of my friends gathered at my place before heading to the Olive Garden for lunch. We were waiting for my aide to come as it was her birthday also. When she finally came, she was carrying the five dresses and couldn't wait to show them off to all of my friends. Needless to say, I had a great birthday. She has made me many more since, for which I am most grateful, even though I much prefer shorts and slacks to dresses.

Shortly after I came home from rehab Diane came down to visit with me. As usual, she asked me if there was any place I needed to go or any errands to run. I told her that I needed a new printer for my computer as I could not operate the original one independently. The ink cartridges were very difficult to replace and I could not do it without help. Diane and I went to Office Depot and found one much smaller and easier for me to use. I looked at many before settling on the one I got. I needed a good printer before I could start work on my book so that I could print out what I had written just in case the computer went down and I lost everything that was in it.

On June 11, 2008 Diane came down for a visit. She often brought Emogene with her, but this day Emogene was busy and could not come. When she got here she asked me the usual question "Any place you need to go, or any errands you need to run?" I told her that for once I didn't have anything I had to do so we just sat and chatted. We talked about her a lot because I was concerned that, since she lived alone, she might not be able to get help in an emergency. I told her about the Life Alert that I wear and told her that she should also wear one because if she should fall and could not get to a phone she might not get help for several days. She said she didn't need one. I told her what I thought and there was nothing more I could say.

We went out to lunch at "Mimi's". We had never been there before but were glad we tried it. One of my neighbors recommended it. We came back to my place and we enjoyed an afternoon of tea and desserts. She asked me if I was getting all the services I needed and I told her that I was. And if I wasn't, it was my fault for not opening my big mouth. She just laughed. Little did I know that this would be our last visit. Diane passed away in August of 2008 and I would never see her again.

Her passing left such a huge hole in my heart. It was so sudden. She was a picture of health and never complained of not feeling well. I never suspected anything was wrong. She came down to see me about every six weeks or so. I didn't see her every day, so I didn't notice any changes in her personality or behavior.

When I got the e-mail from her granddaughter Jeni telling me that Gram was in the hospital in Tampa, I was very concerned that it was something quite serious. Jeni said Gram had undergone emergency surgery to remove a brain tumor that day and that the operation went well. The only thing anyone could do now was to wait and see how well she pulled through the ordeal. I knew enough about this type of surgery to know the dangers that could follow it.

When I talked with Diane's son Mark and her daughter Heidi who were staying at their mother's house to get a progress report that next day, they gave me the bad news that their mother had a massive stroke and there was very little anyone could do now but wait. She was paralyzed on one side and if she pulled through, she would need extensive rehabilitation. At this point, it was very doubtful that she would ever be able to live independently again. To someone who had dedicated her life to helping others, this would have been devastating.

A few days later, Mark took me to the hospital so I could say my final good bye to my lifelong friend of fifty-seven years. We rode back to my apartment in silence. I knew it wouldn't be long now before she would be joining her husband Johnny, and her three children, David, Arlyn, and Rusty in Heaven.

Another Big Move

One day when my friend Darlene came to Tampa for her usual two-week early morning visit, she told me that she was seriously thinking about selling her house and moving into an apartment. She said that the house was getting to be too much work for her to handle with the yard work and upkeep that goes with owning a house. She told me that there were two new senior citizen apartment buildings near completion within walking distance of each other in Spring Hill and that she had seen both of them. She said that because it has about three hundred more square feet of floor space than the Madison Reserve, Vista Grand was her choice. She told me that the rent is reasonably affordable for senior citizens on fixed incomes but that they were not income adjustable.

That was the end of February. When she came down again two weeks later, she brought the floor plans of both places with her for me to take a look at. She thought it would be nice if I could move into one of them. She said that both places had a few ADA approved handicap accessible units. She pointed out that both the kitchen and the bathroom were at least two and a half times larger than mine, and there was plenty of room to navigate with my wheelchair. I think she was tired of listening to my complaining about how difficult it was for wheelchair users to function in these two rooms. There is no turning space for my wheelchair and I have to back out of both rooms. The kitchen is even worse than the bathroom. Because of the way it is laid out, I not only have to back out of it, but I have to make a ninety degree turn in about three feet of space between the laundry area and the sink, very tricky to say the least.

I told Darlene that even as low as the rent would be, that I could not afford to live there. As much as I wanted to move out of where I am, with my income as low as it is, I would have no money to live on after the rent was paid. I reminded her that I am receiving help through the federal government's housing program and that a large portion of my rent is paid for under the "Section 8 Voucher Housing Program", and that unless Vista Grand and Madison Reserve participated in the program, there was no way on earth I could live at either place. Like it or not, I am stuck right where I am for now.

In the meantime, my annual re-certification packet arrived from the Tampa Housing Authority (THA). I was dreading the task of filling out all of the papers. In the past eleven years, no matter how careful I was to include **all of the information** that THA asked for, I would always get a threatening letter back stating that unless this or that wasn't in their office within X number of days, I would be terminated from the program. This occurred even when I had the paperwork double checked by Williams Landing's office staff. One time there was a new girl in the office. When I ask her to check my papers, she told me that she knew nothing about the Section 8 program and I would have to wait until her co-worker got back from vacation. I left the office very disgusted to say the least. I couldn't understand why she was hired if she knew nothing about the federal housing programs associated with the job.

The papers always come in March from THA. Not only would I have to fill out and sign these papers at this time, Williams Landing had its own set of lease renewal papers to be dealt with which required slightly different information. The renewal date on my lease was always June 1st, so I assumed THA used the same formula and there was never any problem with it.

One morning in mid-March, Darlene phoned to inform me that both places welcomed Section 8 vouchers and that the two managers would work with THA to make sure I got into one of the four handicapped accessible units. With this news, I filled out and mailed my application to Vista Grand apartments. The one thing that sold me on Vista Grand over Madison Reserve is that it included the washer and dryer in each unit, which meant that my aide and I wouldn't have to worry about taking my laundry to a coin operated machine each week.

With this information at hand, I contacted my THA counselor to see just what I had to do to transfer my voucher to Hernando County so I could move to Vista Grand in Spring Hill. I told her that I had a chance to get a completely ADA approved handicapped accessible apartment with a low kitchen sink, a refrigerator with a freezer that I could reach and the bathroom has a roll-in shower and a high toilet. All of these features would make my life a lot easier and safer.

At this point, she told me that my lease wasn't up until June 30th and that I would not be able to move before then.

I was very upset with this. Housing for wheelchair users is very difficult to find in the first place and when an apartment becomes available, it is spoken for almost immediately. I knew that if I had to wait until my lease expired, my chances of acquiring one of the four handicap accessible apartments was nil. I wanted to pay for two months rent in advance to Vista Grand to hold one of the four apartments. THA would have no part of this idea.

On March 21 the property manager at Vista Grand at Spring Hill had contacted my counselor at THA regarding my transfer. She was advised that I currently have a lease that does not end until 6/30/2012. She told THA that she might not have a unit available at this time. This was when I learned that my lease dates with Williams Landing and THA were not the same. My lease expiration date with Williams Landing was 5/31/2012, a month earlier than with THA. I really didn't know how to handle this situation.

Looking back, I know how it came to be. I moved into Williams Landing on 6/1/2001 and paid the first two months' rent out of my own pocket. By the time THA picked up its portion of the rent on 7/1/2001, I had already been living there a month. I was reimbursed for July's rent by Williams Landing and didn't think any more about the date until I tried to move. According to Williams Landing, my new lease began on the first of June each year.

My counselor told me that if I could afford to pay the full rent to hold a unit, I could afford to pay it indefinitely, and my voucher would not be renewed because I no longer needed the federal program. I wrote the following letter to my counselor:

"I very much disagree with your office. I think it is very **unfair and inhumane to hold a severely disabled tenant to a lease.** When I moved here eleven years ago, this apartment met my needs just fine. I could stand up unaided and could even take a few steps using a walker. I had a bad accident in 2006 and had to have a hip replacement from which I never fully recovered. As a result, I am totally dependent on my motorized wheelchair."

"The kitchen here is **impossible** for me to function in. I **cannot** reach to turn on the water at the sink to wash dishes, and neither can I reach the controls on the stove to do my own cooking as they are at the back of it. I am limited to using my microwave oven to heat up food my aide prepares for me. The refrigerator's freezer is also off limits to me. My bathroom does not have a roll-in shower, so I have to wait for two or three days for my aide to assist with getting in and out of the bathtub. I say a prayer every time I use the toilet that I don't land on the floor because there is no grab bar for me to pull myself to a standing position to make my transfer to and from the toilet SAFELY. The bathroom is NO bigger than a closet and has NO turning space for my wheelchair. As a result, the wall and door are badly damaged from having to BACK out."

"I have been searching for a HANDICAPPED ACCESSIBLE apartment that is within WALKING distance of a shopping area and near a medical facility, should I ever need it, for quite some time. When a friend told me about Vista Grand in Spring Hill, I thought my prayers were at last being answered."

"If your office will not consider my request to move to Spring Hill, I will contact my congresswoman, Kathy Castor. I don't think I am being unreasonable."

The reply to this letter was that "If we allow one person to break a lease, we would have to let everyone else do the same. We can't do that." At this time, I was unaware of the laws of the Fair Housing Act dealing with "reasonable accommodations" pertaining to disabled tenants and apparently nobody else in the rental office at Vista Grand or THA was either, or THA chose to ignore it. I needed to give Williams Landing a 60 day written notice to vacate no later than 4/1/2012 and to provide THA with a copy as well. I was to contact Vista Grand at Spring Hill in regards to this letter. This would put me out of Williams Landing by 5/31/2012, a month ahead of the date that THA originally set. And at the rate things were progressing at this time, the paperwork with THA just would not be ready for them to issue me the voucher so I could transfer it to Hernando County Housing Authority. Without this voucher, Vista Grand could not assign a unit to me. I now knew that the earliest possible date I could move, if at all, would be 7/1/2012. I knew that all of the handicap accessible apartments were spoken for. But by now, I began to worry that by the time I would be issued a voucher that Vista Grand would be filled to capacity and I would not be able to live there at all.

The months of April, May and June were very stressful. By now, my counselor at THA and I were communicating via E-mail at least three times a week. We both found this much quicker and far more effective than using the telephone or postal mail.

On May 7, I received an E-mail from my counselor at THA telling me that she could not issue me a housing voucher until I paid off a balance of $597.00 I owed to Williams Landing Apt. I was very upset about this. I knew I had always paid my share of the rent on time each month. My first thought was, just maybe, my share of the rent was not calculated correctly and I hadn't been paying the right amount for the past year. In this case, I would have to pay it. This made me angry to think that a whole year had passed and nobody in the rental office had caught the error. When I checked with the rental office to find out what was going on, the girl at the desk pulled up my records from the computer. It showed a balance of **ZERO.** She told me I had nothing to worry about. I then checked with the property manager. What she told me didn't make any sense, but she assured me that I didn't owe them anything. While I was quite relieved to learn that my balance was zero, I was puzzled as to how the error was made in the first place. Somebody was very careless. It could have taken a long time to resolve, and I could have lost my Section 8 housing voucher. It is hard enough to deal with a federal program. But when somebody makes mistakes, it is very time consuming to straighten them out and makes a lot of extra work for everybody concerned.

When I finally got a written notice to go to the THA office to sign for the voucher it was mid-May. I knew the worst was behind me. Vista Grand still had units available. They were on the fourth floor, but at this point, I really didn't care. By now I knew Vista Grand was where I wanted to be. My friend Ester had driven me to Spring Hill twice. The first time was to look the place over to make sure it was more handicapped accessible than where I was currently living. Because Darlene had mentioned to me several times that the one up the street also had handicapped accessible units, I thought it best to leave no stone uncovered. I didn't want to get moved and settled into one, only to discover that I should have moved into the other.

When we visited the Madison Reserve and talked to the property manager I knew right away that I didn't want to live there, even though I could have had the last available handicapped accessible unit. When we got back to the car, we both knew my answer. Vista Grand, here I come!

Now all I had to do was get my hands on the voucher. I had already been in touch with Hernando County Housing Authority, (HCHA) several times by telephone as had the property manager at Vista Grand, to make sure we followed proper steps to transfer the voucher from one county to the other once I had it in my hands.

When I received the written notice telling me that I had to come to the THA office to sign for it, I was very concerned because of its location. I had only been to that office once before, and that was eleven years ago, just before I moved to Tampa. It did not appear to be a place where a disabled person should travel alone and I didn't know just how far the bus stop was to my destination. I could see that it was too far for a wheelchair user and I would have had to cross a very busy street. When I told my friend Lou of my concerns, he gave me the name on one of his neighbors who has transported him to medical appointments. It would be well worth whatever the amount of money I gave him to get me there and back home safely and with the voucher in my possession. As it was, it took an hour and a half to get to THA's office due to a traffic jam on I-4 and we had just five minutes to spare before the appointment. We were in there less than fifteen minutes. When we got back to the car, I told my driver I had just signed for a 'pot of gold'. I was so relieved that I wouldn't have to deal with that office ever again. I knew now that I was on my way to Spring Hill.

When I got home that afternoon I wasted no time. I faxed a copy of my new voucher to Vista Grand Apartments so the manager could assign a unit to me. Then I phoned HCHA to let them know that I had finally been issued the voucher from THA, and set up an appointment to transfer it to HCHA. By now I had less than fifteen days to finish packing, get out of where I was and get moved.

As if I didn't have enough to deal with at this time, my wheelchair conked out and needed to go to the shop to have a new motor installed. It took a few days to get the prescription for wheelchair repairs approved before the parts could be ordered. In the meantime, the company I was dealing with gave me a loaner chair until mine was returned to me. The loaner was much too big for my small body. It was made for a three hundred pound person and I only weigh about eighty-five pounds. But it did get me around in my apartment and that was all I needed for now. Little did I know the problems that I would encounter while I was using it. Because it did not have a seat lift, I had a very difficult time transferring to and from the toilet and the bed, and my left leg started hurting. I tried to use less pressure on it during my transfers but the pain just got worse with every transfer until I could no longer tolerate it.

One night the leg hurt so much, I could not sleep, and I decided to go to the emergency room at Brandon Regional Hospital to find out what was going on and hopefully get some relief from the pain. I was sent for x-rays, only to be told that there was nothing wrong. By now, it's 2:30am. I was given something for the pain and was sent home. A few hours later the hospital phoned me and said they had an ambulance on the way to bring me back in because the x-rays they took showed that I have a hairline fracture and they needed to do more tests. I was very angry that they hadn't read them right in the first place. This wasn't the first time this had happened to me. It happened seven years earlier when I fractured my hip. I was sent for more x-rays and a CAT scan. The results confirmed that I had a hairline fracture and I was told that there was nothing anyone could do for that. I was given a prescription for pain pills and once again sent home. I knew from OT school that hairline fractures took a long time to heal and there is really nothing that can be done to speed up the process. It will take anywhere from four to eight weeks if I didn't use the leg at all. I knew this would be impossible, as I had to get on and off the toilet. There was nothing I could do about that. I had to pay my night aide to come to get me up in the morning as well as put me to bed. This was an inconvenience but it worked out okay. I would be moving in a few days and I would have my own wheelchair back from the shop. Then everything would be back to normal–or so I thought.

There was just so much to do that last week before I moved. I had to get to Brooksville on Friday to sign the papers to transfer the voucher to Hernando County Housing Authority. Darlene said she would see to it that I got there. This meant that she would need to make two round trips to Tampa, a good four hours on the road. I was very worried that she couldn't drive this long trip since she had all she could to get back home from her bi-monthly visits. When she phoned to tell me that her niece would do the second half of the trip, I felt a little better about it. I knew I had to get there to sign the papers to transfer the voucher from Tampa to Hernando County and Darlene was my only means of transportation.

The day before the appointment, I collected all the papers that I would need. My leg was hurting even with the pain pills and I was very concerned about how I was going to get into the car, but somehow I managed. I told Darlene that I really didn't want to have to get out of the car again until I got home. When we got to the office, Darlene took all of the papers in and explained to the counselor the situation. A few minutes later, they both came out to the car with all the paperwork ready for me to sign. Everything was finally completed. I was so relieved that everything went so smoothly here, and I think Darlene was too. This was Friday. All that was left to do was the apartment inspection, which I was told would be done on Monday and I could plan the move for Tuesday. Darlene said she wasn't at all tired and she would take me home. It was to be the last trip she would make to Tampa and I think we were both very relieved.

The weekend was very busy. When I got home, the first thing I did was to call the mover in the hope that there was an opening for Tuesday. This was the only day my friend in Tampa had free to drive my cat Gabby and me to Spring Hill. There was a lot of last minute packing and cleaning to be done that goes along with moving out. My caregiver did most of that when she came in to put me to bed. I wasn't feeling up to par. The medicine I was taking for the pain in the leg was making me feel very woozy and grumpy and I really wanted to be left alone and stay in bed. I knew I couldn't because I couldn't get up unassisted to use the bathroom during the day. The oversized wheelchair I was using really didn't help my disposition any, either. I kept bumping into everything, as there was so little floor space due to all of the packed boxes everywhere.

On Monday afternoon Darlene phoned to tell me that the housing inspector did not have time to do the inspection of my apartment until the first thing Tuesday morning and there was no way I could move my things in until after he had done his job. This meant that I had to reschedule the mover for Wednesday or Thursday. At this point, I was so upset that I broke down in tears. Darlene told me not to worry, that she would drive down to get Gabby and me on the morning of the move. I told Darlene that I would have to call the mover to reschedule the move for Thursday. I prayed that he had an opening for some time that day. If he didn't, I really don't know what I would have done.

I had to ask my caregiver to come for three extra days. The agency had discontinued all services as of Sunday night. So whatever services I needed now, I would have to pay for out of my own pocket. It was an added expense that I hadn't planned on and I really couldn't afford it either. But there was no way around this problem. My leg was hurting even when I was quiet and I had all I could do to use the toilet during the day. I knew I needed help getting in and out of bed. There was just no way around it.

The night before the move was a real nightmare. A friend came in to put me to bed and disconnect my computer and pack my television and whatever else needed doing. I was having a very difficult time using the toilet all day, and by now the pain in the leg had become unbearable to the point of tears. It was apparent to the both of us that the medication I was taking to ease the pain was not working, and I really needed medical attention. I did not want to go back to Brandon Regional Hospital's emergency room after being misdiagnosed two times only to be told there was nothing wrong and sent home. Seeing that I really needed treatment, my friend and I decided to call 911 and let the ambulance driver take me to University Hospital.

By the time I got to the hospital, it was close to 11 o'clock. I was pleased with the good bedside manners of those who attended me. I was sent for x-rays and a slew of other tests to make sure it wasn't a blood clot that was causing the severe pain. With all that was going on with the leg and the moving, my blood pressure shot up. I knew once the pain was managed, the blood pressure would return to normal, so I wasn't worried about that. By the time I got back to the emergency room the medicine I was given two hours earlier had begun to take effect and the pain began to lessen a little, but it was making me nauseated and very groggy. Finally, after three hours, someone came in and told me the hospital was releasing me. The leg was badly bruised and there was nothing more they could do for me. I was given a prescription for oxycodone, a very powerful narcotic and told to see my orthopedic doctor if the pain lasted for more than a week.

When Darlene and her friend Ann came down at 8:30 in the morning to take Gabby and me to my new apartment, I was up and sitting in the oversized wheelchair apparently in a lot of pain and very groggy and swaying from side to side unable to sit up straight. The seatbelt was holding me in so I wouldn't fall forward and land on the floor. I asked Darlene to get the prescription for pain medicine filled before we left Tampa.

When the movers finally arrived, Darlene told the men to put the bed in the van last so that it could be set up as soon as we got to my new apartment. She knew I would need to be put to bed as soon as we got there. I was so sick from the medication and not sleeping much the night before. Her friend Ann managed to get Gabby into the carrier before the movers arrived so the cat wouldn't get frightened and try to get out. Darlene put my portable wheelchair in her car as she knew I would need it when we got to Spring Hill. When the movers had the van packed and ready to hit the road, she asked one of them to lift me into her car. I really don't remember much about the events of the rest of the day and the next two or three weeks were very patchy. Darlene said I slept most the way and Gabby cried a lot.

The week before I moved, my social worker in Tampa contacted the Department of Children and Family in Hernando County to make certain that the homemaker and personal care services I was receiving in Tampa would be carried over as soon as I got to my new apartment in Spring Hill. The day after I moved, a very nice social worker came to see me. I explained to her all of the services and supplies I would need in order for me to function independently. Under ordinary circumstances, the number of hours I was receiving for the past few years was sufficient.

However, at this time I was unable to get in and out of bed by myself and my motorized wheelchair was still in the repair shop and wouldn't be back for at least another week. This meant that I would have to stay in bed all day with no food and wet pants until help arrived in the afternoon. For now, Darlene was coming up to make certain that I had food and took care of my personal needs. Before I left Tampa, I had my caregiver fix me enough meals to last me for two weeks. I figured by then, things would be well organized here. I was really too sick to care who did what at this time. The medication I was taking for the pain made me very dizzy and lightheaded and I slept a lot. When I was half awake and tried to change positions to avoid getting bedsores, the leg would go into muscle spasms and hurt worse than ever. By now I knew what was happening. The doctor in the ER had treated the pain, but overlooked the fact that I have cerebral palsy. What I really needed now was a muscle relaxant to help control the spasms. I had Darlene call my doctor in Tampa and tell her what happened and what I needed. As soon as I got the right medicine, my leg began to feel better and I was able to cut back on the powerful pain pills. It would be another two weeks before I could replace them with an over-the-counter pain medicine,

By now an aide had been sent to help me, and my motorized wheelchair was back. There was only one problem, the aide came in at

11 o'clock in the morning to tend to my personal needs. I was still not able to transfer to and from the bed and toilet alone. This meant I had to be put back to bed before she left two hours later and I wouldn't see anyone until the next morning. Darlene was still the go-between. I did not like this at all. I felt that it would ruin our long–time friendship of 60 plus years. After all, she was a friend, **not** my caregiver, and I wanted to keep it that way. Late on the evening of July 5, Darlene came up to tell me she was leaving on the next flight to Boston, MA. Her brother had passed away. He had been sick for quite some time. So I was not surprised at the news. However, this event changed everything for the both of us–I think for the better in the long run. However, getting to the point where I needed to be, in order to function as independently as I could before I developed a hairline fracture was very difficult and frustrating to say the least.

When my aide came in the next morning at her usual time to tend to my basic needs, I told her about what took place the night before. I was very scared. I told her that after she left at 1 o'clock Friday, I wouldn't see anybody until she returned on Monday. This meant that I would be in bed without food or water and have to lay in wet and soiled pants for three days or until she returned on Monday.

Being the caring person she is she knew this was not acceptable. She said she had a friend, Jane Doe, (not her real name), who used to be a caregiver. She would ask Jane to come to help me over the weekend. My aide, Jane, and I came to an agreement that Jane would come in at ten dollars an hour for two hours twice a day for the weekend. I knew I could not afford this very often, but this was an urgent need and I had no choice in the matter. Jane did not drive but my aide's sister who was living with Jane would do the driving. I really don't remember very much about that weekend. I was still feeling the effects from the pain medication and I guess it left many blank spots on my brain.

I do remember that Jane was a very mannish person and a workaholic. By the end of the second day she had most of my boxes unpacked and my things put away. Most of my pictures were hung and my apartment was quite livable. It felt really good to be up in my wheelchair for a few hours. But by the time she came back to give me my supper, I was exhausted and needed to be put back to bed.

I remember one time that weekend when I tried to use the computer, I got very dizzy and fell onto the keyboard. I knew I had to get off the potent prescription drugs, at least during the daytime hours. I decided I would take an over-the-counter pain reliever and the muscle relaxant during the day, and take the powerful one at bedtime so I would get a good night's sleep.

One night after I had been put to bed, my aide's sister came in to tell me that Jane had fallen and broken her big toe and needed money for pain medicine. I think I gave her ten dollars. She wanted more. I told her I didn't have any more. She didn't seem very satisfied, but she took it and left.

The next morning when Jane came in to get me up, she didn't seem to be in any discomfort at all. I inquired about her fall the night before. She said she was fine. I didn't say any more. But I had a feeling something wasn't quite right. I could have misunderstood her roommate. After all, I was half asleep and quite groggy from the medicine when she came in. I believe this night was the beginning of a real nightmare for me.

I phoned my social worker and told her about what had happened over the weekend. I told her that my aide came in in the morning to get me up and tend to my personal needs and put me back to bed. I told her that the number of hours the aide was given per week was sufficient but the way they were being used was wasted and did not meet my needs at all. For now what I really needed was for someone to come for an hour in the mornings to get me up and then leave. Then I needed someone to come for another hour to put me to bed in the evenings seven days a week, not just five days. My aide did not work on weekends nor did she work after 5pm. I was still not able to get out of bed unaided because the leg wasn't completely healed and I still could not put much weight on it. My social worker and the home health agency finally worked things out to resolve this problem.

Just when I thought things were going fairly smoothly, my motorized wheelchair started giving me trouble again. It hadn't been back three weeks from having over one thousand dollars of repairs on it. I thought, this can't really be happening. But when I couldn't get it to go in reverse, I was devastated. I turned the power off and turned it back on and was able to back up to get turned around. It worked this way a couple of times. Then it conked out altogether.

When a repairman came out to look at the wheelchair he put a tester on it. He said it was the batteries. I told him I just had new batteries put in two months ago and couldn't see how they could have died this soon.

They are supposed to last up to two years, not just two month. He got sort of 'pissy' with me and told me he knew his business better than I did.

The next day he brought new batteries and installed them. He wanted me to pay for them right then and there. I told him the company could bill me and I would pay it as soon as the bill came in. He left. The chair did work. So maybe he was right after all.

I decided to try the lock on my door to make sure I could use it safely. The manager was going to see about having a different kind put on if this one was too difficult for me to use.

I got to the door and guess what? I could use the lock fine. But my wheelchair conked out and I was stuck at the door and could not move an inch. I managed to get the door opened a crack and yell at the top of my lungs for help. "I am stuck. I can't get out". A neighbor heard me. I sent her to get the manager. She and the maintenance man came up to see what the problem was. The two of them together could not push me and my wheelchair back far enough to get the door open. The manager decided to call 911 to get the fire department's help. At this point, I thought how stupid I was. I wear a medic alert and I didn't think to use it. Oh well! When the two firemen arrived, between them they managed to push the door open far enough so that the slim feller could squeeze through the opening to rescue me. So it wasn't the batteries after all! I never saw that wheelchair repairman again to tell him, "See, I told you so".

The next morning I called the company to tell them that my wheelchair conked out again even before he drove away and that I was not going to pay for the batteries the repairman put in the day before. Another repairman was sent out. I told him what had happened the day before. He knew I was very upset. He checked the wheelchair over. He said the controls were worn out. The wheelchair looked pretty beat up from where my cat Lucky had clawed the seat and the back. He told me that it would cost too much to fix it. The chair was just too old, maybe eight years. The life of a chair like mine is about five years. He said that I was long overdue for a new one. I had hoped to get one more year's use from this chair before retiring it. I knew I was going to have to put out at least one thousand dollars on the lift seat for a new wheelchair as that is not covered by any medical insurance and I cannot function independently without it. For me, the lift seat is a **need**, not just a want. I knew he was right.

The repairman said the new wheelchair would be exactly like my old one. We filled out the paperwork, and I let him order it.

He said it would take two to three weeks to come in because of the lift seat. In the meantime I would just have to use my portable wheelchair.

When I finally got a call saying my new wheelchair had come in and it would be delivered right away, I was delighted. I thought, now I can be independent again.

However, it did not turn out that way at all. The seat was much too large for my 85lb body, my feet could not reach the footboard, and the seat lift was already higher than my old wheelchair without even using the lift. I was very upset. I think I told the man he could send the wheelchair back. He said he could build up the footboard. I told him that wasn't going to do much good because the seat was just too big and too high for me. He said they didn't make anything any smaller. This is a standardized wheelchair and it is the only size Medicare would pay for. I told him I wasn't a standard sized person and I needed something to fit my small body.

When John, not his real name, came back the next day, he said he could order me a customized smaller seat to replace the one that came with the wheelchair, but it is going to cost me $1600, and he needed the money before he ordered the seat. I told John that I didn't have that much to give him. But I would pay him nine hundred dollars now and find a way to pay the rest when the seat came in. He agreed to this. He said he would replace the thick leather seat with a two-inch foam cushion. This would lower me about two inches. This was enough to allow me to use the toilet safely, and with the lift seat, I would be able to reach my microwave oven.

I wasn't very happy with having to spend so much money for a smaller seat. And it bothered me to think that the seat that came with the wheelchair would just be thrown out. What a waste of money! If I gave it to the wheelchair company, they, no doubt, would sell it to some poor soul and make a bundle on it. I wasn't about to let this happen.

About a week later John called to tell me that rather than try to fix the oversized wheelchair, they decided to order a new one and for me to be careful not to damage the one I was using.

When John came with the new wheelchair, he said I didn't owe any more money. For this I was quite relieved. While this new wheelchair is not as small as my old one, it is functional

I wasn't feeling quite up to myself yet, but almost. My head had begun to clear up from all the medicine I was taking. I decided to clean out the drawer of my bed side table. It was a mess from where people had taken things and hadn't put them back in their proper places. I discovered my bankcard was missing. I emptied the drawer onto the bed and double-checked everything before I put it back into the drawer. The bankcard just wasn't there.

I went to my computer and checked my bank statement. To my horror, the balance read minus over nine hundred dollars. I almost panicked. Right away, I thought I knew who had done it. I just had no proof. That afternoon, my aide's sister phoned to say that she was coming to help me get into bed. I mentioned to her that my bankcard was missing. She said she would look for it when she came. I hoped I had set a trap. I was on the computer in the bedroom when she came in. When she came into the bedroom, she said, "I found the card you were looking for. It was on your dining room table". I knew that was a lie and I had her right where I wanted her. When I checked my statement again the next morning, there was still more money missing. I knew this would be the last of it. I phoned my friend Lou in Tampa as soon as I discovered money missing and ask for his advice.

I knew I needed help with the phone call to the police. Darlene hadn't returned from Duxbury, Massachusetts yet and I didn't know anyone in the building. While Darlene was away, her friend was dog sitting. I went downstairs and told Ann what had happened. She was as upset about it as I was. I asked her to come to my apartment to help me with the call to the police. I use a speaker phone with the volume turned up to accommodate my hearing impairment.

We didn't know whom to call, so we dialed 911, and the dispatcher connected us to the right department. Within half an hour a sheriff was sitting at my dining table asking all sorts of questions and taking down the information. I did not know my aide's sister's name. It's an odd name, one I had never heard before. Neither did I know Jane's last name or where they lived. The sheriff waited for my aide to come in so he could question her and get whatever information he needed. I could tell that she was very upset, but there was nothing I could do at the moment. When the sheriff was satisfied, he left.

I told my aide that she had nothing to do with what her sister did and not to worry. She had just gotten her CNA license and I think she was afraid of losing her job.

The sheriff must have contacted the agency that my aide works for. That afternoon I received a call from my aide's supervisor wanting to know if I wanted her back. I made it quite clear that what happened had nothing to do with my aide's job performance. She is a very good and caring worker. And yes, I wanted her back, tomorrow. She worked with me for several weeks more, until I no longer needed morning help.

A private investigator was called in within a week. She came to see me several times. One time when she came in, she had pictures taken from the surveillance cameras at the bank where my bankcard was used. I was asked if I could identify the person in question. I had no doubts. Yes, it was the right person. That was what was needed to get her arrested.

Dealing with the bank was a nightmare I never want to experience again. I was the victim and I was treated as though I was the criminal. I think either the police or the private investigator notified the bank that my bankcard was stolen and the account was broken into. The bank insisted that I was at fault for **giving** this person permission to use it (which I did not). And therefore I would have to pay back every dime of the over-draw. The bank refused to let me close out the account. I wanted to open a new one and transfer my social security check to it. The bank said, "Nothing doing".

When Darlene came home from Massachusetts I told her what was going on. She couldn't believe what the bank was doing to me. She had to take me to the bank so that they could match my Florida ID card to me. Darlene went in to ask them if they could come out and identify me. Because of my injured leg I couldn't get out of the car to go into the bank. They made us sit in the hot car for forty-five minutes before coming out. The representative identified me and then told me that the bank, not only would not reimburse me, but would not close out my account so that I could start a new one for the month of August. She said they would continue taking those checks until all the overdrawn money was replaced. I was devastated. This meant that I would have no money for at least three months. How was I going to pay my rent and other living expenses?

Darlene couldn't believe what the bank was doing to me. Her friend gave her the phone number of a legal aide she thought would be able to help us. And she did! Within an hour of telling the legal aide what was happening to me, Darlene got a call from a representative at the bank telling her that the bank had "reversed their decision and that they would reimburse her for all monies taken from her account unlawfully and that her August Social Security check would be deposited into a new account". Darlene set up an appointment with the bank for the next morning so that I could sign the papers to activate the account.

When Darlene and I arrived for the appointment, Darlene went in to tell the person in charge I was there. She told Darlene that the papers weren't quite ready and that she was busy at the moment, and for us to go get a cup of coffee. I told Darlene that I thought this was a trap and we weren't leaving the bank until I signed those papers. If we left and the lady came out and found us not there, she would have had an excuse that I missed my appointment. I wasn't about to let this happen. We waited for over two hours in the boiling sun. Darlene finally had to cut the air conditioner off so we wouldn't run out of gas. That last hour was very uncomfortable to say the least. We drank water, but that really didn't help much. By now it was 90 degrees and in the sun, it felt like 110.

I sent Darlene in a second time. When she came back to the car, she told me that there were no other customers in the bank and the lady who was supposed to be helping me gave her the cold shoulder and told her she would get to me in a few minutes.

Darlene told the lady that I was writing an autobiography and that after today's experiences Arlene planned on writing another chapter. Darlene said that the surprised look on the representative's face was worth a million dollars. All's well that ends well!

The representative did come out in a few minutes with papers for me to sign. It took no longer than five minutes for the whole process of signing.

In February 2013 I was called to the public defenders' office at the county courthouse to tell them what had happened. On the way into their office, I met the private detective on the case. She said to me, "They are going to take good care of you." And they did. One of them told me that my aide's sister would be spending a very long time in jail for this crime. I was pleased with the outcome.

One afternoon in mid-February, I received a phone call from the property manager to come to the office. I had no idea what she wanted to talk to me about, and I wasn't too concerned. The first question she asked me was, "Are you planning to renew your lease?" When I told her that I was, with a big grin, she said, "Good. How would you like to move down to the first floor?" She said she had an ADA approved unit available and when she saw it, it had my name on it. She took me to have a look at it. Right away, I knew this was just where I needed to be. There was only one concern. It is a two-bedroom unit and I had been approved for only one bedroom. She thought **we** could work around this problem. I wasn't so sure. But I was willing to give it my best shot, as I really did not like being up on the 4th floor. My biggest fear is being trapped if there ever was an emergency and the elevators were not working. Even if I am rescued, my six-thousand dollar wheelchair would surely get left behind.

I had to make the initial contact to the Hernando County Housing Authority (HCHA) to tell them what I wanted and why I **needed** the ADA approved unit. From here on in, it would be teamwork. HCHA requested a letter from my doctor stating the reasons I need the ADA unit. Together, the property manager, the doctor and I composed a letter for the doctor to send to HCHA. I had recently studied the part of the Fair Housing Act pertaining to reasonable accommodations for disabled tenants, so I knew the wording HCHA was looking for in order to make this move a reality. Within a few days, I was notified by HCHA that the unit was mine as of the first of the next month, and I signed for a new voucher. I hope to live here happily ever after.

Writing This Book

For the past twenty years, I had been thinking about writing my autobiography but I really didn't have the tools to work with, nor did I have the time to devote to it.

In 1987 when my electric typewriter burned itself out, my Uncle Phil introduced me to the modern age of writing with a word processor. I was quite amazed at just how much this little machine could do. It wasn't long after that that I was introduced to the modern day computer at the Endependence Center where I was teaching. It wasn't until 2000 that I bought my first computer, a rebuilt one, through the Center.

I was so excited that I was *on line* at last. One of the first things I did was to find out where I could play my favorite card game of **bridge**. I still enjoy playing it when I am too tired for anything else. I really had no idea of the unlimited things that are available to me through the internet, and I am still amazed by all that I have found and the way I am able to work in more than one program at the same time. Without the use of the word processor and the internet, I doubt very much that I would ever have attempted to write my story.

My friends, Lorraine and Karen had been bugging me to get started on writing this book for about three years. I think they were very disappointed when they were here in 2008 that I hadn't yet started work on it. I knew I didn't have the proper equipment nor did I have enough experience with the word processor to undertake such a big project. I also knew that when the time was right and I would finally start writing it, I would want to work on it without interruptions until it was completed.

In April of 2008, I decided to start writing. At that time I was also 'saving' my work by printing it out. I soon found that my disability prevented me from installing new ink cartridges in the printer that came with my computer. This was when I asked Diane to take me to get a new one – one that I could *physically* operate.

The new printer (an HP 'all-in-one') that Diane helped me purchase is also a 'scanner'. I quickly realized I would need to 'scan' the pictures I was sending to my cousin Lorena, so I used it for that purpose also.

(I sent the *original* pictures to Lorena. I wanted 'insurance' in case something happened to them or they got lost in the mail.)

At this point, I needed my new printer to be properly installed. Diane tried to connect it the day I brought it home but she really didn't have enough computer knowledge to finish the job. I asked around the complex and Lou came to my rescue. He had it in working order in no time. Not long after that he started working with me to get my story ready for publication.

I never realized the enormity of the task of writing an autobiography. I thought that all I had to do was to write short stories and then tie them together. How wrong I was. There are so many aspects to writing my story including choosing pictures from my past and then deciding where to place them in my story. Some of the pictures I would write stories for and then decide where their permanent home would be in my book. Many of the pictures needed to be cropped and edited and I had no idea how to do that. But luckily, my cousin Lorena, who had just graduated from college where she majored in graphics arts, was a tremendous help to me. I sent all my old family photos that I thought I might use in my book to her and she spent timeless hours working her magic touch on them, preparing them for publication. Some of them were really old and in very poor condition. When I got them back, they looked like they were recently developed.

Not being a 'computer whiz', I needed help setting up the format and organizing the materials for my new project. I realized the importance of getting it right to start with. I started out by writing my life stories, with little concern for what the finished product would look like. Then along came Lou. What a God-send he has been. He is very computer literate and knows his way around the programs, which I do not. I write the stories and then Lou checks them out and edits them as my typing leaves something to be desired. When I run into a problem, whether it is with the program or the computer, he is most always available to help me. He spent countless hours putting the pictures into my book after I got them back from Lorena.

I am not able to physically work the computer well enough to put the pictures in their proper places. Together Lou and I spent hours sizing and placing the pictures for the best perspective. Lou also took the picture of me for the cover of my book with his own camera. Together we worked on getting it ready for publication.

Lou spent hours and hours going over the main text for spacing and other typographical errors of which I have very little control because of my disability. He put all of my edited scripts on CD's so that if my computer went down I would not lose everything that we had worked so hard on. I also printed out everything as I went along for this same reason. It paid off because I lost a whole chapter somewhere along the line. Darlene took my printed copy home and retyped it and then put it onto a CD so I could put it back into my computer in its proper place.

I had a really difficult time with the double-click using the mouse. My finger just could not work fast enough on the mouse, and most of the time the computer registered my 'double clicks' as single clicks. Lou tried slowing the 'time response', but this didn't help any. Finally he told me he could turn my computer into a 'single-click' machine. The day he did that, it relieved a lot of my frustrations. It has made using my computer a whole lot easier and more enjoyable. Now, when he comes to do some editing for me, he sometimes forgets he's changed it. I don't know why anyone would want to use a double click when a single click can do the job just as well.

Well, here I am, three years later and somewhat wiser having told my story as it really happened. As I started out my story I told of how I was born with cerebral palsy and my parents were told to put me in an institution. They should not even bring me home as I would not live to see my tenth birthday. They were told I would never walk or talk and would not even be able to sit up unaided. My mother told the doctors that she was not leaving the hospital without me. So after ten days in the hospital I came home with my parents and I stayed. As you read in my story, how ***wrong*** the doctors were. It is now seventy-nine years later and I am still going strong. I live my life one day at a time. I will always be an advocate for people with disabilities. Whenever I am invited to a speaking engagement regarding disability issues, I would never turn it down.

Made in the USA
Middletown, DE
10 December 2014